IMAGES
of America

THE UNITED STATES MINT IN PHILADELPHIA

Congreſs of the United States:

AT THE THIRD SESSION,

Begun and held at the City of Philadelphia, on Monday the ſixth of December, one thouſand ſeven hundred and ninety.

RESOLVED *by the* SENATE *and* HOUSE *of* REPRESENTATIVES *of the United States of America in Congreſs aſſembled*, That a mint ſhall be eſtabliſhed under ſuch regulations as ſhall be directed by law.

Reſolved, That the Preſident of the United States be, and he is hereby authorized to cauſe to be engaged, ſuch principal artiſts as ſhall be neceſſary to carry the preceeding reſolution into effect, and to ſtipulate the terms and conditions of their ſervice, and alſo to cauſe to be procured ſuch apparatus as ſhall be requiſite for the ſame purpoſe.

FREDERICK AUGUSTUS MUHLENBERG,
Speaker of the Houſe of Repreſentatives.

JOHN ADAMS, *Vice-Preſident of the United States,*
and Preſident of the Senate.

APPROVED, March the third, 1791.

GEORGE WASHINGTON, *Preſident of the United States.*

DEPOSITED among the ROLLS in the OFFICE of the SECRETARY of STATE.

Th: Jefferson Secretary of State.

The United States Mint was authorized by a joint resolution of the Senate and House of Representatives on March 3, 1791, signed by Secretary of State Thomas Jefferson. The US Mint was established in Philadelphia by an act of Congress on April 2, 1792. (Courtesy of the National Archives and Records Administration.)

ON THE COVER: Mint employees inspect new dimes in the Philadelphia Mint press room in 1916 before the freshly struck silver coins are distributed into circulation. (Courtesy of the Library of Congress, Francis B. Johnston Photograph Collection.)

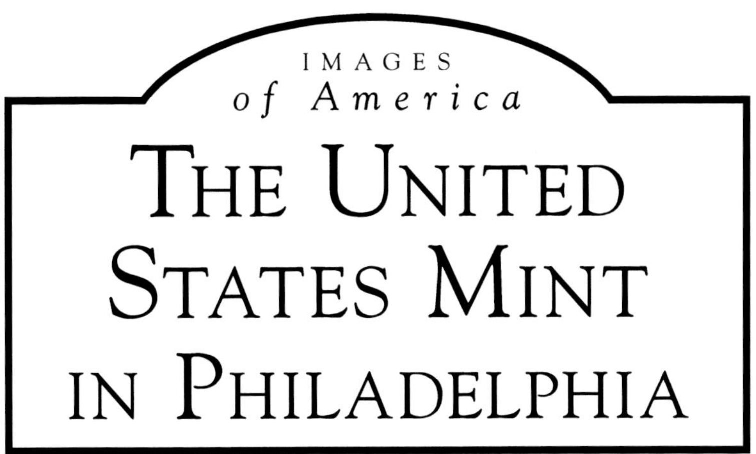

Joshua McMorrow-Hernandez

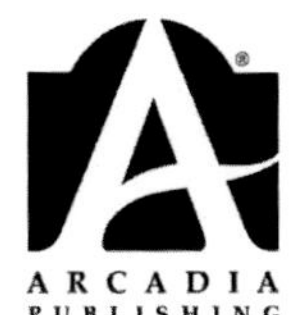

ISBN 978-1-4671-2919-0

Published by Arcadia Publishing
Charleston, South Carolina

Printed in the United States of America

Library of Congress Control Number: 2018936847

For all general information, please contact Arcadia Publishing:
Telephone 843-853-2070
Fax 843-853-0044
E-mail sales@arcadiapublishing.com
For customer service and orders:
Toll-Free 1-888-313-2665

Visit us on the Internet at www.arcadiapublishing.com

In memory of Mom, with gratitude to my loved ones for their support, and for the late, great Ed Reiter, who opened many doors in my numismatic writing career.

Contents

Acknowledgments

My work on Images of America: *The United States Mint in Philadelphia* would not have been possible without the arduous efforts of many individuals who provided their time, energy, and resources. Among these, I must first thank the team at the US Mint, including Thomas V. Johnson, Todd Martin, Gwen Mattleman, and Tim Grant.

Also critical to this project were historians Leonard Augsburger of the Eric P. Newman Numismatic Portal, Roger Burdette, and David W. Lange, who took much of their time to review this book and provide me with their incredible feedback and insight. Augsburger, Burdette, and Joel Orosz offered several dozen photographs, which greatly contributed to this book coming to fruition. Also gracious with providing much historical photography were Bill Gibbs and Jeff Starck at *Coin World*. Others who lent photographs for this project include Ron Brackemyre at Heritage Auctions; John Zieman and Alexandrea Zieman of Z-Man's Coins in Florida; numismatic historian Robert W. Julian; John Frost of the Liberty Seated Collectors Club; Saint-Gaudens National Historic Site in Cornish, New Hampshire; and Alex Doty.

Many others shared their time, knowledge, and support, including renowned US coin expert Scott Travers, Dr. Michael Fuljenz at Universal Coin & Bullion, Lynnette and Jim Walczak at TheFunTimesGuide.com, John Feigenbaum and Patrick Ian Perez at *Coin Dealer Newsletter*, Charles Morgan and Hubert Walker at *CoinWeek*, Lynn Varon of *COINage*, Karen Lee of the National Park Foundation, Karie Diethorn at Independence National Historical Park, Erin Beasley at the Smithsonian Institute, Michael Seneca at the Athenaeum of Philadelphia, Ed Moy, John Mercanti, Don Everhart, and Heidi Wastweet.

Last but not least, I extend my heartfelt gratitude to my beloved Jeanine Baker for putting up with the many, many long hours I spent researching and compiling information and photographs for this project. I also thank my dad, Frank "Rudy" Hernandez, and Michele Hernandez for their loving parental guidance and support. My sister Kelly McMorrow-Hernandez must also be recognized for her efforts in keeping reading alive at the local library where she works, and my heartfelt thanks go to her fiancé, James Libengood, for his support.

US coin images appear courtesy of United States Mint and are used with permission. The United States Mint does not endorse nonfederal providers of goods or services.

INTRODUCTION

The United States was a young nation when Congress approved An Act Establishing a Mint and Regulating the Coins of the United States (widely shorthanded as the "Mint Act" or "Coinage Act") on April 2, 1792. Throughout the nation's first years, Americans purchased goods and services mainly by exchanging copper and silver coins struck by individual states, or private trade tokens placed into circulation by merchants. Many who have a general awareness of early American money may have also heard of wampum, consisting of whelk-shell and clamshell beads. Wampum was primarily traded among Northeastern Native Americans and early American colonists, but it had mostly withered away from usage by the early 18th century, long before the United States became an independent nation. Foreign coins from nations such as England, Germany, France, and Spain were also legal tender during the Colonial and early Federalist eras. Among the most widely circulated foreign coins was the Spanish milled dollar, or "pieces of eight," upon which the value of the US dollar was based.

By the early 1780s, many great thinkers proposed concepts for a US monetary system, leading to the production of several privately minted proposal coins. The earliest known among these, the Plain Nova Constellatio quint, was struck in Philadelphia under the authority of the US government in 1783. This experimental, or pattern, coin is made from silver and would have been worth 500 units in a decimal system of coins ranging in value from 5 to 1,000 units. A second pattern, additional to the plain piece mentioned here, features the words "NOVA CONSTELLATIO," a Latin phrase meaning "a new constellation."

Other privately minted pattern coins were struck in the following years, and many remain popular today with numismatists (those who study money). Among these pieces is a particular type of gold coin struck by Ephraim Brasher, a New York jeweler who was a friend of George Washington. In 1787, Brasher produced a coin now known as the Brasher doubloon, which was valued at $15 in New York currency and roughly equal to the value of a Spanish doubloon, or 16 Spanish dollars. Another widely known coin that was struck in 1787 is the fugio (a Latin word intended here to mean "time flies") cent, a copper piece featuring an image of a sundial. The legends on the coins, which bear the phrase "MIND YOUR BUSINESS," are generally credited to founding father Benjamin Franklin.

Hopes for an official US coinage system became a reality after the ratification of a revised US Constitution in 1789. Two men who helped lead the charge for creating a US monetary system were Alexander Hamilton and Thomas Jefferson. Hamilton, a man who never served as US president, was chosen by Pres. George Washington to become the nation's first secretary of the treasury. Hamilton proposed ideas on monetary policy to Congress on January 28, 1791. In his report, which is partly based on findings made by Jefferson, were proposals for an official government mint.

Hamilton's vision for a national mint included the groundwork for the types of coins that would be produced at such a facility, including his concept for the US dollar, which was based largely on the Spanish silver dollar.

A few weeks later, on March 3, Congress passed a resolution to establish a national mint but failed to appropriate necessary funding. These matters were resolved the following year with the passage of the Mint (or Coinage) Act of 1792, which established the US Mint in Philadelphia, a city that from 1790 through 1800 served as the nation's capital and was among the largest cities in the English-speaking world. Also authorized with the Mint Act was the nation's official coinage system. These included $10 gold coins or "eagles," $5 gold coins or "half eagles," $2.50 gold coins or "quarter eagles," a dollar coin minted from silver and worth 100 cents, half-dollars with a face value of 50 cents, quarters worth 25 cents; dismes (now called "dimes") valued at 10 cents, half dismes (or half dimes) of 5 cents, copper one-cent coins, and copper half-cent coins, which were discontinued from production in 1857. The US Mint took several years unrolling the first official circulating examples of each denomination, and others not mentioned here came along in later years with additional legislation.

July 1792 was a pivotal moment in the history of the US Mint. Renowned Philadelphia scientist and public official David Rittenhouse became the first director of the US Mint following his appointment by President Washington on April 14, 1792. His position was one of five originally listed in the Coinage Act of 1792. By the end of July 1792, construction was also underway on the first US Mint, which was located adjacent to the present-day intersection of Seventh and Arch Streets in Center City.

The original US Mint facility consisted of several buildings tightly positioned near one another on property purchased by Rittenhouse on July 18, 1792, for $4,266.67. The original US Mint facility in Philadelphia, anchored by a three-story structure, also included what was by some accounts the first federal building ever constructed under the authority of Congress. By the end of 1792, the first official US pattern coins struck under the Coinage Act were made in Philadelphia and included a variety of copper and silver coins. Among these early US coins were a silver one-cent coin, copper cent (widely known as the "Birch" cent, an ode to its engraver, Robert Birch), half disme, disme, and quarter.

The first circulation coins to be released by the US Mint came in March 1793 with the introduction of a large one-cent coin bearing the likeness of Liberty on the coin's obverse (or "heads" side) and a chain encircling the words "ONE CENT 1/100" on the reverse ("tails" side). Before the end of 1793, the one-cent coin, measuring approximately 27 millimeters wide—wider than a modern-day quarter—underwent various design changes. The only other US denomination officially issued in 1793 was the half-cent coin.

The last years of the 1790s proved eventful for the US Mint, which hired its first women in 1795 as adjusters. A yellow fever epidemic was particularly burdensome in 1797, forcing the mint to close during the summer and autumn, as the health of its employees came first in the wake of the deadly, flu-like mosquito-borne illness.

By the early 1800s, a variety of denominations had entered circulation, though the new US coins were hardly plentiful. While the US Census of 1800 counted 5,308,483 Americans, the US Mint had produced barely more than 10 million coins by that time. Of these, nearly 8.2 million were either copper half-cent or one-cent coins, mostly the latter, leaving relatively few silver or gold coins available for use in larger transactions. As a Philadelphia day laborer could earn an average of one dollar per day in 1800, the amount of federal coinage available at the time represented barely a pittance, even in the economic picture of the early 1800s. To help remedy the persistent coin shortages, US law permitted Spanish silver dollars and other foreign coins to continue circulating as legal tender throughout the states; that practice finally ceased in 1857.

Production of gold and silver coinage was temporarily interrupted in 1816 by a fire that destroyed the Philadelphia Mint's critical rolling machinery and other equipment. However, overall production of coins was on a steady increase as the 19th century continued onward. Still, the minting operations barely kept pace with the rapidly increasing and spreading population of the United States. The US Census of 1830 recorded a population of 12,860,702 which was no longer mostly concentrated in the original 13 states. By then, America was geographically and demographically growing westward.

In 1833, a new US Mint facility opened at the corner of Chestnut and Juniper Streets. The second Philadelphia Mint, a much larger and statelier structure than the previous facility, could hardly keep up with coin demands due to outdated minting technology. In 1833, Philadelphian Benjamin Franklin Peale was hired by the US Mint to study advanced steam-powered minting technology already in use in Europe. His innovations helped dramatically increase coin production at the Philadelphia Mint during the remainder of the 1830s and were later adopted at US Mint branch facilities that opened throughout the 19th century and afterward as the US population swelled.

The first of these branch facilities opened in 1838 in New Orleans, Louisiana; Dahlonega, Georgia; and Charlotte, North Carolina. Coins produced at these facilities and other US Mint branches are denoted by the presence of a tiny letter (or set of letters) known as mintmarks. These include "C" for Charlotte (gold coins only minted from 1838 to 1861); "CC" for Carson City, Nevada (gold and silver coins minted from 1870 to 1893); "D" for Dahlonega (gold coins minted from 1838 to 1861), and again for Denver, Colorado (1906 to present); "O" for New Orleans (gold and silver coins minted from 1838 to 1861 and 1879 to 1909); "P" for Philadelphia (most coins without a mintmark were struck at the Philadelphia Mint, which did not place its first mintmark on a coin until 1942); "S" for San Francisco, California (1854 to present); and "W" for West Point, New York (1984 to present).

Even with the addition of several branch mints throughout the latter decades of the 1800s and the relocation of main administrative offices to Washington, DC, when the US Mint became a bureau of the Department of the Treasury in 1873, primary coining operations were still located in Philadelphia. As the 19th century wore on, coin production increased further to accommodate booming populations on the East Coast and beyond. By 1900, Philadelphia had 1,293,697 residents, and other nearby metropolises, such as New York City and Baltimore, counted 3,437,202 and 508,957 inhabitants, respectively. By the dawn of the 20th century, a new, modern US Mint building was already under construction at 1700 Spring Garden Street in Philadelphia; it opened in 1901. The iconic landmark, bearing a likeness to a Roman temple, measures nearly a full city block in size and opened as the third Philadelphia Mint. By 1910, the US Mint in Philadelphia was striking nearly 200 million coins per year, which is a figure presumably unfathomable to US Mint officials just a couple decades earlier. By this time, the US Mint produced a variety of coins other than those used day to day by ordinary American citizens, including proof and commemorative coinage for collectors, and specially contracted circulating issues for various nations around the world.

The US Mint enlarged its operations in the 1930s to include bullion depositories in Fort Knox, Kentucky, and West Point, New York. These facilities, known respectively as the Fort Knox Bullion Depository (or colloquially just "Fort Knox") and West Point Bullion Depository (which officially became a branch mint in 1988), were operating by 1937 and have served administrative duties for the Philadelphia Mint. Advancing technology and expansions at the Philadelphia Mint helped bring unprecedented coin production figures for the facility during World War II. In 1944, the number of one-cent coins produced at the Philadelphia Mint exceeded 1 billion for the first time (to be exact, 1,435,400,000 circulating one-cent coins were minted in 1944 at the Philadelphia Mint), and all told, more than 1.9 billion one-cent coins, nickels, dimes, quarters, and half-dollars were made in Philadelphia that year.

Beginning in 1945, officials with the Bureau of the Mint began requesting Congress to approve funds for a new mint facility in Philadelphia. By the early 1960s, a nationwide coin shortage spurred the need for a larger Philadelphia Mint, and on August 20, 1963, Congress passed Public Law 88-102, which gave the green light for a new mint. Local architect Vincent G. Kling, who designed many iconic Philadelphia buildings, including Five Penn Center and the Annenberg Center for the Performing Arts, was commissioned for the new US Mint. Following some three years of construction, the fourth and current Philadelphia Mint opened in 1969 at the corner of Arch Street and North Independence Mall East, just a few blocks from the site of the original US Mint. The current Philadelphia Mint, which opened as the world's largest mint, can strike nearly two million coins per hour. In a typical year, the Philadelphia Mint will pump out six to eight billion coins or more.

While earlier coinage from the Philadelphia Mint does not bear a "P" mintmark, it is much easier these days to tell newer Philadelphia coins from those produced elsewhere in the United States. Following the temporary appearance of the first "P" mintmark on the Jefferson nickel from 1942 through 1945, the "P" reappeared in 1979 on the Susan B. Anthony dollar and has been used on all other Philadelphia-minted coins (except the one-cent coin) since 1980. On December 21, 1981, Secretary of the Treasury Donald Regan moved the Bureau of the Mint, along with the Bureau of Engraving and Printing (which manufactures "paper" currency), under the responsibility of the treasurer.

The 1980s and 1990s were a particularly busy period for the mint. Commemorative coinage, which was produced from 1892 through 1954, was reintroduced in 1982 with the launch of a special half-dollar honoring George Washington on what would have been his 250th birthday. Dozens of other commemorative coins paying homage to various people, places, and events have since followed. A 1984 secretarial order changed the name "Bureau of the Mint" to simply "United States Mint." The Coinage Act of 1985, signed by Pres. Ronald Reagan, authorized the production of precious metal bullion coins, which debuted the following year with the release of the first silver and gold American Eagle bullion coins. Platinum bullion coins followed in 1997, and in 1999, the US Mint embarked on the wildly popular 50 State Quarters program.

The 21st century has been an exciting period for the US Mint. The first decade of the new century brought several major coin programs, including the Westward Journey nickels in 2004–2005 to honor the bicentennial of the Lewis and Clark expedition, the Presidential $1 Coin program in 2007, and the Native American $1 Coin program begun in 2009. Following up on the 50 State Quarters program, which ended in 2008, was the one-year D.C. and US Territories Quarters series in 2009, with the America the Beautiful Quarters program commencing in 2010. In 2014, the National Baseball Hall of Fame commemorative coinage became the first pieces struck by the US Mint to feature curved surfaces, which, in this case, are a concave obverse and convex reverse.

The US Mint turned 225 years old in 2017, and the occasion was marked in grand fashion. Notably, the Philadelphia Mint struck Lincoln cents with a "P" mintmark for the first time in the history of the denomination. Other firsts also occurred in 2017, including the striking of the first US palladium bullion coins, which were produced at the Philadelphia Mint. Meanwhile, the first US coin to feature a representative visage of Liberty with distinctly African American features was struck in 2017. While this coin, a 24-karat gold issue with a face value of $100, was made at the West Point Mint, silver medals featuring this same design were struck at the Philadelphia Mint.

While the US Mint has become an infinitesimally larger, more nationwide effort since its earliest days, the Philadelphia Mint still serves as the "Mother Mint" and the sentimental heart of coin production in the United States. Meanwhile, tens of thousands of visitors tour the Philadelphia Mint each year, making the facility one of the most popular attractions in the City of Brotherly Love.

One

How Coins Are Made
From Conception to Circulation

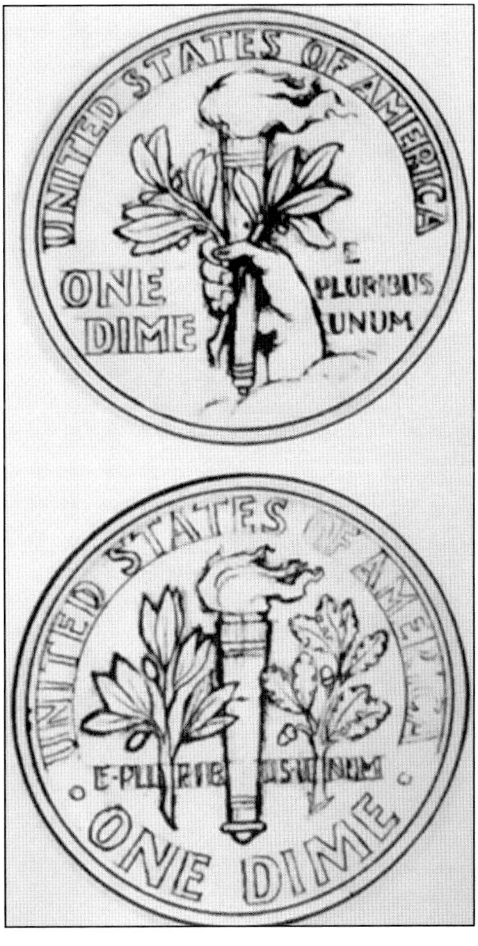

Every coin starts as an idea. These ideas are traditionally expressed on paper by a coin designer, as seen with these two conceptual sketches of the Roosevelt dime reverse (tails) by chief engraver John R. Sinnock, who designed this dime in honor of Pres. Franklin Delano Roosevelt shortly after his death in 1945. Today, much of the coin design process takes place on computers. (Wikimedia Commons.)

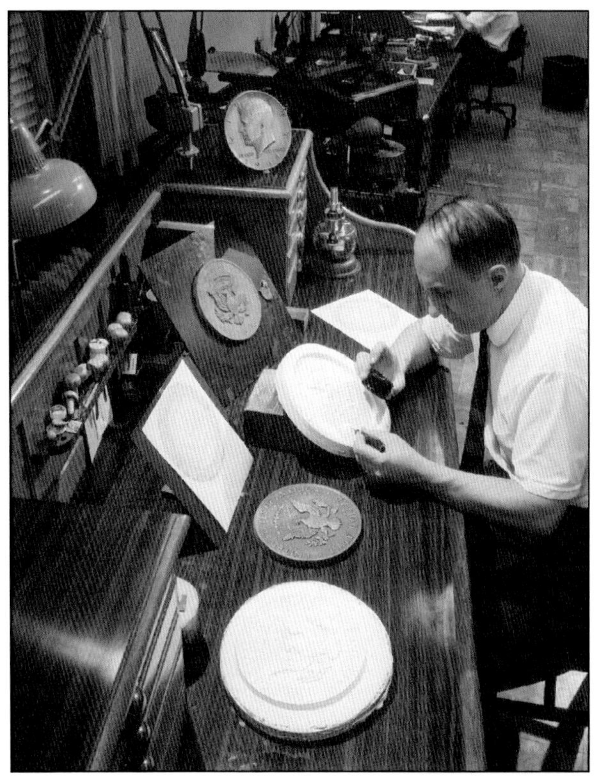

After a coin design has been created, the artistic concept is modeled in plaster. Here, engraver Frank Gasparro is working on a three-dimensional model of the Kennedy half-dollar reverse, which depicts the Seal of the President. While many modern coin designers use computer technology to design and sculpt models, some still prefer more traditional methods, as seen here in the 1960s. (Courtesy of the Athenaeum of Philadelphia.)

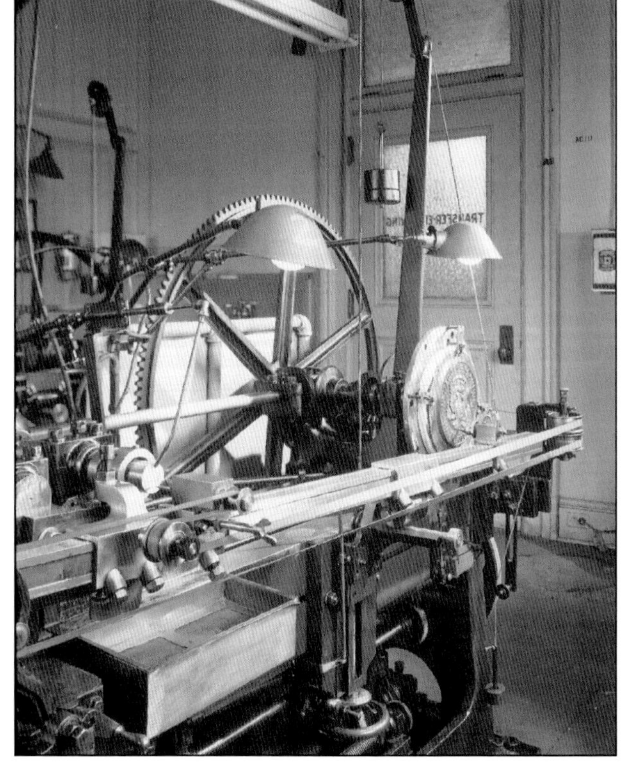

Until recently, the design on the three-dimensional model has been faithfully replicated in coin-size miniature form, right down to the minutest detail, by use of a reducing lathe seen here in the 1960s. This machine, also known as a pantographic reducing machine or transfer lathe, creates a master hub. The master hub is generally used to create working hubs, which are used to produce working dies, though sometimes the master hub makes the working die. A die is the device that strikes designs on the blank pieces of metal, known as planchets, that become coins. Computer-aided milling machinery has replaced the reducing lathe in the coin-making process. (Courtesy of the Athenaeum of Philadelphia.)

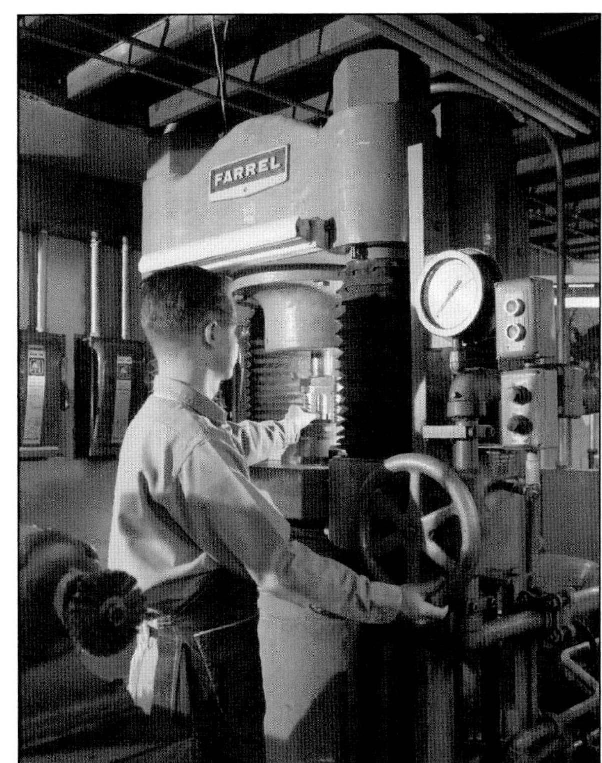

Pictured at right in the 1960s, an employee at the Philadelphia Mint is using a press to work with a hub, which is seen in the close-up below. The hub creates dies, which may strike hundreds of thousands of coins before becoming too worn to use. Old, worn dies are replaced with new dies. Meanwhile, retired dies are destroyed so that they cannot be used for unofficial purposes. (Both, courtesy of the Athenaeum of Philadelphia.)

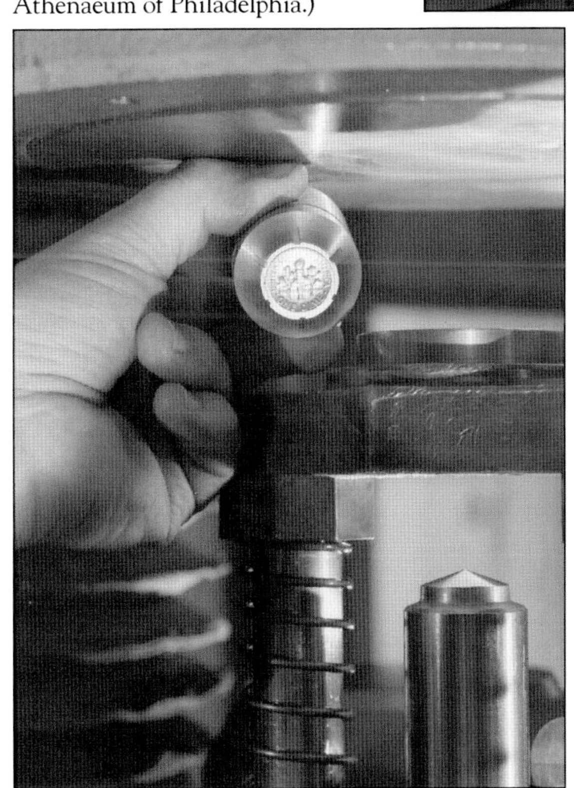

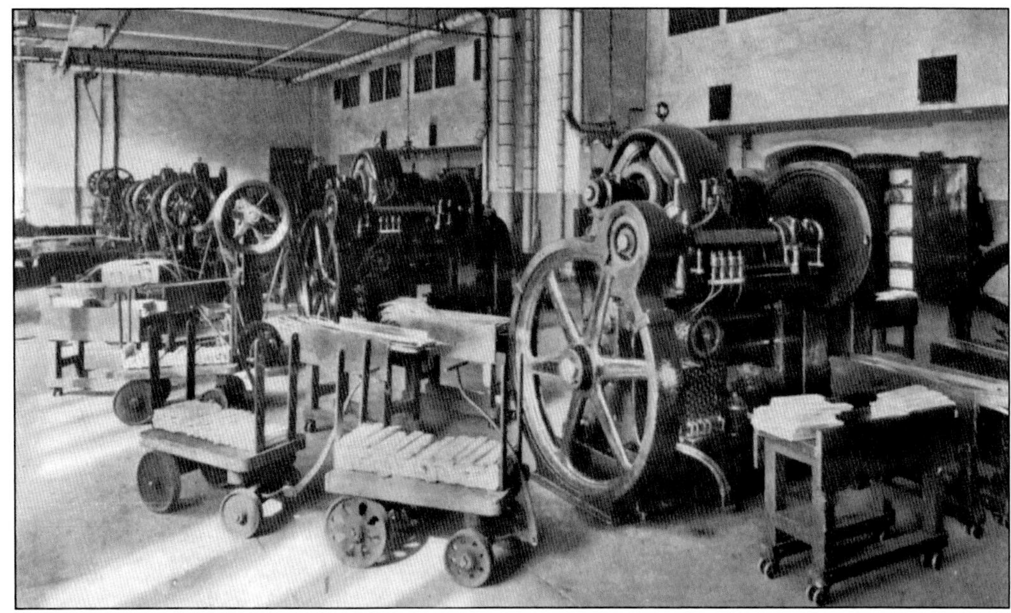

Once a coin has been designed, its hub created, and dies made, the physical minting process can begin. A new coin begins as metal ore, which is refined per government specifications. The metal often arrives at the mint as bars of metal, known as ingots, which are rolled and pressed into long, thin sheets. This early 1900s photograph shows wagonloads of bars that will be flattened into strips, which are seen at center piled on a small table between two rolling mills. (Courtesy of the Library of Congress, Francis B. Johnston Photograph Collection.)

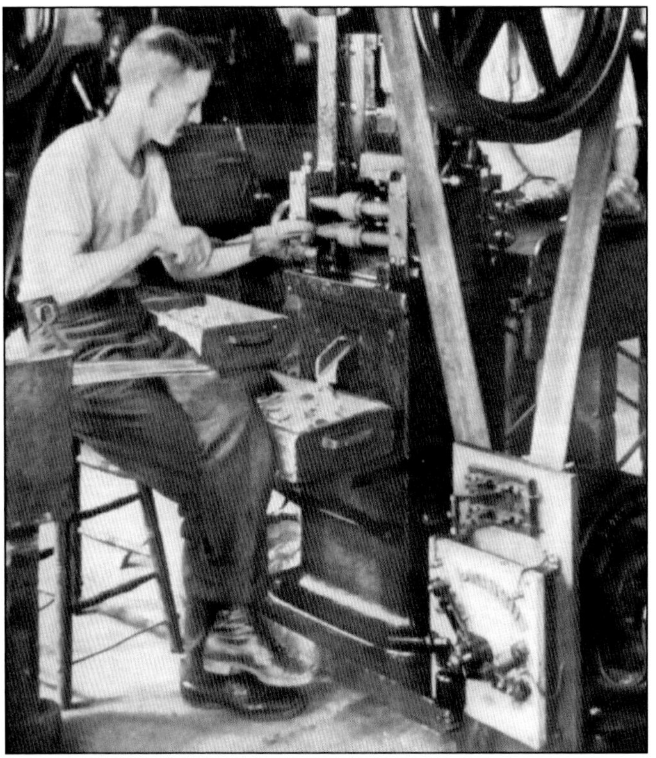

In the early 1900s, this Philadelphia Mint employee is blanking strips of metal into disc-shaped pieces of metal, which will soon become coins. After the round coin blanks are cut from strips of metal, softened with heat in an annealing furnace, washed, and dried, they are sorted through a riddler to filter out any that are misshapen or the incorrect size. (Courtesy of the Library of Congress, Francis B. Johnston Photograph Collection.)

Coin blanks are then processed in an upsetting mill, seen here in the early 1900s. The upsetting mill raises a lip of metal, or rim, along the edge of the blank. At this point, the coin blank becomes a planchet. The planchet is then fed into a coin press, where it is struck between two dies to create the obverse (heads) and reverse. (Courtesy of the Library of Congress, Francis B. Johnston Photograph Collection.)

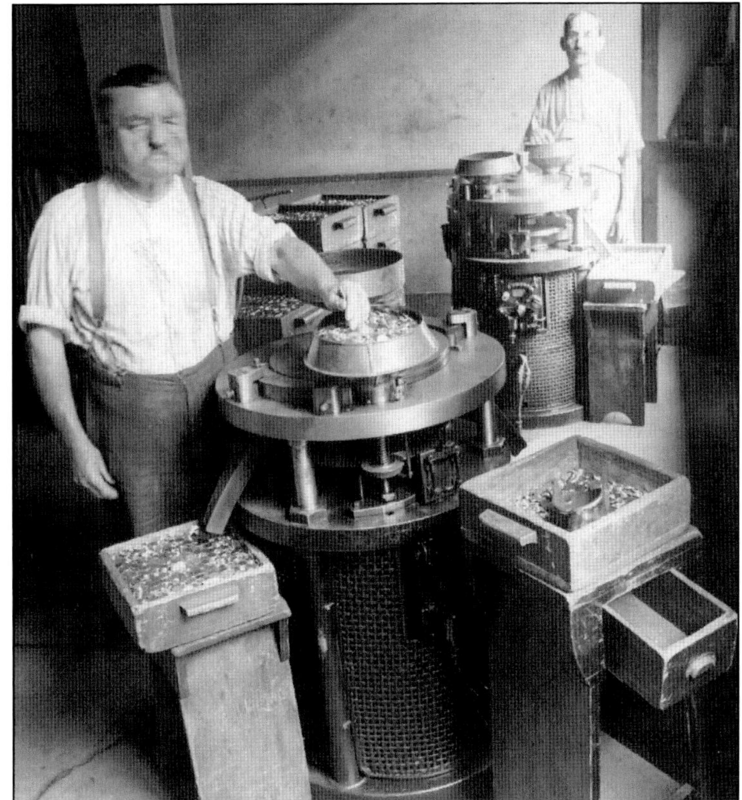

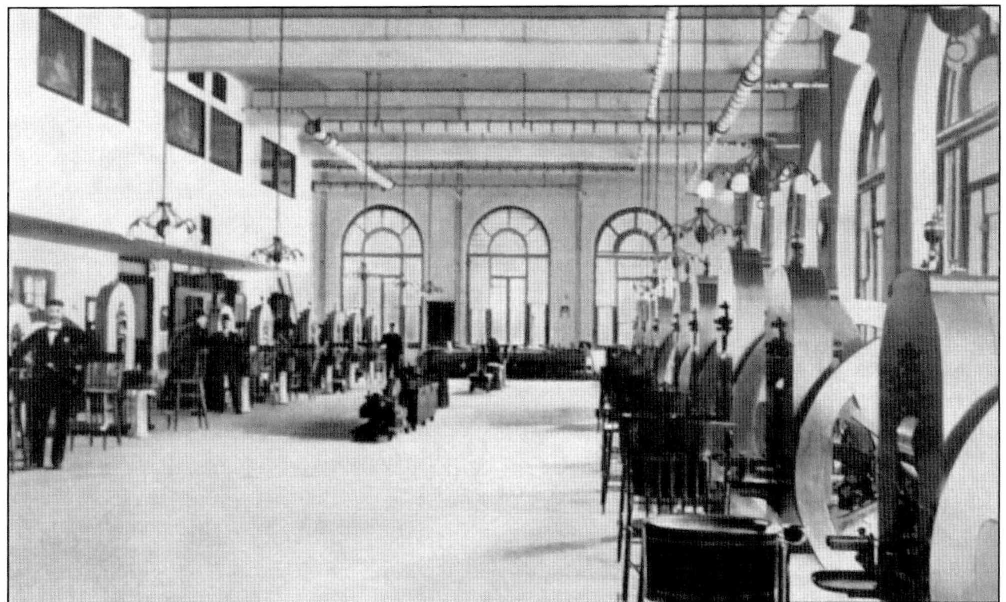

Once a blank's rim has been upset and the disc of metal has been transformed into a planchet, it heads off to the mint's press room, seen here in the early 1900s. At the time, a typical coin press might have struck 60 to 120 coins per minute, whereas today's presses can strike about 750 coins per minute. (Author's collection.)

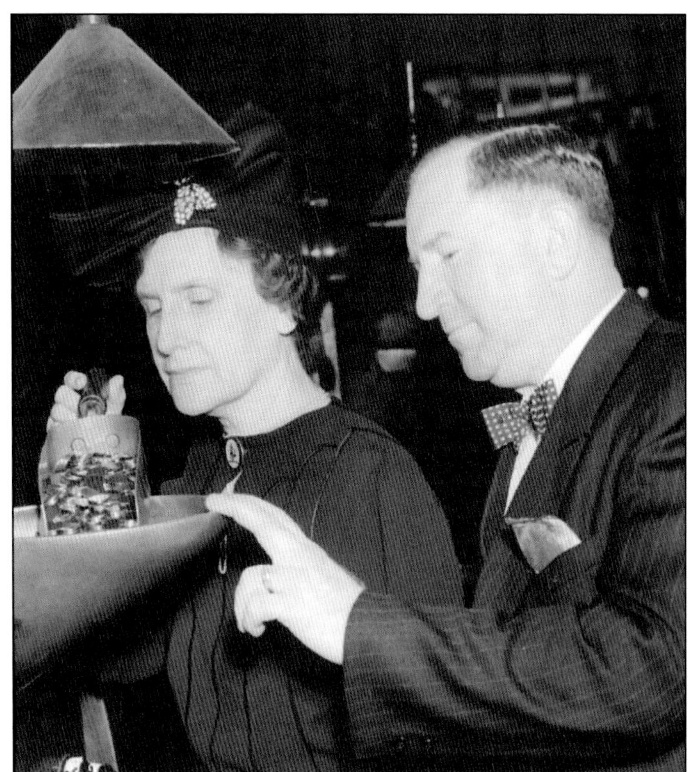

Planchets are fed into the coin press, where the obverse, reverse, and any edge details (such as lettering or reeding) will be added. In this 1938 photograph, Director of the US Mint Nellie Tayloe Ross places a scoop of nickel blanks into the coin presses to make the first Jefferson nickels as Philadelphia Mint superintendent Edwin H. Dressel looks on. While planchets are sometimes still hand-fed into presses during ceremonial strikings, such as the one pictured here, day-to-day operations of processing planchets into coin presses is performed automatically with machinery. (Courtesy of the Historical Society of Pennsylvania.)

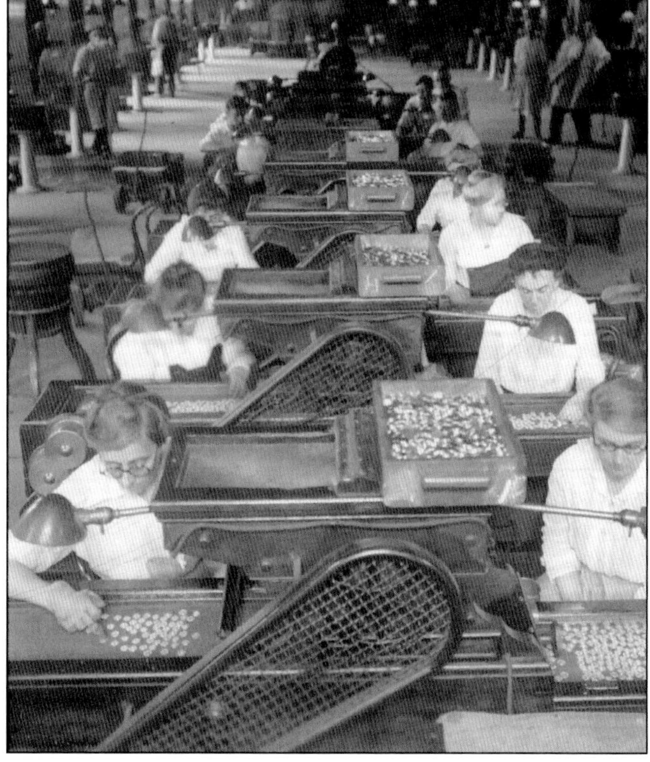

These Philadelphia Mint employees carefully inspect silver dimes in the press room, where the new coins have just been struck. While operations at the US Mint are much more technologically advanced and automated than they were when this 1916 photograph was taken, the coin inspection process still requires the human eye, aided by a magnifying glass. Once batches of new coins have passed inspection, they can be bagged and shipped off for distribution. (Courtesy of the Library of Congress, Francis B. Johnston Photograph Collection.)

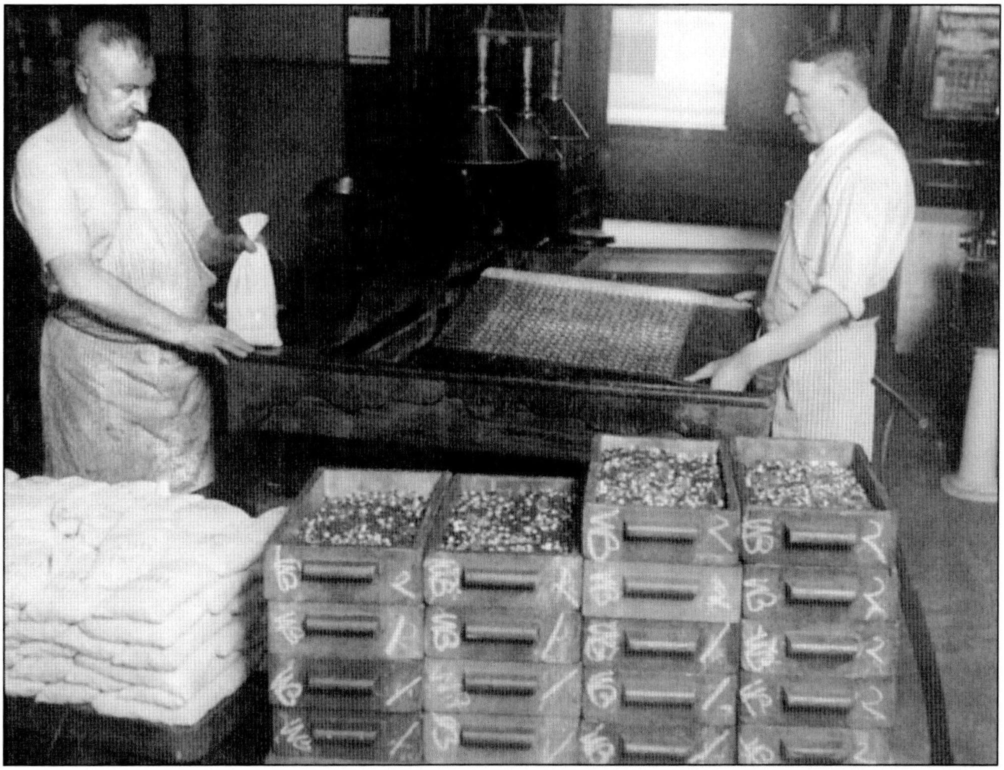

These two Philadelphia Mint employees are counting and bagging dimes in 1916. As with many other steps, this part of the process involves more automation today than it did when this photograph was taken. In many cases, bags of new coins leave the US Mint for the Federal Reserve, the nation's central banking system, which manages the money supply in the United States. (Courtesy of the Library of Congress, Francis B. Johnston Photograph Collection.)

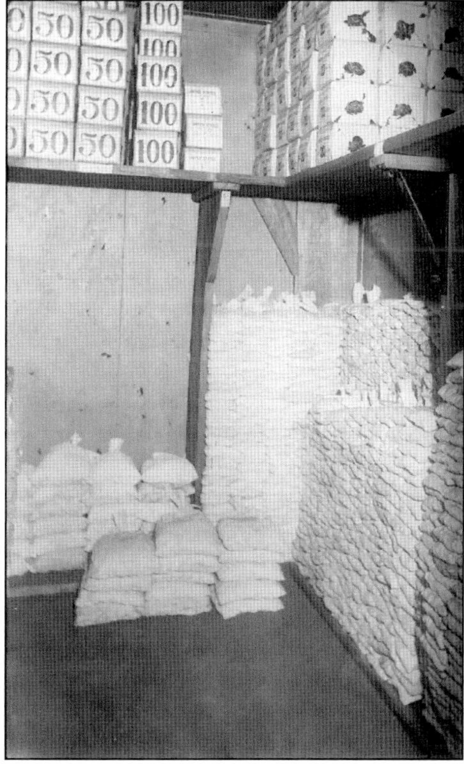

Bags of new coins from the US Mint await distribution inside a Federal Reserve vault in 1914, along with stacks of "paper" currency notes (actually made from a mixture of cotton and linen) produced by the Bureau of Engraving and Printing. While coinage generally enters circulation by way of the Federal Reserve, new coins may also be shipped from the mint directly to private banking institutions, stores, and other destinations. Meanwhile, most bullion coins are delivered to authorized precious metals dealers, while collectible coins are shipped to those who order them, including coin collectors and coin dealers throughout the world. (Courtesy of the Library of Congress.)

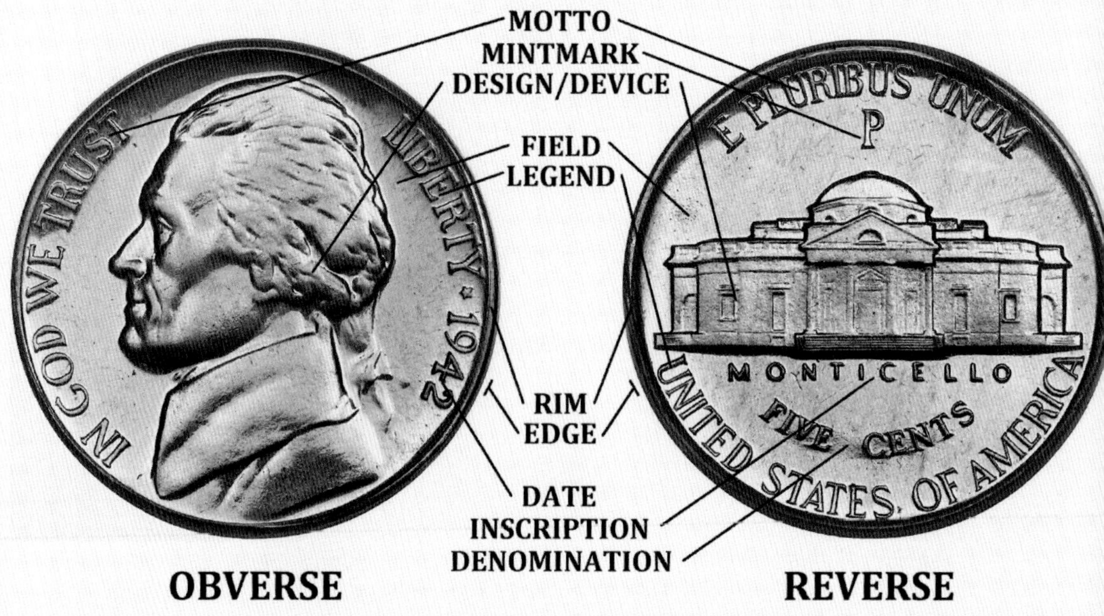

The lexicon of a numismatist is filled with terminology that may be unfamiliar to most people, but they are words that are important to know for anyone who wants to better understand coins. Some of the terms above have already been used in this chapter, and will appear elsewhere in this book. Those who familiarize themselves with these terms and their meanings will more easily navigate this book and become more knowledgeable about coins and the world of numismatics. (Courtesy of Heritage Auctions, www.HA.com, and Kelly McMorrow-Hernandez.)

Two

The First Philadelphia Mint

In Operation from 1792 to 1833

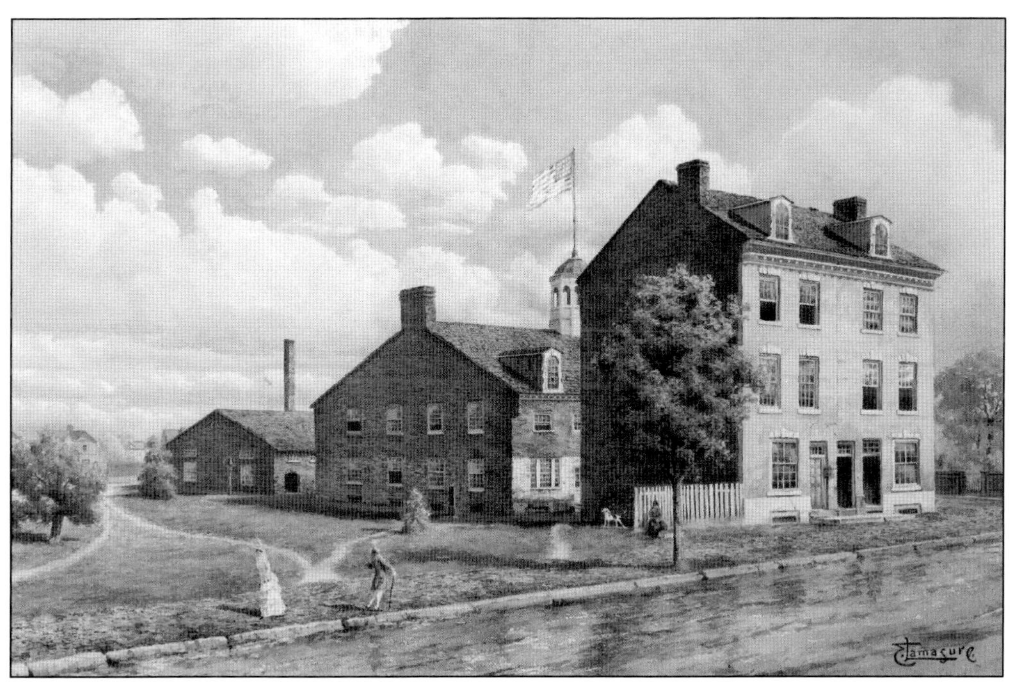

Philadelphia-born artist Edwin Lamasure Jr. (1866–1916) painted this 1914 watercolor titled "Ye Olde Mint." This is the image of the first Philadelphia Mint that many have carried in their minds and hearts for generations. Featuring three buildings on a bucolic spread, the painting is more of a whimsical representation of the early US Mint. In fact, the original mint consisted of several buildings tightly packed on a small lot that was eventually surrounded by tall, urban buildings. (Courtesy of Leonard Augsburger and Joel Orosz.)

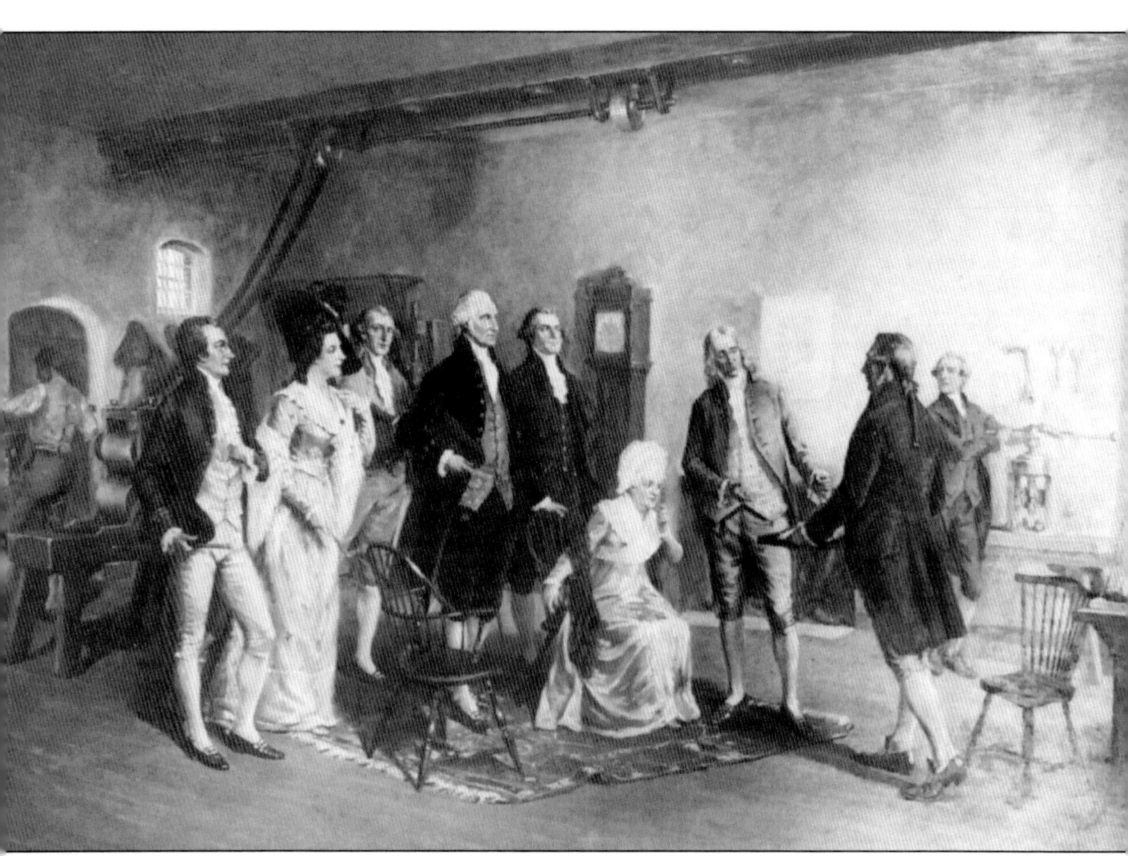

This famous oil-on-canvas painting by John Ward Dunsmore, "Washington Inspecting the First Money Coined by the United States," depicts various US Mint and government luminaries in Philadelphia, including Martha Washington, seated, as she inspects half dismes that many scholars say were made from the Washingtons' own household silver. Other figures prominently featured are, from left to right, Alexander Hamilton, Elizabeth Hamilton, Tobias Lear, George Washington, Thomas Jefferson, David Rittenhouse, chief coiner Henry Voigt with a tray of coins for inspection, and coin engraver Adam Eckfeldt by the coin press. On the far left in the background is a mint worker whose back is turned. This 1914 painting should be seen as an approximate representation of events, as the work was commissioned more than 120 years after the 1792 striking of half dismes occurred, but it is nonetheless historically significant in the numismatic world and holds a treasured place in Philadelphia culture. (Courtesy of the Library of Congress.)

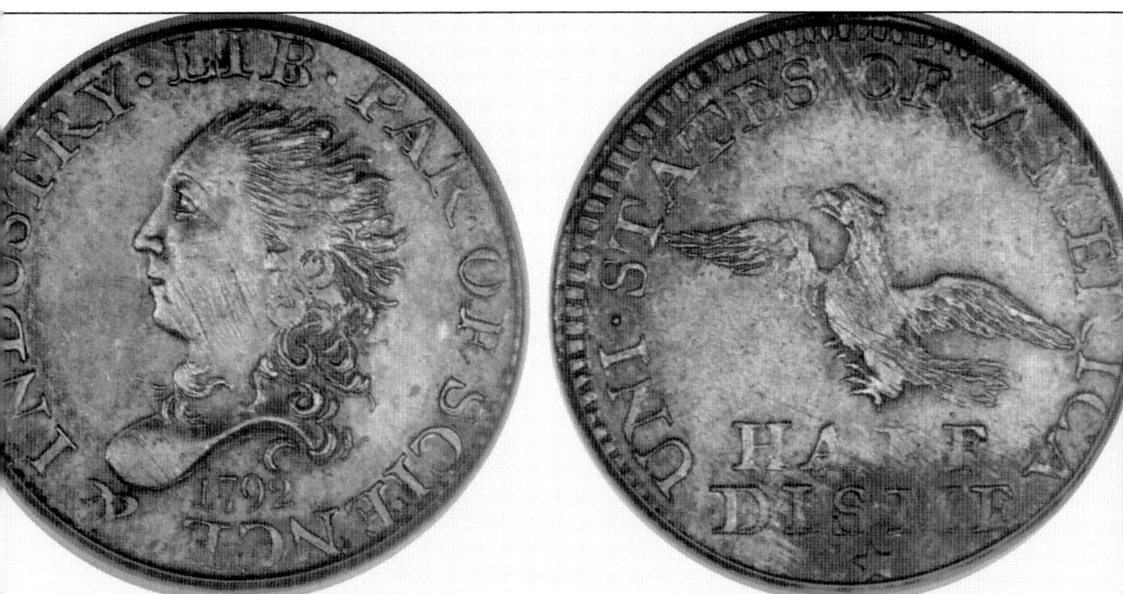

The coin Martha Washington is inspecting in the painting on the opposite page is a 1792 half disme, illustrated here. A representation of Liberty appears on the coin's obverse (left), along with the date 1792. The inscription "LIB [Liberty] PAR [Parent] OF SCIENCE & INDUSTRY" traces the coin's rim. The coin's reverse (right) shows an eagle in flight along with the legend "UNI [United] STATES OF AMERICA" and the denomination "HALF DISME." A total of 1,500 half dismes were produced during a first striking in July 1792, and all were received by Thomas Jefferson, who recorded the transaction in his accounting logbook as "1,500 half dismes of the new coinage." According to his logbook, Jefferson distributed the new coins over the next few days, giving many of them to children and servants. It is estimated that only about 250 of these 1792 half disme exist today. Each is worth many thousands of dollars, and all are considered important relics of American history. (Courtesy of Heritage Auctions, www.HA.com.)

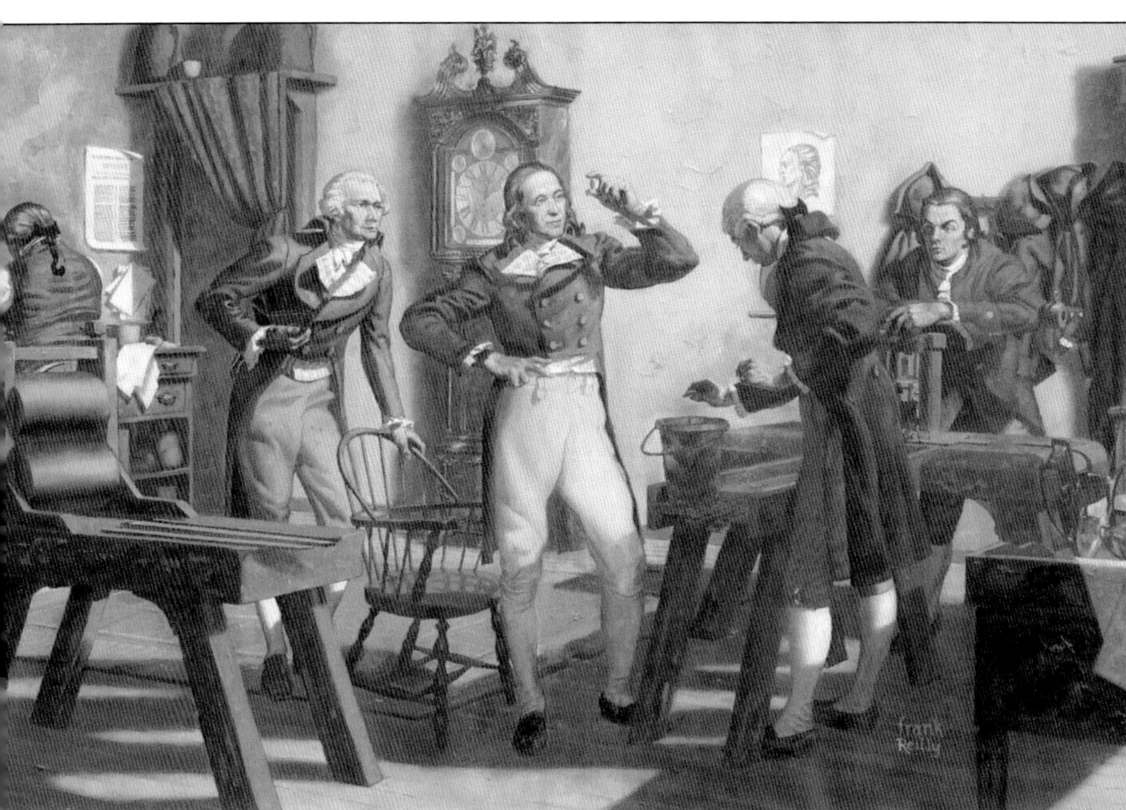

Artist Frank Reilly created this 1947 work, "Director of the First US Mint, Inspecting Initial Coinage, Philadelphia, 1792." Depicted are a coin-rolling machine on the left and a coin press in the background. Despite a few technical inaccuracies in the representation of the minting equipment of the era, this painting captures David Rittenhouse, center, inspecting a new half disme, represented here in proportions much larger than its actual size. Other figures in this image are less recognizable, though the man holding the purse for the new coins may be George Washington or Alexander Hamilton. (Courtesy of Leonard Augsburger and Joel Orosz.)

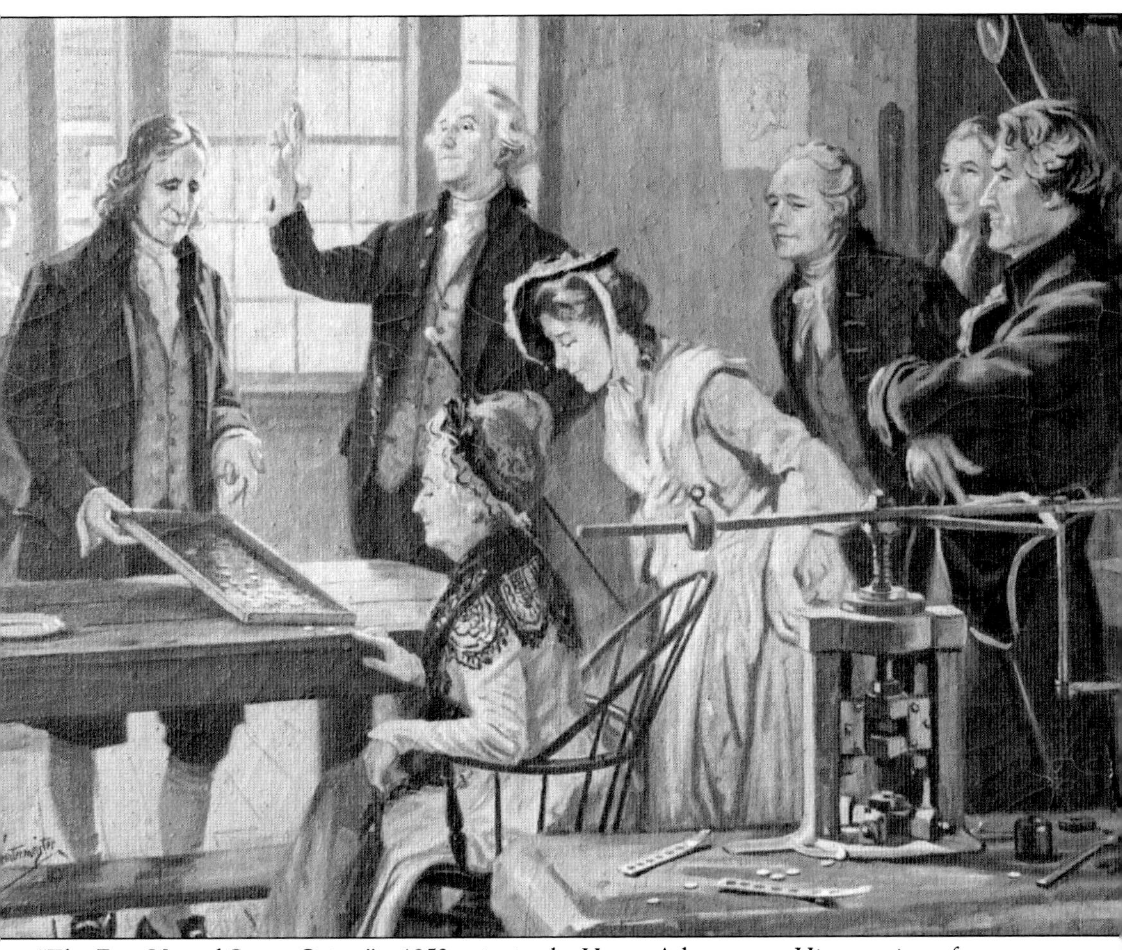

"The First United States Coins," a 1953 painting by Henry Adamaugust Hintermeister, features George Washington, center and standing, inspecting a coin, as his wife, Martha, sits poring over coins in a tray held by David Rittenhouse. Chief coiner Henry Voigt stands in the background at left, while Elizabeth Hamilton peers over Martha Washington's shoulder at the coins in the tray. Directly behind Elizabeth Hamilton is her husband, Alexander, and behind him in the background is a figure numismatic scholars identify as either mint contractor Adam Eckfeldt or George Washington's personal secretary, Tobias Lear. While the various images presented on these pages portray differing perspectives on how the initial presentation of US coinage may have unfolded, all of these paintings depict many of the same figures, while the latter portraits by Reilly and Hintermeister borrow various elements from Dunsmore's work. (Courtesy of Leonard Augsburger and Joel Orosz.)

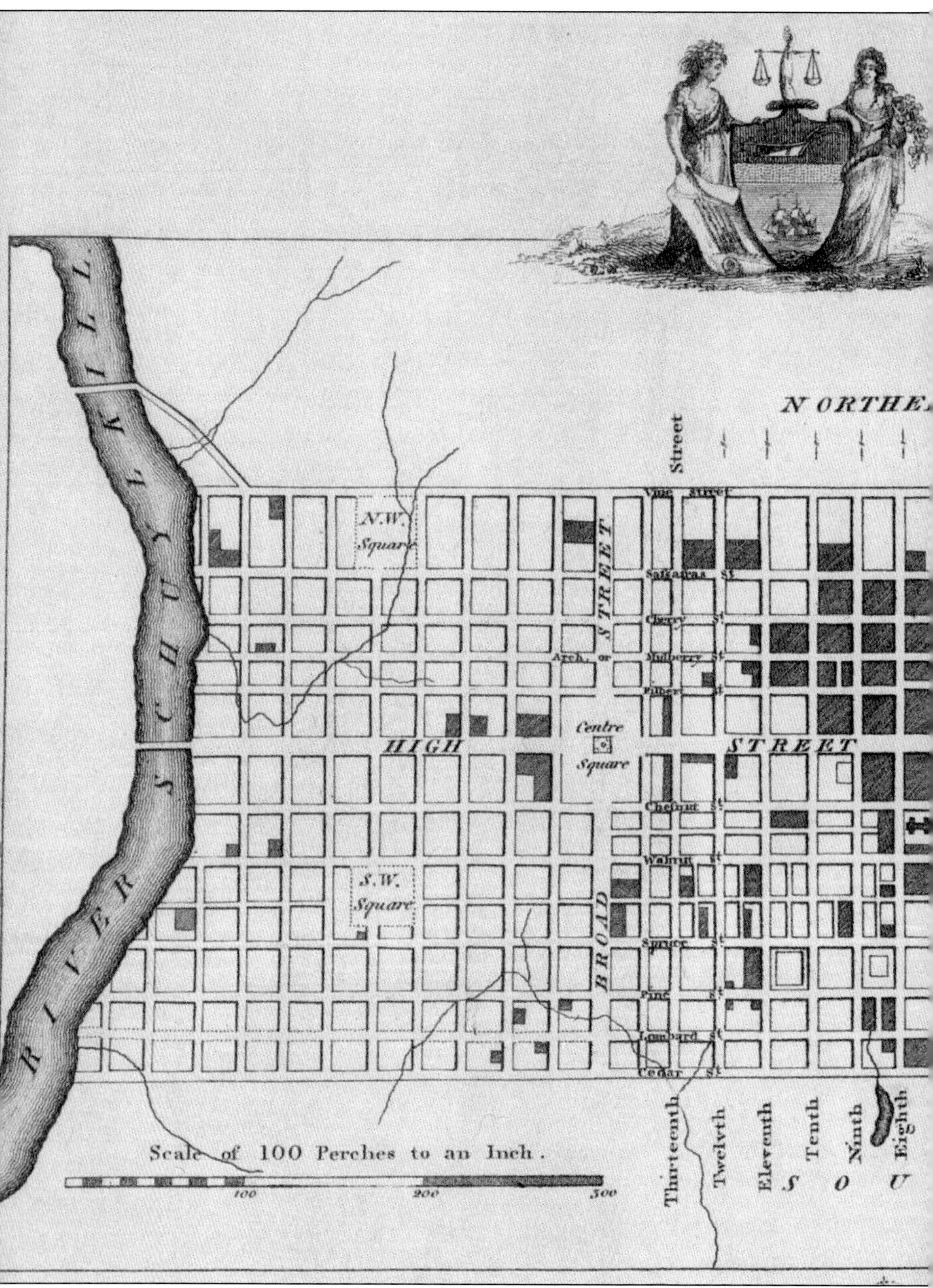
RIVER SCHUYLKILL
N.W. Square
S.W. Square
Centre Square
HIGH STREET
BROAD STREET
NORTHE
Vine Street
Sassafras St
Cherry St
Arch or Mulberry St
Filbert St
Chesnut St
Walnut St
Spruce St
Pine St
Lombard St
Cedar St
Thirteenth
Twelvth
Eleventh
Tenth
Ninth
Eighth
S O U
Scale of 100 Perches to an Inch.
100
200
300

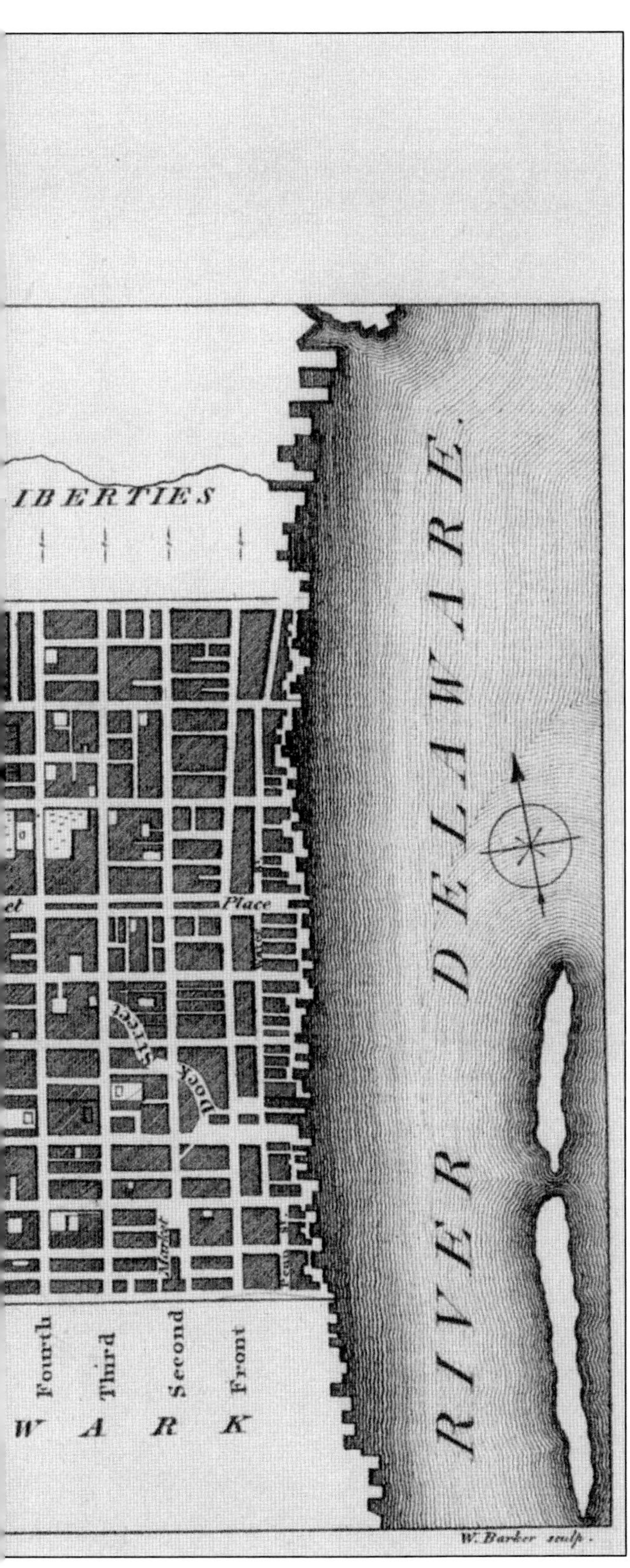

This c. 1804 map of the city of Philadelphia sets the scene for the surroundings of the US Mint during its early years. While a bustling metropolis by measures of the early 1800s, the city's proportions at the time look quaint by today's standards. Noteworthy in the version of Philadelphia depicted on this map is that the city's boundaries are depicted running east to west from the Delaware River to the Schuylkill River, and north to south from Vine Street to Cedar Street (present-day South Street). While the additions of Interstate 95 along the Delaware River and Interstate 676 across Center City have vastly altered the landscape since the early 1800s, the overall street grid as presented on this map remains today, along with the original naming and numbering of most streets. The original US Mint was located nearest to the intersection of Filbert and Seventh Streets in the upper right of this map. (Courtesy of Leonard Augsburger and Joel Orosz.)

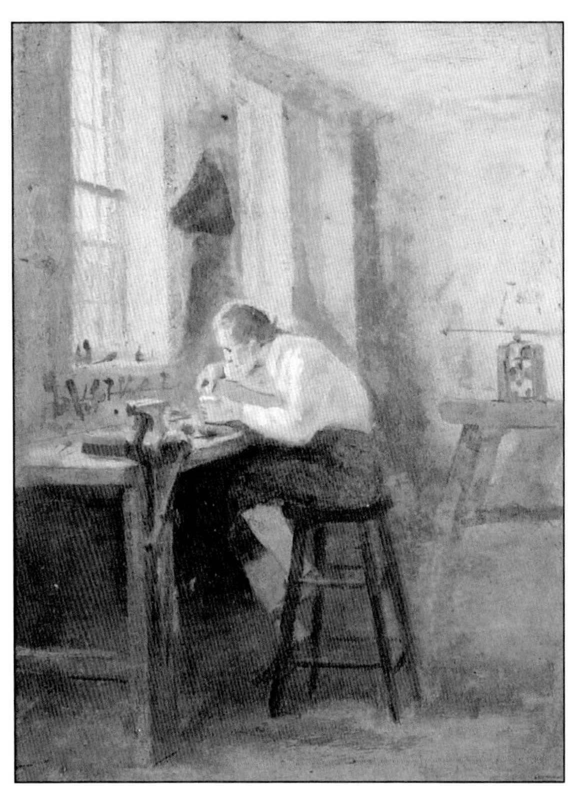

The portrait at left by John Ward Dunsmore depicts a solitary coin engraver sitting on a stool as he works at his desk with many engraving tools scattered about the work area. In the background stands an early coin press atop a workbench. The press depicted here is an artistic rendering of the "first press" seen in the 1930s photograph below. The handpress is one of several types of equipment used at the first US Mint. (Left, courtesy of Leonard Augsburger and Joel Orosz; below, courtesy of the Pennsylvania State Archives.)

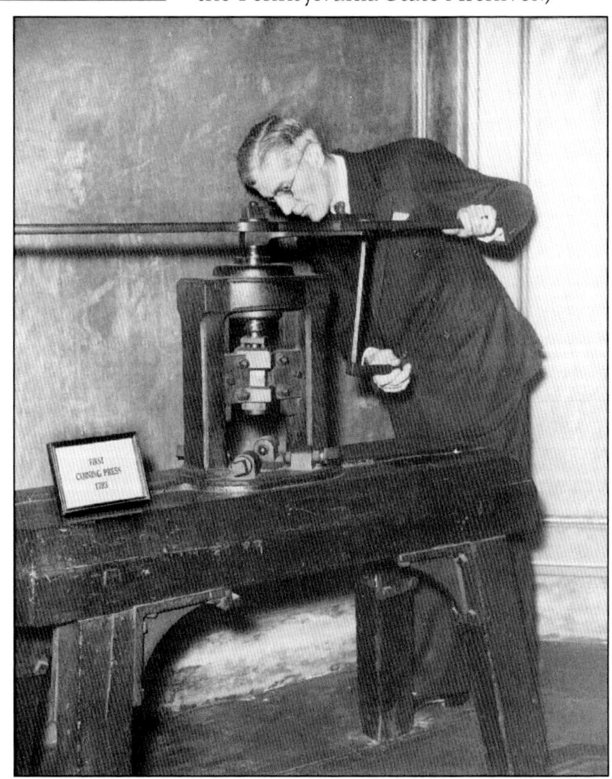

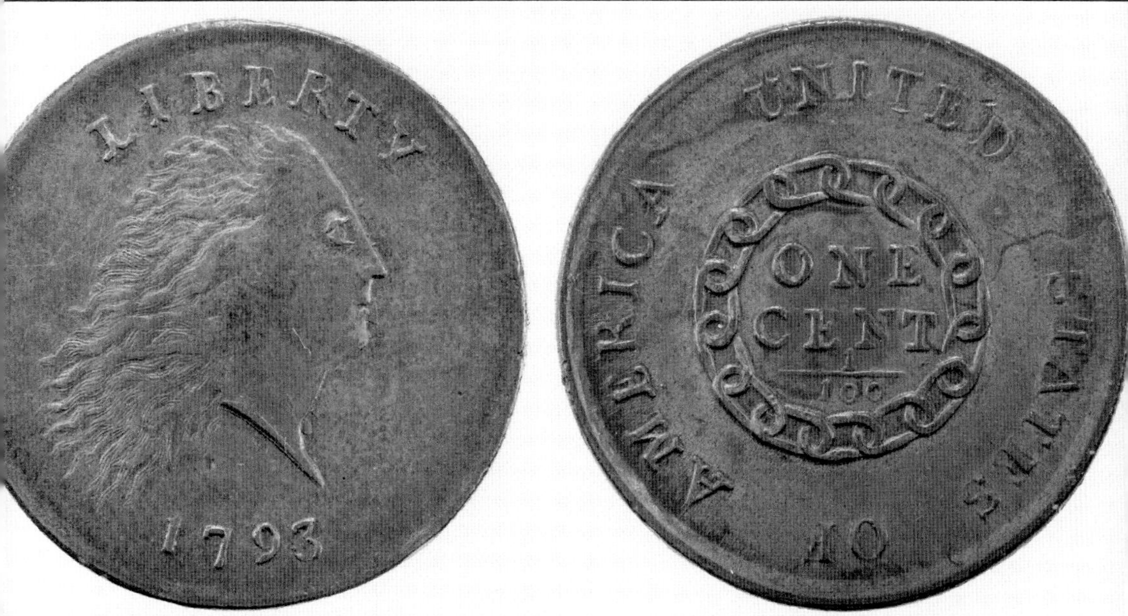

This 1793 one-cent coin was among the very first coins officially produced at the US Mint in Philadelphia for circulation. The coin, generally known by numismatists as the "Flowing Hair with Chain Reverse" type, was produced for only a very short time in 1793 before changes were made to both sides of the coin, including the replacement of the chain on the reverse with a wreath. The US Mint made 36,103 of these coins, which are often dubbed "large cents" by coin collectors because these early "pennies" measure 26 to 27 millimeters in diameter, or about 7 millimeters wider than the current "small" one-cent coin. The United States has never struck a coin denominated as a "penny." Only Great Britain and its commonwealth nations use coins officially known as the penny. In the United States, the official name of this denomination is simply "one cent." (Courtesy of Heritage Auctions, www.HA.com.)

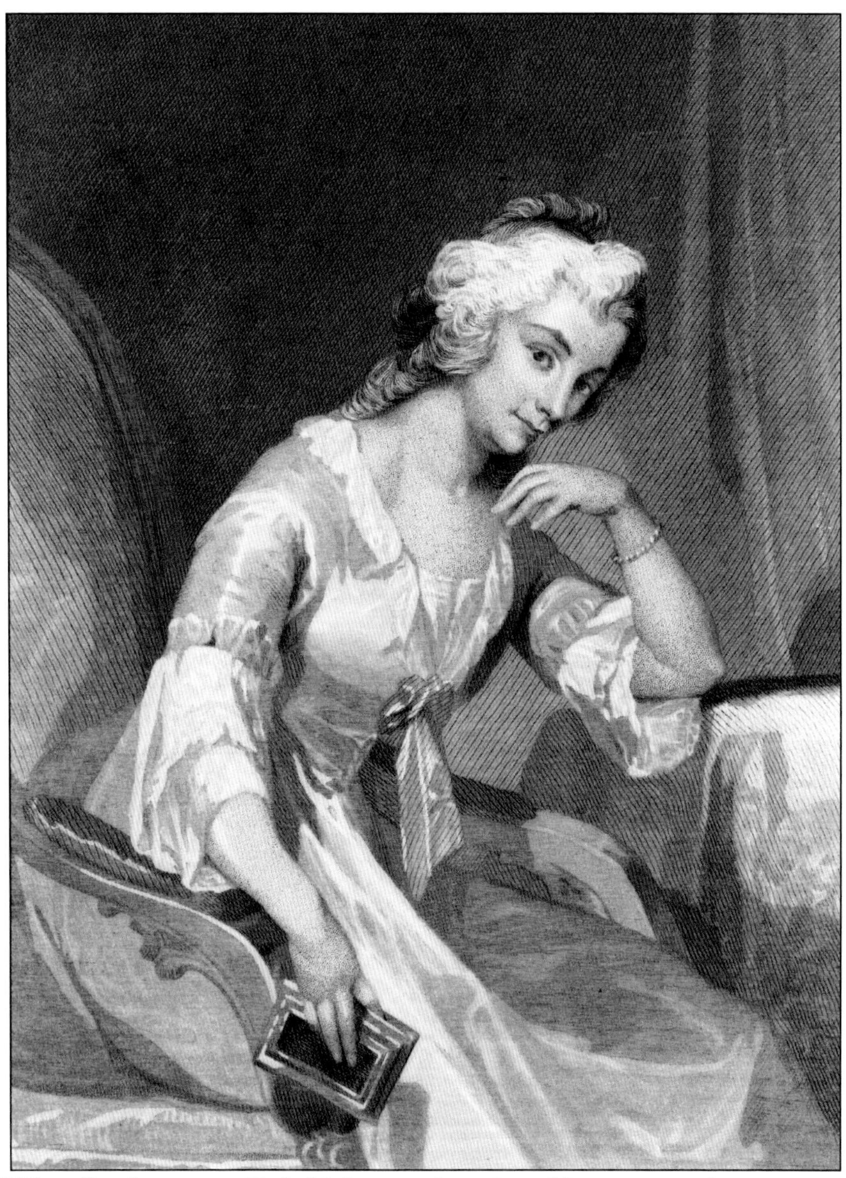

Anne Willing Bingham was a Philadelphia socialite whose likeness, according to a popular but widely refuted legend, appears on several famous early US coins. She was born on August 1, 1764, the oldest daughter of Thomas Willing, the president of the First Bank of the United States. She was married to American statesman William Bingham and regularly corresponded with Thomas Jefferson, with whom she shared concerns that an individual's rights needed greater protections than those promised in the US Constitution alone. Jefferson incorporated her ideas within the framework of the Bill of Rights, which Virginia representative (later president) James Madison drafted in a document approved by Congress in 1789 and ratified in 1791. Bingham, considered one of the most beautiful women of her day, modeled for many portraits by renowned painter Gilbert Stuart. It is widely believed, but unproven, that Stuart's sketches served as the basis for a depiction of Liberty that appeared on several US coins during the late 1790s and early 1800s. Sadly, Anne Willing Bingham died of an illness while en route to Europe in 1801. She is buried in Bermuda. (Courtesy of the Library of Congress.)

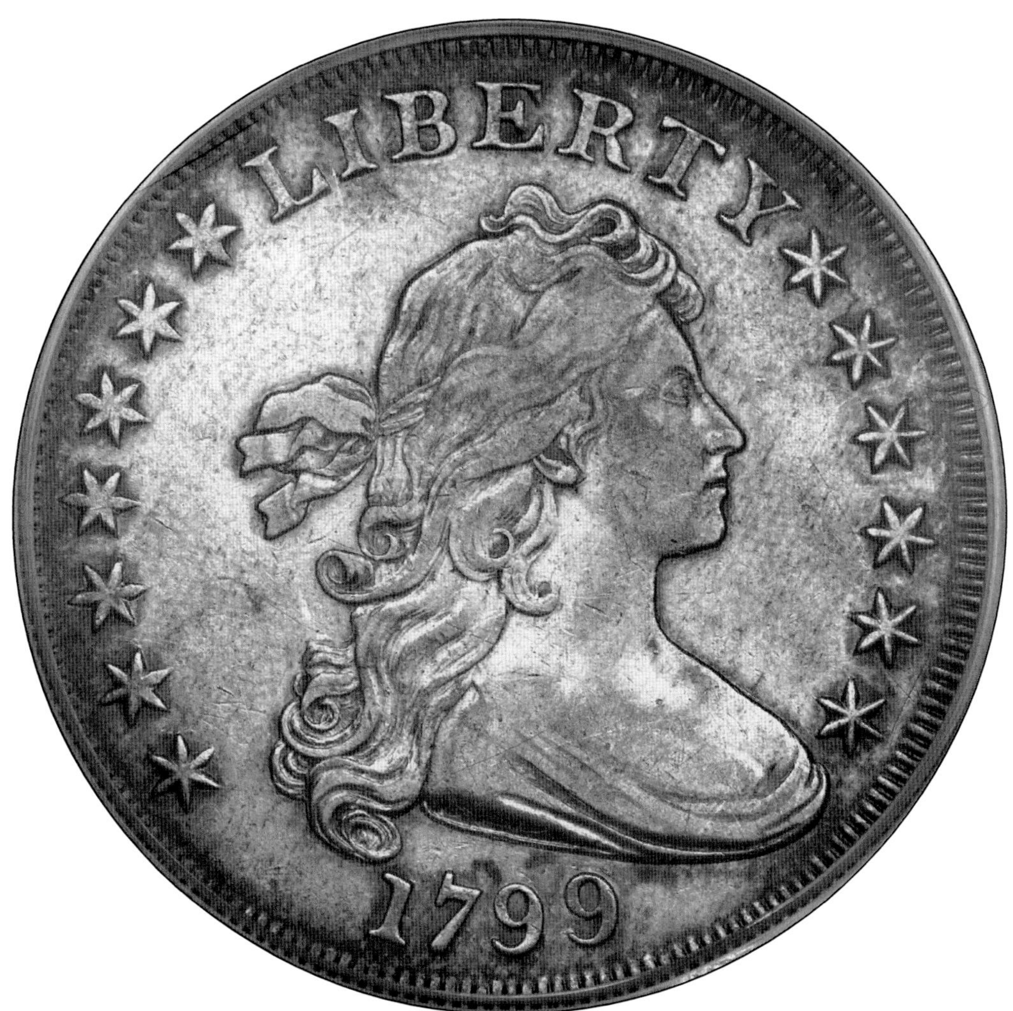

Some claim Anne Willing Bingham was the model for this coin design, known by numismatists as the "Draped Bust" type. The design, artistically translated for use on coinage by first chief engraver of the US Mint Robert Scot, is theorized to have been based on a sketch of Bingham created by Gilbert Stuart. Variations of this design were used on several US denominations around the turn of the 19th century and replaced the widely unpopular Flowing Hair design. The Draped Bust design was generally used on US coinage from 1795 through 1807 and appears on the obverses of the half cent, large cent, half dime, dime, quarter, half-dollar, and dollar (the obverse of the latter is seen here). While numismatists may never know for certain whether Gilbert Stuart's sketches of Bingham were used in designing Draped Bust coinage, there is no denying that Stuart has a significant place in history. Stuart, who produced portraits of the first six presidents and whose "Athenaeum" portrait of George Washington appears on the one-dollar bill, soared to fame while living in Germantown (now part of Philadelphia). The Gilbert Stuart House site is in Philadelphia at the intersection of Chestnut and North Fifth Streets. (Courtesy of Heritage Auctions, www.HA.com.)

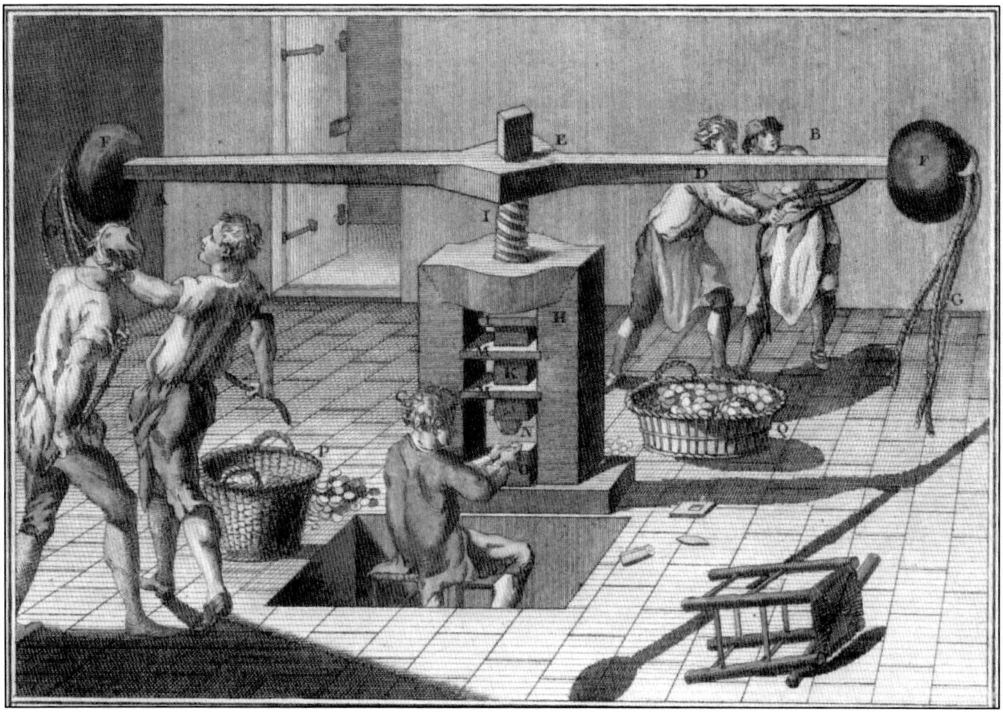

These illustrations from editor Denis Diderot's *Encyclopédie* depict how coins were made when minting equipment was powered by men and horses, similar to the equipment at the first US Mint in Philadelphia. The above illustration features the process of using a screw press to strike coins. Blank coins, known as planchets, are seen in a basket to the left of the person placing the blanks under the die, which is pushed downward by a weighted screw press. Below is the type of horse-powered mill equipment that was originally used at the Philadelphia Mint before steam-powered engines replaced the horses after the fire at the mint in 1816. (Both, courtesy of Leonard Augsburger and Joel Orosz.)

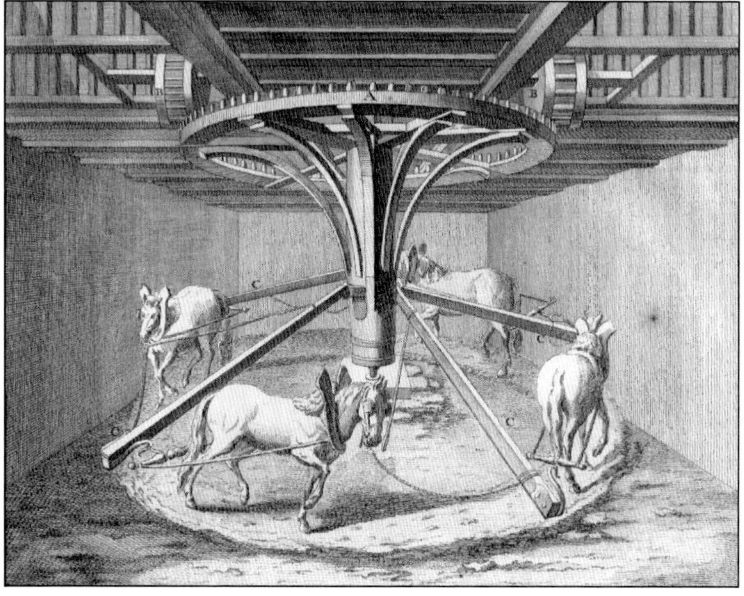

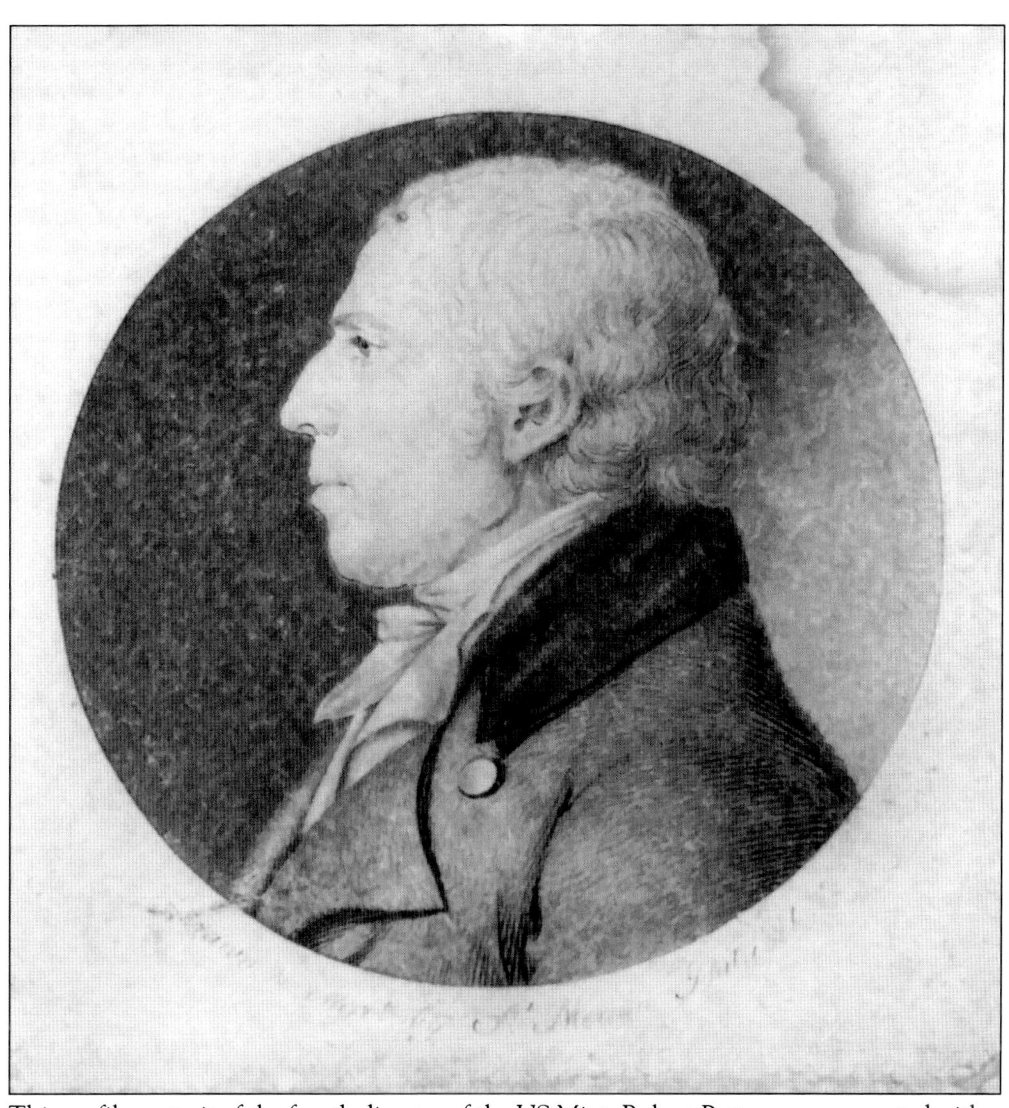

This profile portrait of the fourth director of the US Mint, Robert Patterson, was created with a copperplate that once sat on Patterson's desk. Born on a farm in Ireland in 1743, Patterson came to the United States in 1768 and spent his first days as a new American in Philadelphia. He is mainly remembered by numismatists for his tenure as the mint director from 1806 until shortly before his death in 1824; however; he also dedicated many years of his life to education. In 1774, he became the principal of Wilmington Academy in Delaware, a position he held until the onset of the Revolutionary War caused the relocation of students. Patterson enlisted in the Delaware militia as an instructor before serving in the medical corps and, later, as a brigade major. In 1779, Patterson became a professor at the University of Pennsylvania, where he taught mathematics and natural philosophy. He served as the school's vice provost from 1810 through 1813. Among his many other achievements was helping found the Franklin Institute of Philadelphia, a science education and research center that was established in 1824. His son Robert M. Patterson served as the sixth director of the US Mint from 1835 through 1851. (Courtesy of John Zieman and Alexandrea Zieman.)

Photography was a burgeoning technology during the 1830s when the US Mint transitioned its operations to its second location in Philadelphia. Known as a daguerreotype, this image was taken by mint employee Joseph Saxton around September 25, 1839, from a window in the second US Mint facility in Philadelphia and shows many architectural details of Philadelphia Central High School at Walnut and Juniper Streets. It is believed by many scholars to be the earliest surviving daguerreotype taken in the United States. The image is presented here to represent the early history of the Philadelphia Mint and also to document the evolution of photography itself, a technology that rapidly evolved during the 19th century, when the US Mint was also coming of age. (Courtesy of the Historical Society of Pennsylvania.)

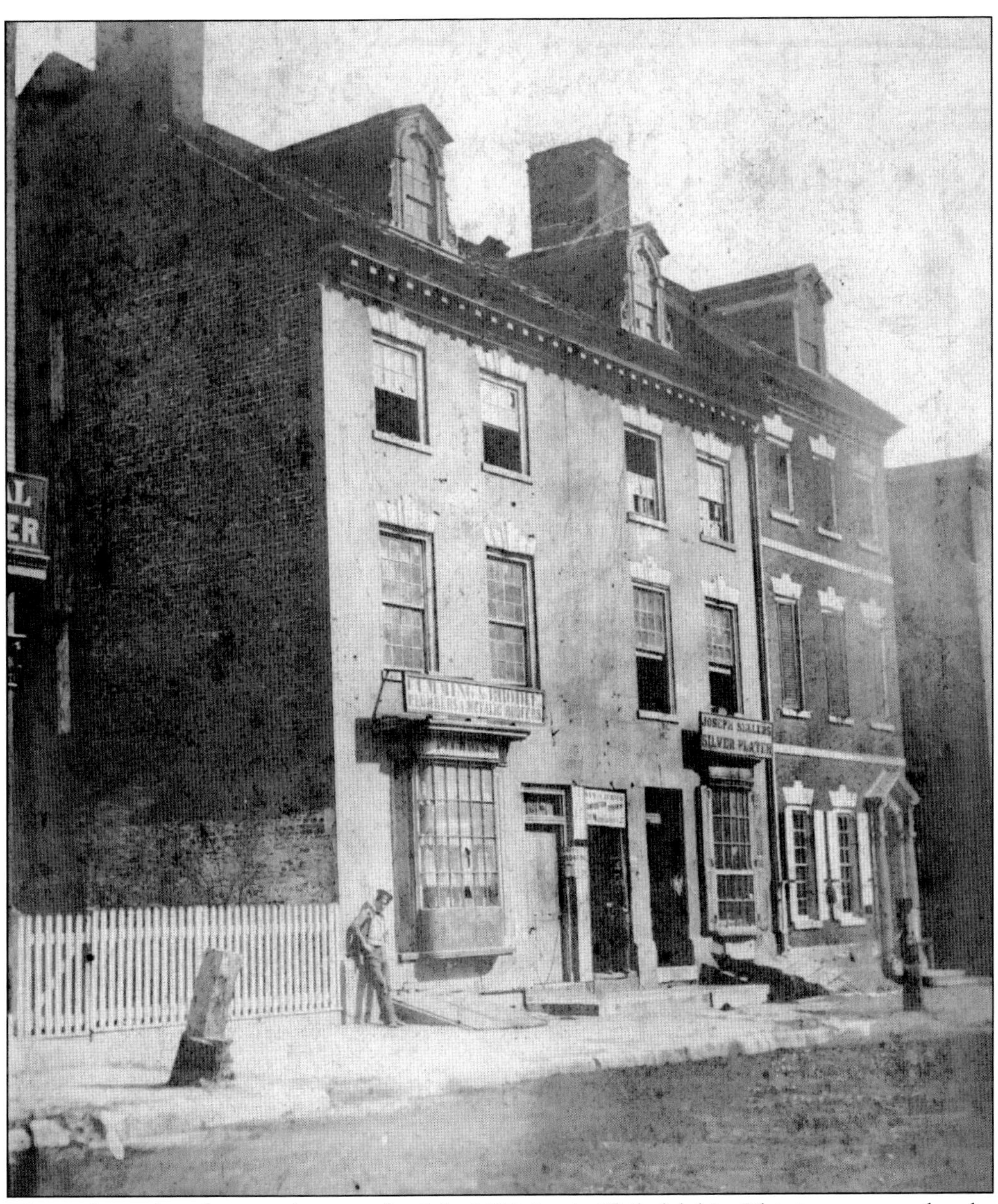

This is the earliest known photograph of the US Mint in Philadelphia. This image was taken by Philadelphia painter and pioneer photographer Frederick DeBeurg Richards in 1854 and shows the Front Building that faced North Seventh Street. The photograph was shot in an effort to capture Philadelphia's 18th-century public, commercial, and residential buildings and was included in a scrapbook of about 120 photographs commissioned by Philadelphia antiquarian Charles A. Poulson. By the time this photograph of the Front Building was taken, the structure was no longer serving as the US Mint, which had relocated to a new building at the intersection of Chestnut and Juniper Streets. The building pictured here would today stand a half-block north of Market Street and a quarter block south of Arch Street, immediately east of where Filbert Street intersects with Seventh Street. Standing on the site today is a complex built by the US government in the mid-1960s that includes a federal courthouse and offices for the Internal Revenue Service and Federal Bureau of Investigation. (Courtesy of Leonard Augsburger and Joel Orosz.)

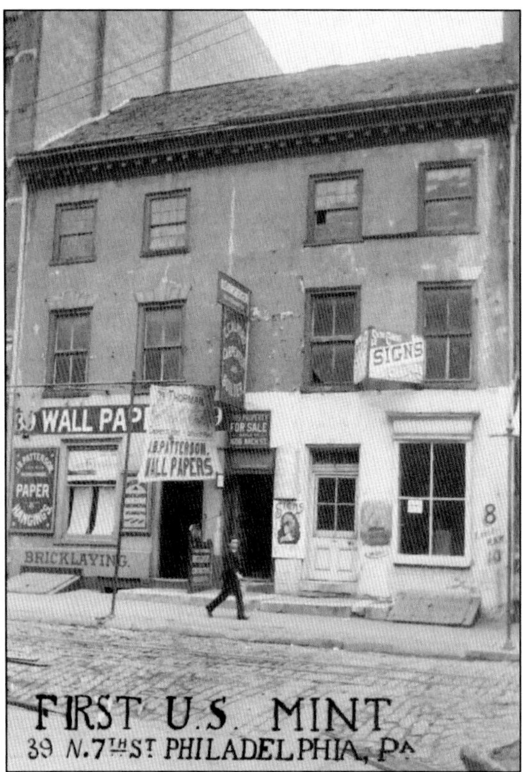

This c. 1898 photograph features the former US Mint's Front Building. The structure evidently served many purposes during its post-mint existence; here, it is the location of a wallpaper merchant, bricklayer, and sign-maker. (Courtesy of Leonard Augsburger and Joel Orosz.)

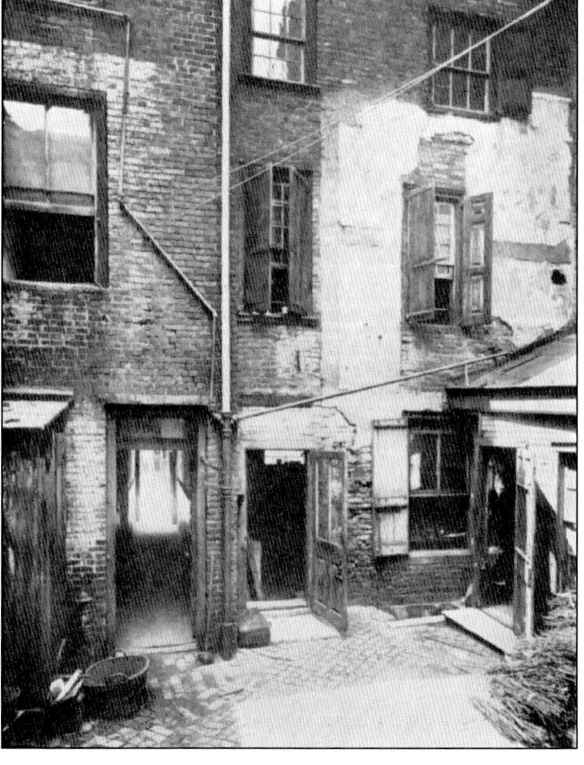

This image features the back side of the Front Building, a perspective rarely seen in photographs. The interior area of the first floor is visible, and one can see straight through the building, measuring only 33 feet deep and about 37 feet wide. Also seen in this photograph is the courtyard area between the rear of the Front Building and the other buildings in the back of the property. On the right is part of the structure that once served as the watch house for the mint's security personnel. (Courtesy of Leonard Augsburger and Joel Orosz.)

The building that served as the original US Mint continued evolving in appearance as businesses came and went. In this 1903 photograph, the Front Building houses an umbrella store and cigar shop. A few years later, Philadelphia historian and electrician Frank H. Stewart bought the former US Mint property. (Courtesy of Leonard Augsburger and Joel Orosz.)

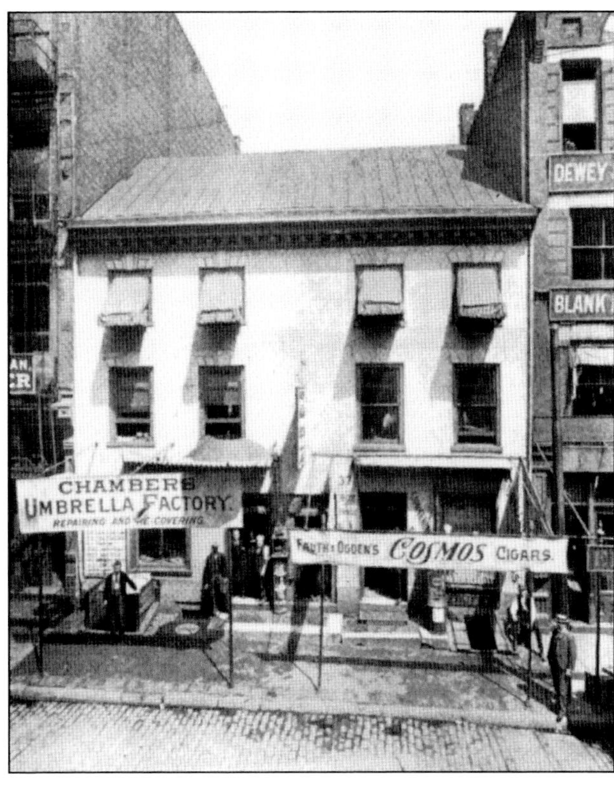

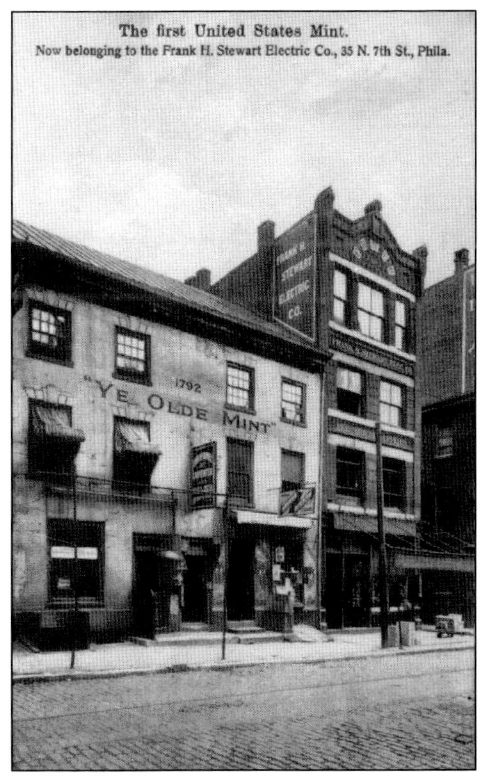

This 1908 postcard declares, "The first United States Mint. Now belonging to the Frank H. Stewart Electric Co." Stewart's building, the one standing taller on the right, had existed for many years prior to its purchase by Stewart. Ever the historian, Stewart painted "1792 'Ye Olde Mint' " on the facade of the Front Building in 1907. At this time, "Ye Olde Mint" housed Chambers Umbrella Factory and Lipschutz 44 Cigar Company, addressed, from left to right, as 39 and 37 North Seventh, respectively. (Courtesy of Leonard Augsburger and Joel Orosz.)

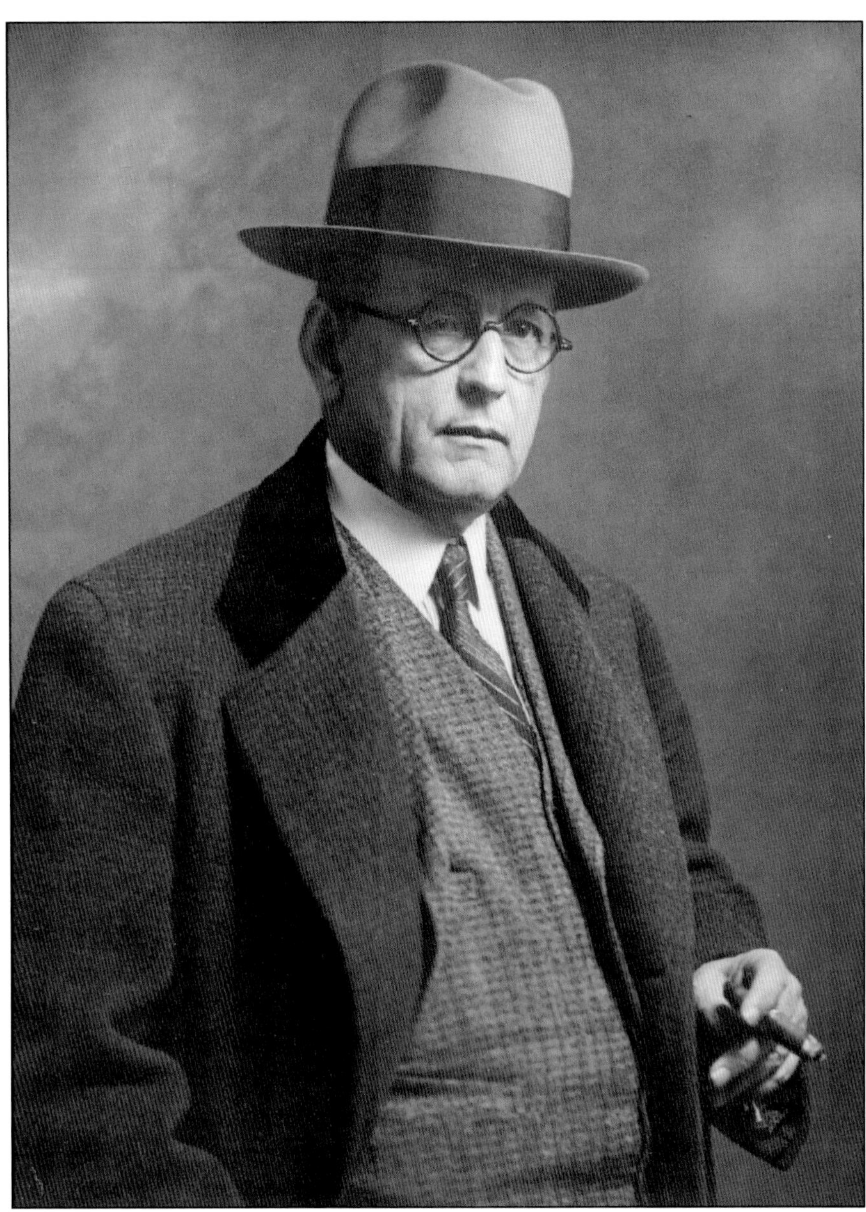

Frank H. Stewart (1873–1948), photographed here around 1945, founded Frank H. Stewart Electric Company in 1894 and eventually rented the building at 35 North Seventh Street. As the use of electricity boomed throughout Philadelphia in the first years of the 20th century, so did Stewart's thriving business, which outgrew its original quarters. In 1907, Stewart purchased the adjoining property and the three buildings on it that had once served as the first Philadelphia Mint. Stewart labored to find preservationists who could save the former mint buildings and remove them from the property, but he was unsuccessful in his efforts. Disappointed, he removed many relics from the original mint buildings prior to razing the structures in 1911 to make way for a new building to house his growing electrical supply business. In the years following the demolition of the original mint buildings, Stewart commissioned Edwin Lamasure's "Ye Olde Mint" and John Ward Dunsmore's "Washington Inspecting the First Money Coined by the United States," both featured earlier in this chapter. (Courtesy of Leonard Augsburger and Joel Orosz.)

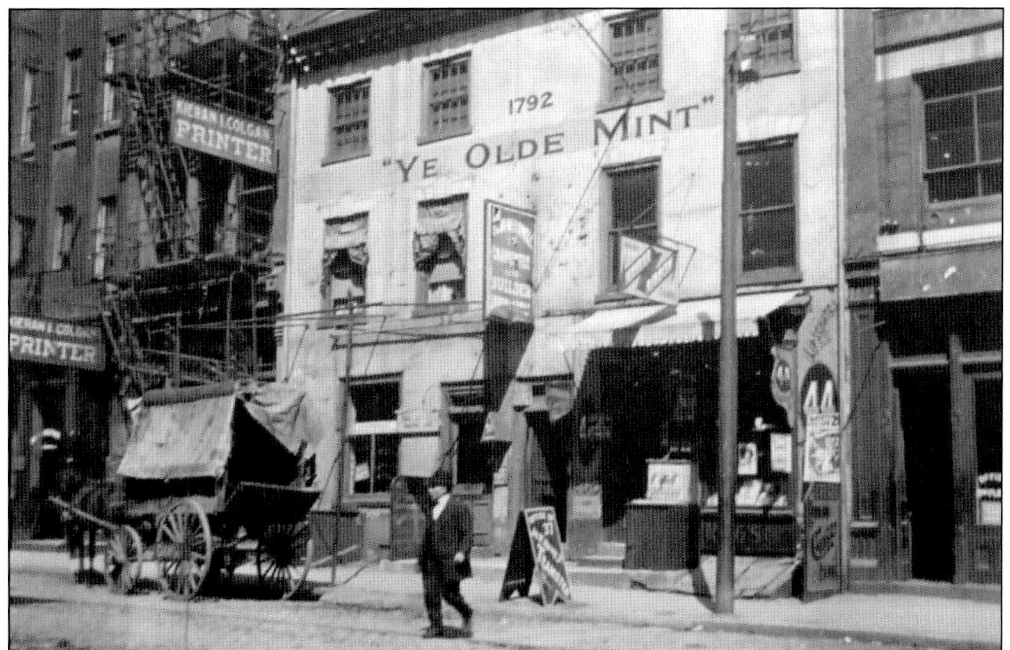

This c. 1910 photograph shows the original US Mint building in its waning years. At this point, the former mint building was occupied by a cigar company and carpentry workshop. Meanwhile, Stewart's electrical supply firm was booming next door on the right. (Courtesy of Leonard Augsburger and Joel Orosz.)

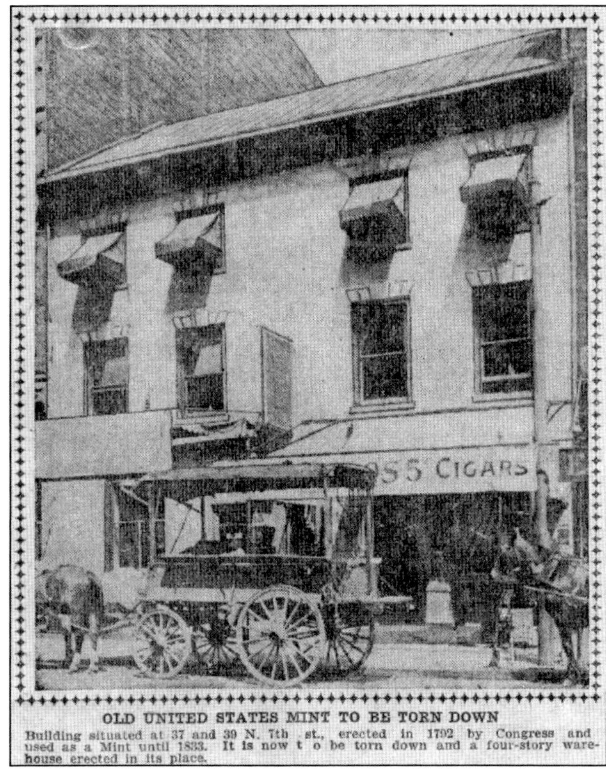

OLD UNITED STATES MINT TO BE TORN DOWN

Building situated at 37 and 39 N. 7th st., erected in 1792 by Congress and used as a Mint until 1833. It is now t o be torn down and a four-story warehouse erected in its place.

This clip from the April 24, 1907, edition of the *Evening Bulletin* forewarned of coming doom for the old mint building. "Old United States Mint To Be Torn Down," declares the headline. "Building situated at 37 and 39 N. 7th St., erected in 1792 by Congress and used as a mint until 1833. It is now to be torn down and a four-story warehouse erected in its place," reads the caption. In actuality, what replaced the former mint structures was an ornate six-story building erected by Frank H. Stewart and completed by 1914. (Courtesy of Leonard Augsburger and Joel Orosz.)

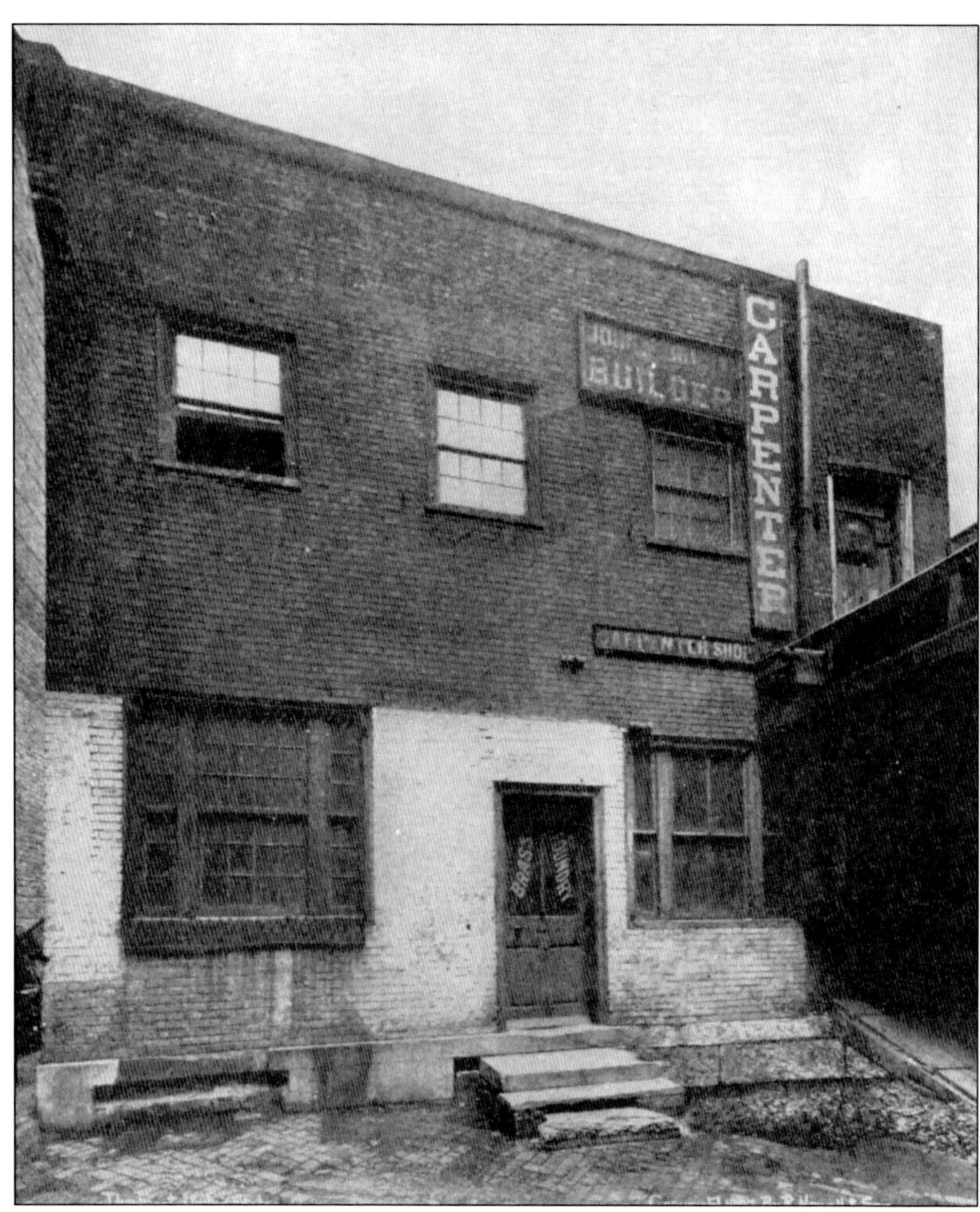

While the building that fronted Seventh Street has become to historians and others the most familiar aspect of the original Philadelphia Mint facility, there were other smaller structures on the property, with the largest of these being the "Middle Building," or as some historians call it, the "Coinage Building." Originally, the site of the Middle Building was a wood-frame structure that served as a horse-drawn mill, but this edifice and an adjoining rear building used for smelting were destroyed in an 1816 fire that temporarily interrupted minting operations. The Middle Building was reconstructed in 1816, and at this time, the horses, which powered mills for rolling metal, were replaced with more efficient steam-powered equipment. After the US Mint vacated the premises in 1833, the Middle Building and the adjoining structures were utilized by various occupants. Among these was a carpenter, as seen in this c. 1909 photograph of the Middle Building. (Courtesy of Leonard Augsburger and Joel Orosz.)

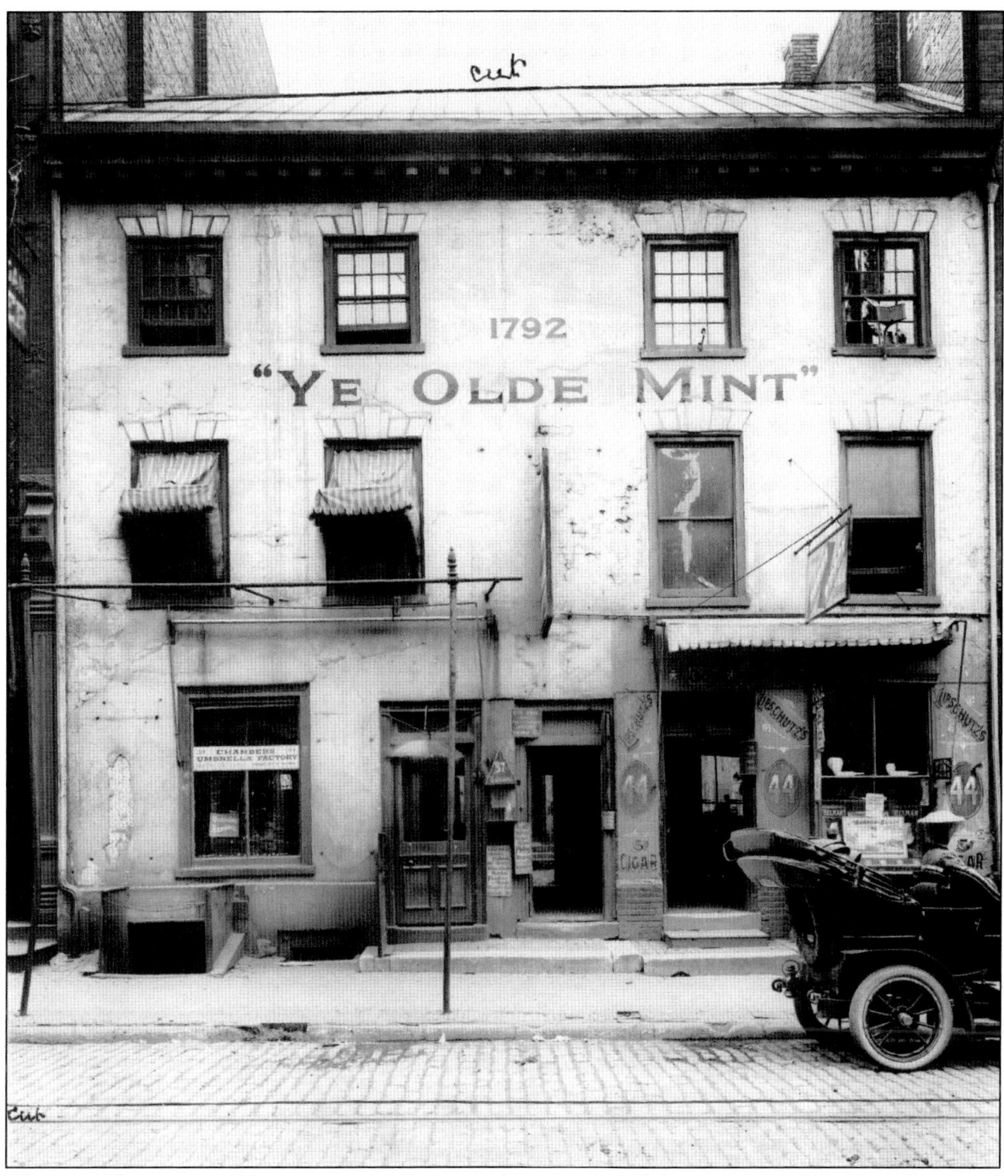

This is perhaps one of the most widely known photographs of the structure that formerly served as the first Philadelphia Mint. Taken during the building's last years before its demolition, the photograph, which is marked with vintage cropping instructions, is credited to Robert Newell & Son, a famous father-son photography company that was based in Philadelphia. Robert Newell was born in Burlington, New Jersey, in 1822 and relocated to Philadelphia as an adult. In 1855, he became a professional photographer, earning acclaim as a renowned portraitist. He opened a studio at 633 Arch Street, not far from the site of the original Philadelphia Mint. Eventually, Newell entered the genre of landscape and commercial photography. He opened a larger, posh gallery in 1865 at 626 Arch Street. In 1872, his son Henry joined his father's business as a professional photographer, and together, they recorded the late 19th-century Philadelphia scene, including the events surrounding the 1876 Centennial Exposition. They also compiled a popular series of photograph books titled *Old Landmarks & Relics of Philadelphia.* (Courtesy of Leonard Augsburger and Joel Orosz.)

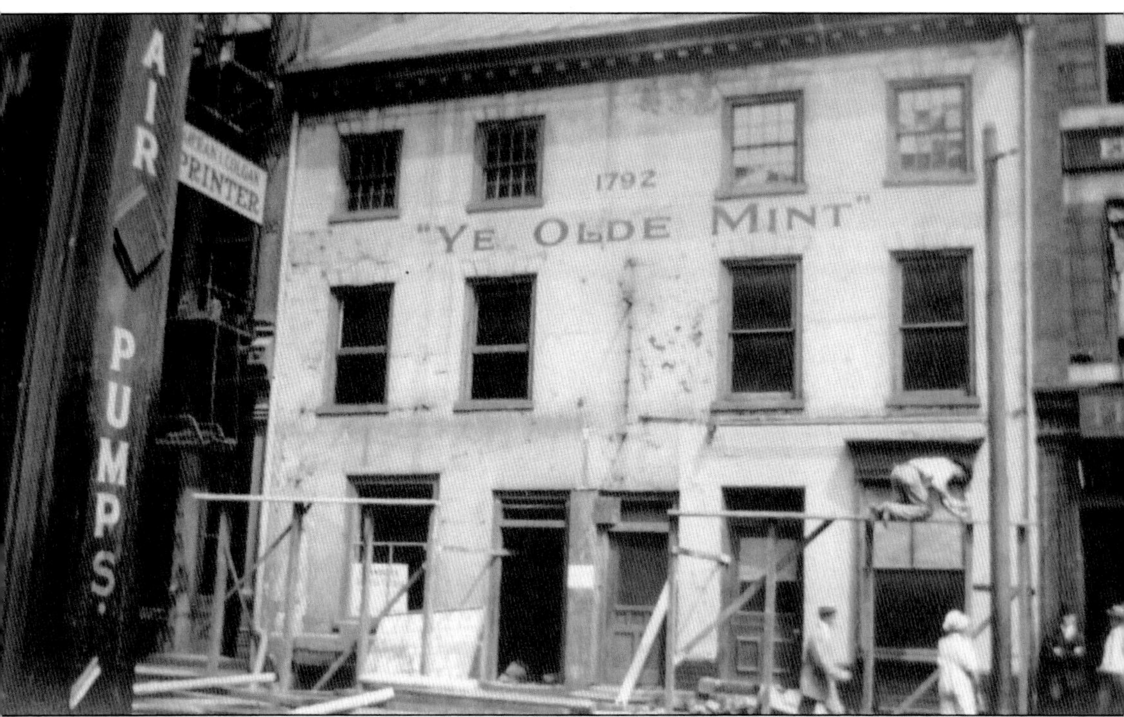

Taken on August 4, 1911, this is the last known photograph of the original mint building. At this point, demolition of the former US Mint structures was already underway. While demolition was the last option Frank H. Stewart considered for the historic landmark, it was also a sad reality, as there was virtually no interest from other organizations at the time to move the buildings elsewhere and preserve them. Meanwhile, Stewart's business needed room to expand. In the years following, Stewart diligently worked to document what he could of the former mint building. In 1924, he authored *History of the First United States Mint: Its People and Its Operations*. Among the information historians know of the original building is how and where operations took place throughout the facility. In the basement of the Front Building were gold and silver vaults. Deposit facilities, weighing rooms, and a press room occupied the first floor. The second floor housed offices for mint officials. An assay laboratory was on the third floor. In the rear areas of the mint's small property were other facilities, including a smelt house and mill. (Courtesy of Leonard Augsburger and Joel Orosz.)

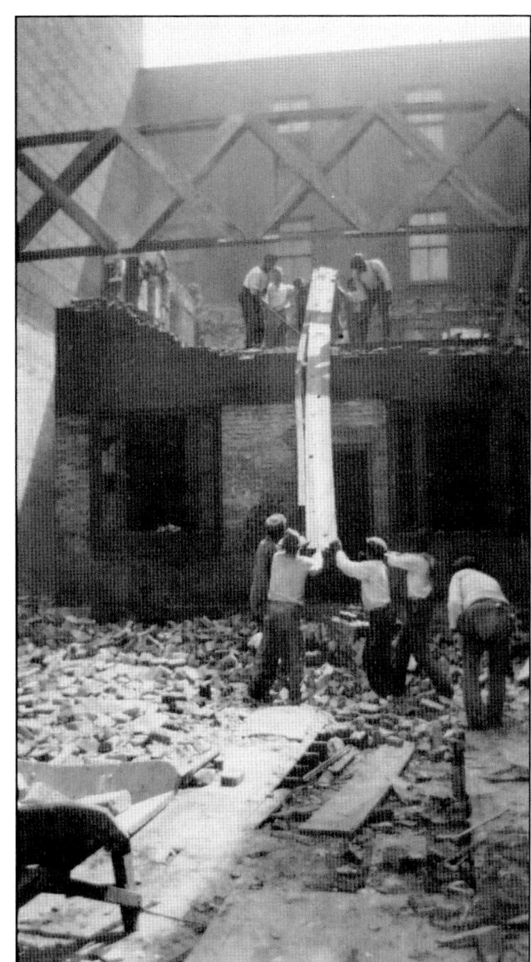

Demolition progressed rapidly on the nearly 120-year-old building. In the image at right, a roof truss from the Middle Building is lowered to the ground, while below, workers appear amid the billowing dust of falling debris as the historic landmark crumbles into piles of rubble. (Both, courtesy of Leonard Augsburger and Joel Orosz.)

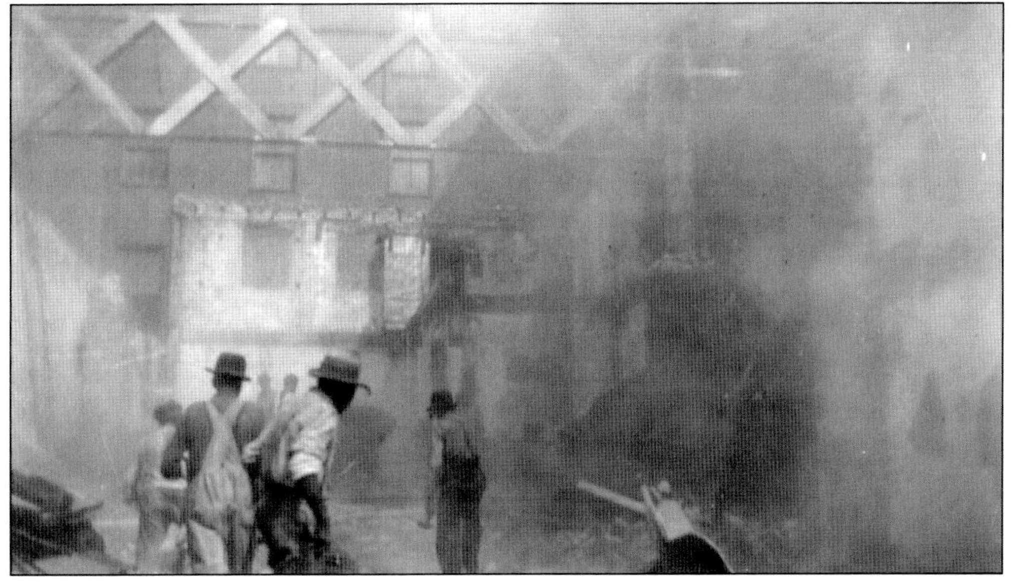

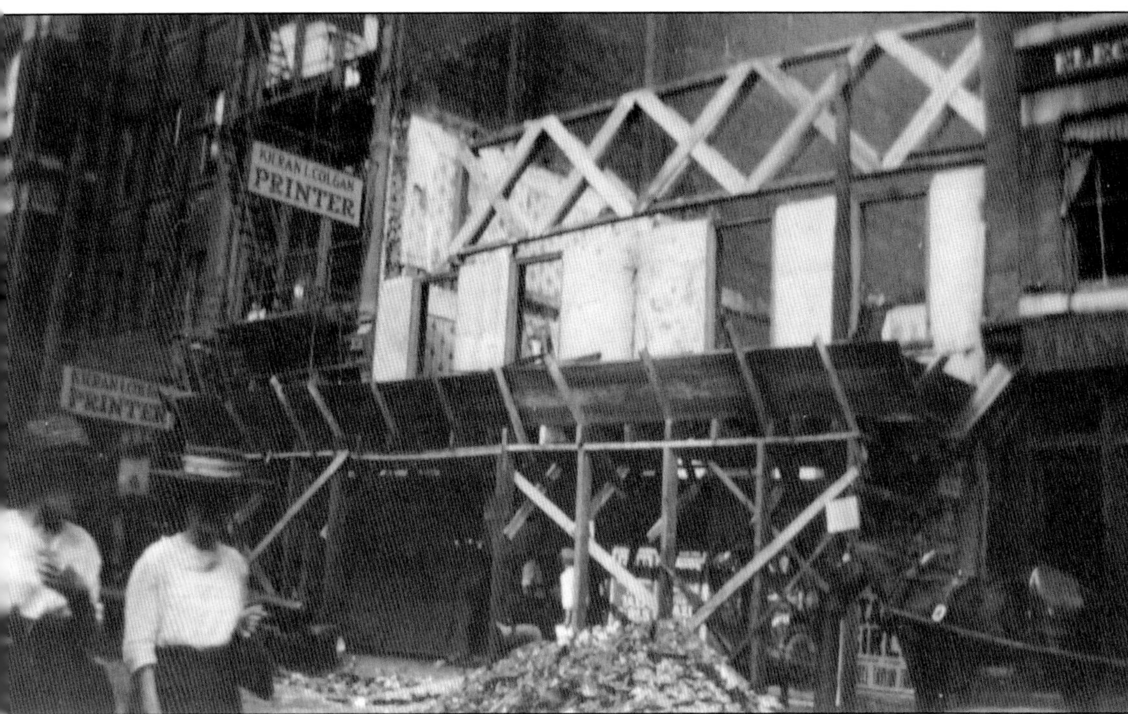

Demolition of the former mint building was swift but happened meticulously, in an almost surgical way. This was necessary given the tight proximity of other buildings in the urban setting. This photograph, taken on Seventh Street, shows two women walking by in the foreground as the mint building is removed in segments. Wooden scaffolding protects pedestrians walking directly below the disappearing facade. (Courtesy of Leonard Augsburger and Joel Orosz.)

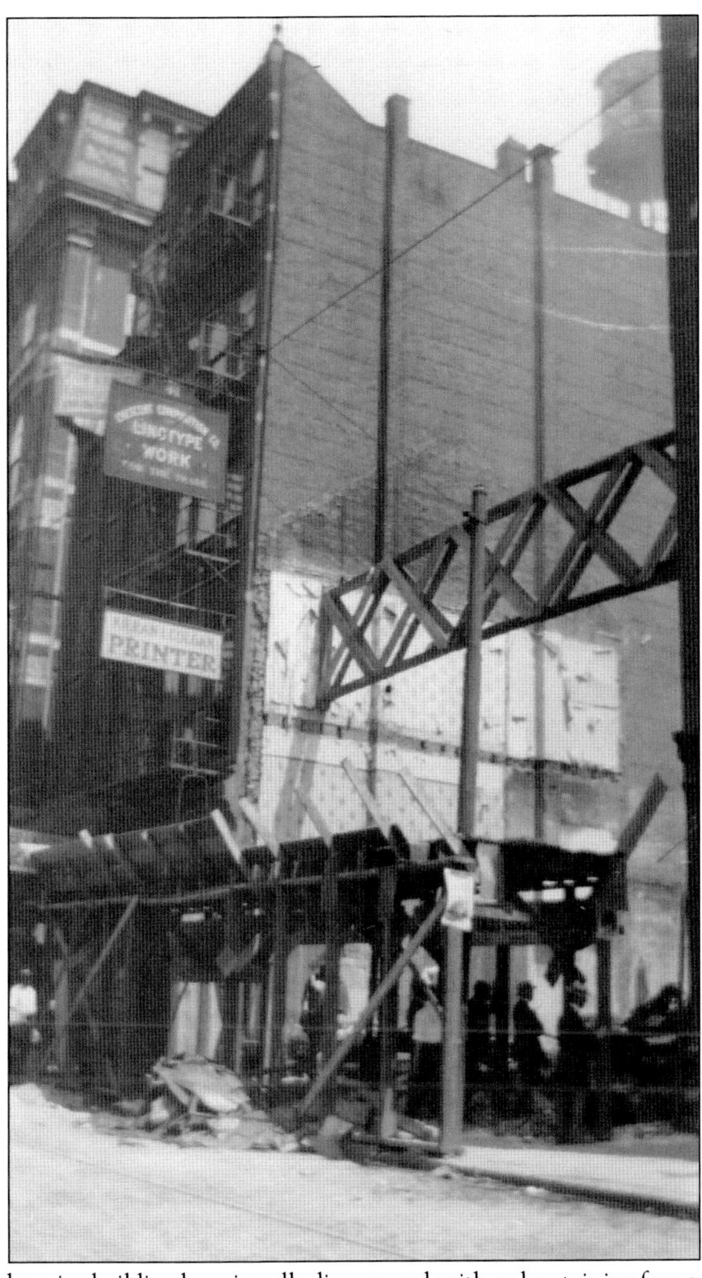

In this image, the mint building has virtually disappeared, with only retaining framework straddling the gaping canyon which "Ye Olde Mint" once proudly filled. The only traces of the mint are three stories of ornate wall coverings that once decorated the inside of the mint's Front Building and a pile of rubble on the right. Passersby can be seen under the protective scaffolding viewing some of the activity still going on at the demolition site. Incidentally, this photograph reveals some insight about the commercial activity along this stretch of Seventh Street. For example, the building at center housed a linotype composer, which at the time was a preferred method for printing newspapers and magazines. Meanwhile, the former mint building fell to make way for Frank H. Stewart's growing electric firm. Many other trade businesses were also prominent along this and adjacent blocks in Center City. (Courtesy of Leonard Augsburger and Joel Orosz.)

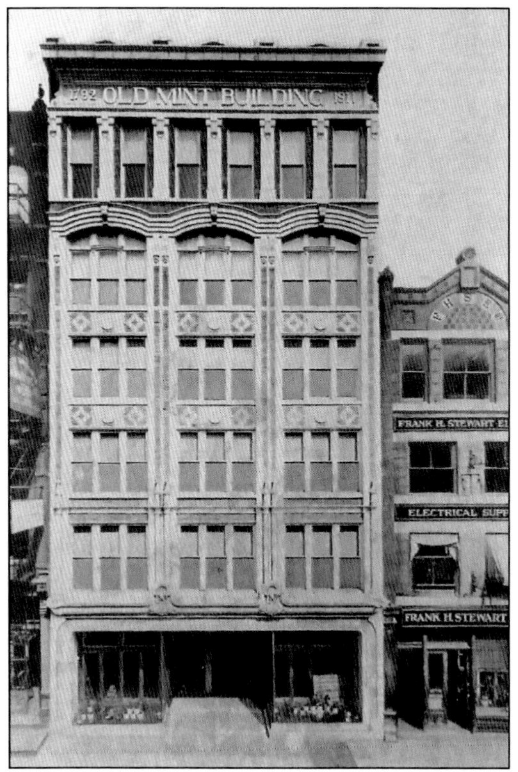

Frank H. Stewart's new building was completed around 1914. While it replaced the former mint facility that had stood along North Seventh Avenue from 1792 through 1911, it was not without a reverent nod to the historic landmark that had previously graced the spot. Stewart's new six-story edifice was officially called the "Old Mint Building." (Courtesy of Leonard Augsburger and Joel Orosz.)

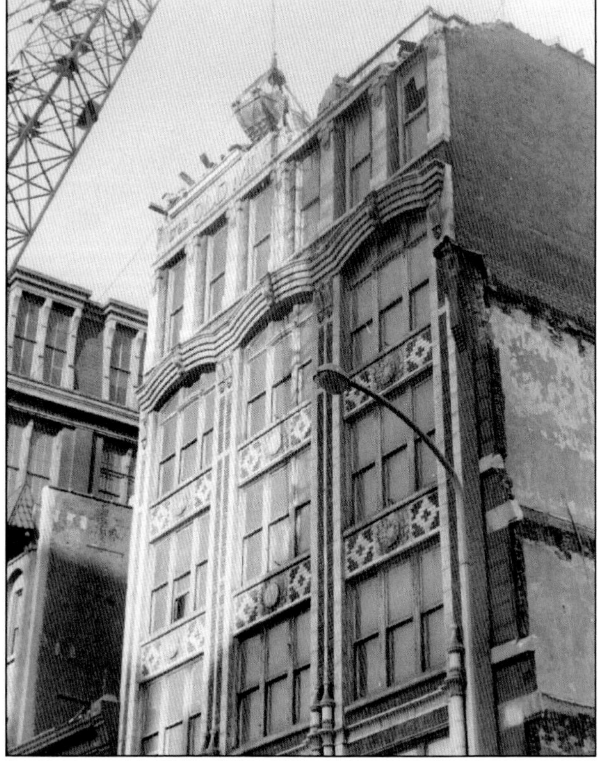

The Old Mint Building that overtook the former mint property in 1911 was itself a victim of urban evolution. In 1965, the US government purchased the land and many adjoining properties to construct what became the largest federal complex in Philadelphia. (Courtesy of Leonard Augsburger and Joel Orosz.)

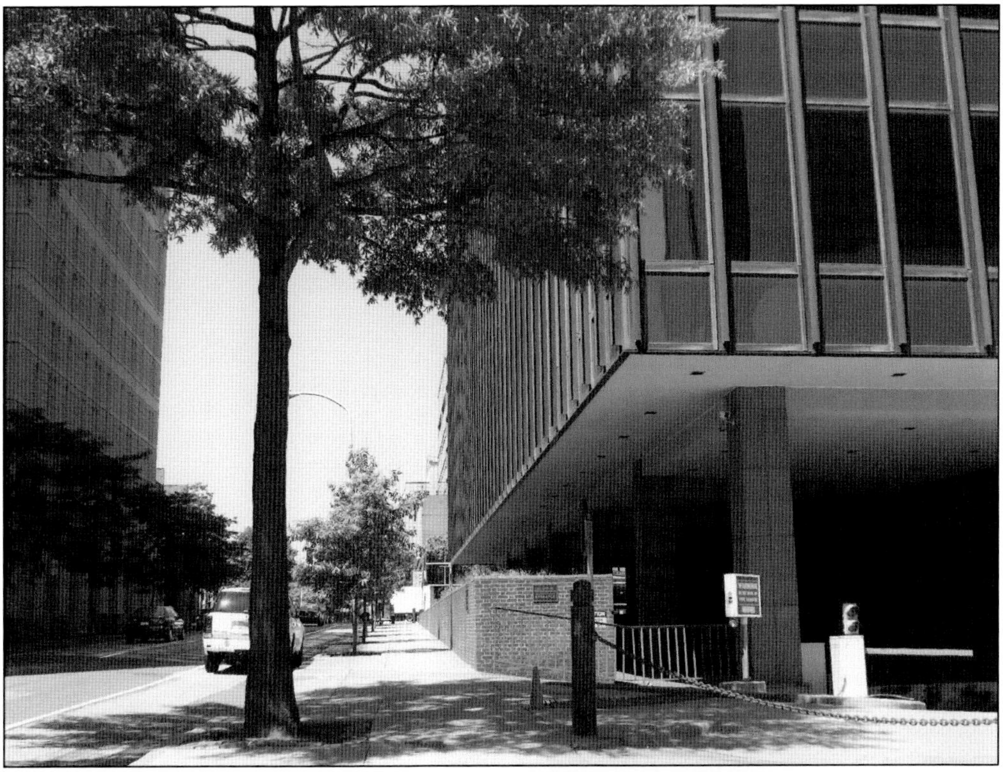

The 1.7-million-square-foot federal complex that now sprawls over the former US Mint property adjacent to Independence National Historical Park includes the James A. Byrne US Courthouse and William J. Green Jr. Federal Building, completed in late 1975 in time for the bicentennial of the Declaration of Independence. Incidentally, the complex houses a massive terra-cotta paver and painted wood sculpture called *Bicentennial Dawn* by Louise Nevelson (1899–1988). *Bicentennial Dawn*, commissioned by the federal government, was dedicated in January 1976, the figurative dawn of the bicentennial year. (Above, courtesy of Leonard Augsburger and Joel Orosz; right, author's collection.)

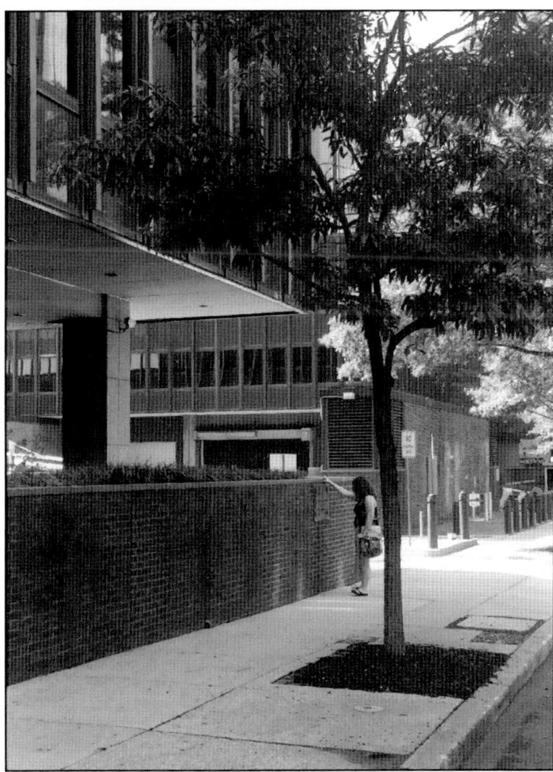

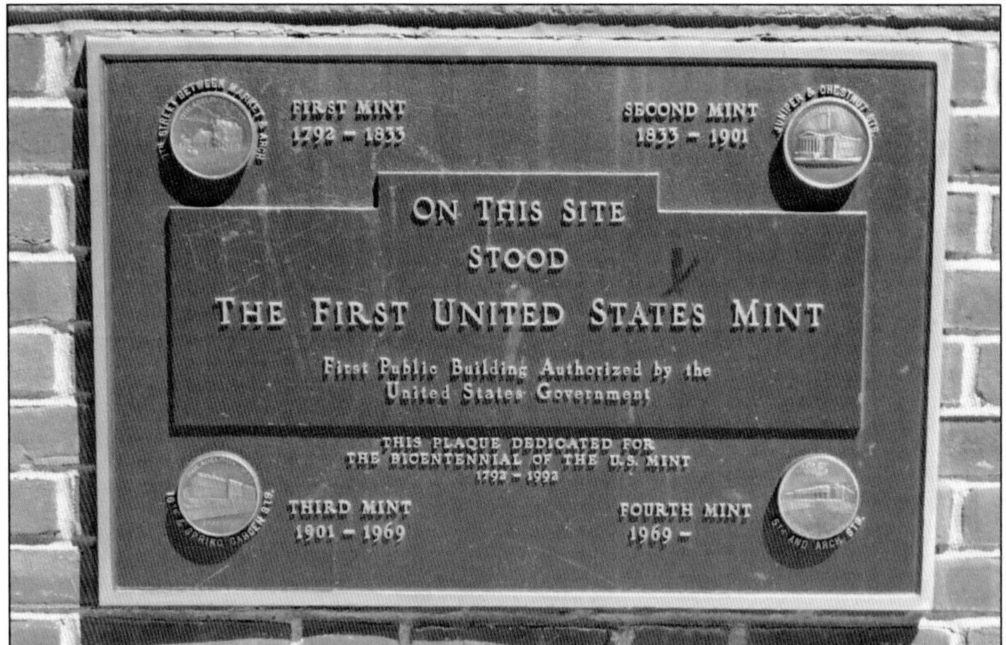

Along a low brick wall that faces the east side of North Seventh Street near its intersection with Filbert Street is mounted a plaque, dedicated in 1992, commemorating the site of the original US Mint, which was built there 200 years earlier. Note the phrase "First Public Building Authorized by the United States Government" on the plaque. Indeed, by many historical accounts, the original US Mint in Philadelphia contained a structure that became the first federally funded building for public use constructed under the authority of Congress. Below is a close-up of the depiction seen on the plaque illustrating the first Philadelphia Mint as painted by Edwin Lamasure in his famous painting, "Ye Olde Mint." (Both, courtesy of Leonard Augsburger and Joel Orosz.)

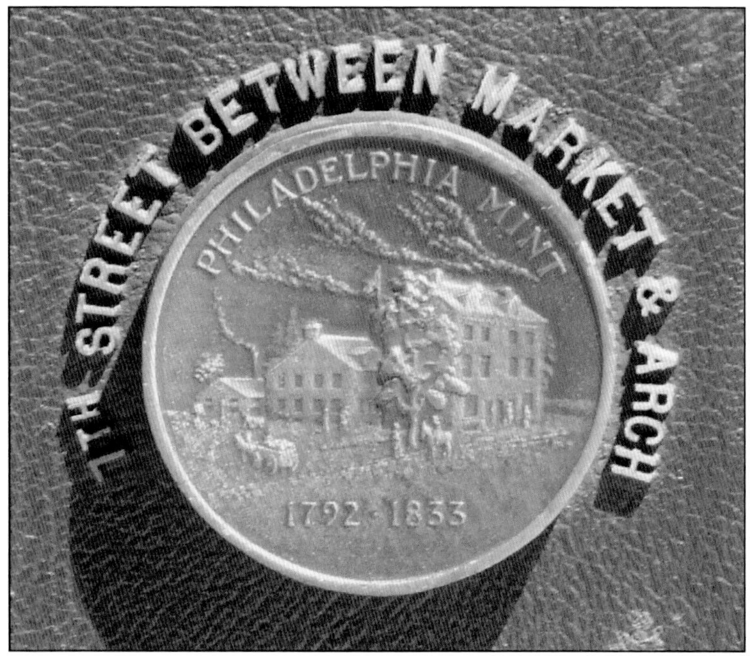

Three

The Second Philadelphia Mint

In Operation from 1833 to 1901

On July 4, 1829, the cornerstone for the second Philadelphia Mint was laid at the intersection of Chestnut and Juniper Streets. The Greek-inspired building, lovingly dubbed the "Grecian Temple," was designed by William Strickland and opened in January 1833. Measuring 150 feet wide and 204 feet long, it was many times larger than the original Philadelphia Mint location, which comprised a few humble buildings. The new mint was architecturally striking, featuring white marble and Greek-styled columns at the front and back of the building. (Courtesy of Leonard Augsburger and Joel Orosz.)

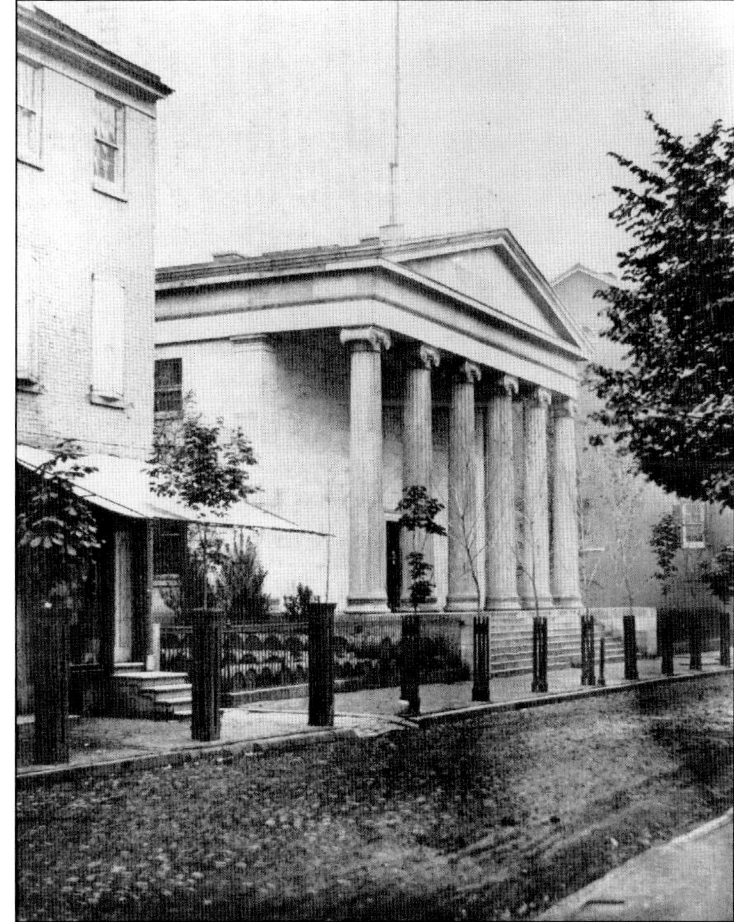

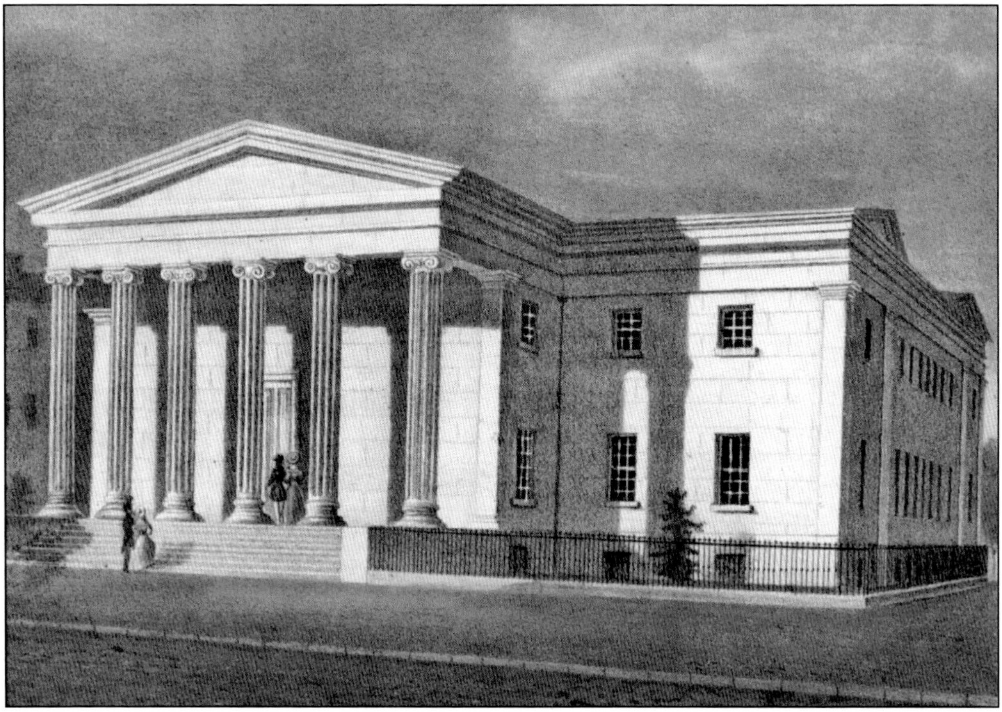

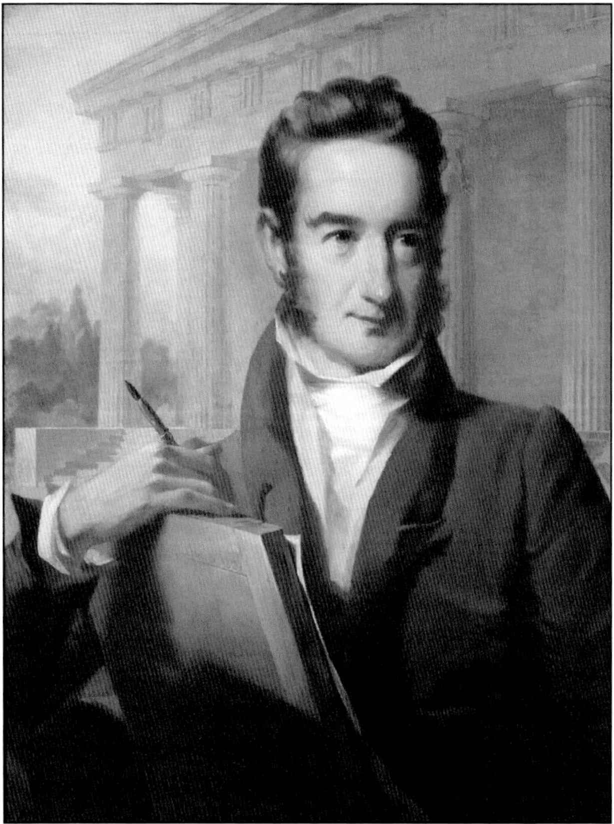

This early 1830s sketch shows the architectural details of the second Philadelphia Mint. The building, which was erected between 1829 and 1833 at Chestnut and Juniper Streets, was a masterpiece of Greek Revival architecture. It was designed by renowned Philadelphia architect William Strickland, seen at left in a portrait by Philadelphian John Neagle. The Second Bank of the United States, which Strickland designed, stands at 420 Chestnut Street and is also featured in the painting. Strickland helped establish the Greek Revival architectural movement in the United States and was also known as an early advocate for the railroad, which revolutionized American industry and tourism during the latter half of the 19th century. (Above, courtesy of the Athenaeum of Philadelphia; left, courtesy of the Yale University Art Gallery.)

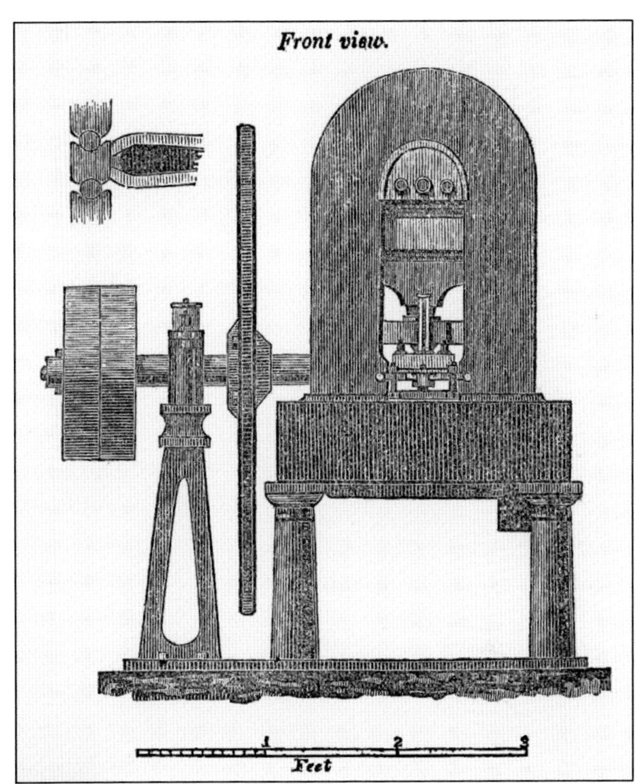

When the Philadelphia Mint relocated to its second location in 1833, operations in the larger facility were still hindered by coining equipment that had become virtually obsolete. This situation changed by 1836, after the US Mint commissioned Benjamin Franklin Peale, who later became the mint's chief coiner (1839–1854), to travel to Europe and study modern coin minting methods there. His design for a steam-driven coin press, illustrated here, was quickly adopted and vastly improved coining productivity at the US Mint. (Courtesy of Roger Burdette.)

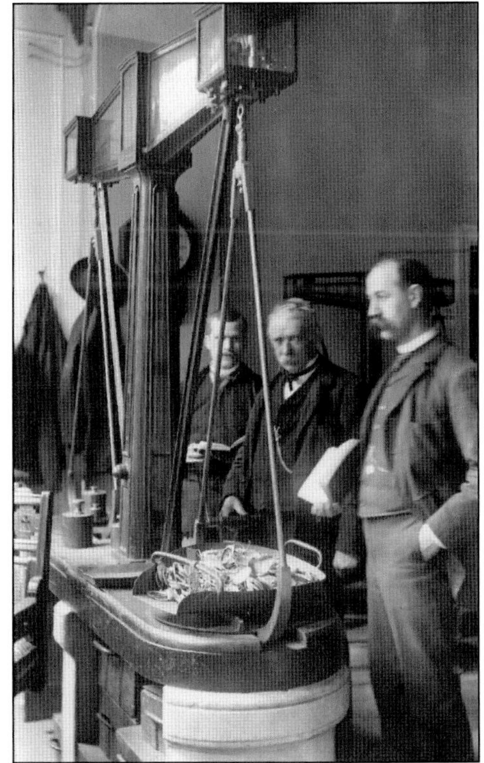

Gold material in the form of jewelry, nuggets, plates, dental fillings, assayed bars, and other items could be hand delivered or sent in by brokers and other members of the public and redeemed for payment from the US Mint. These items, seen here in 1888 being weighed on a large balance in the Philadelphia Mint's receiving room, were melted down and used in coinage. (Courtesy of the Library of Congress, Francis B. Johnston Photograph Collection.)

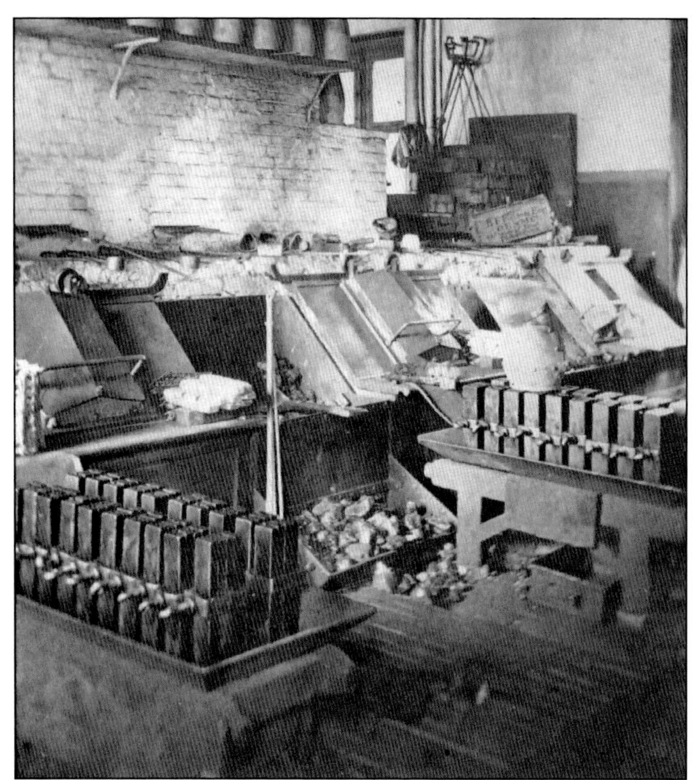

Mint employees are seen making ingots from precious metal deposits that were melted into molten liquid. After the ingots had cooled and hardened, they were taken to the assay office to ensure they met the proper specifications for being turned into coinage. (Left, author's collection; below, Courtesy of the Library of Congress, Francis B. Johnston Photograph Collection.)

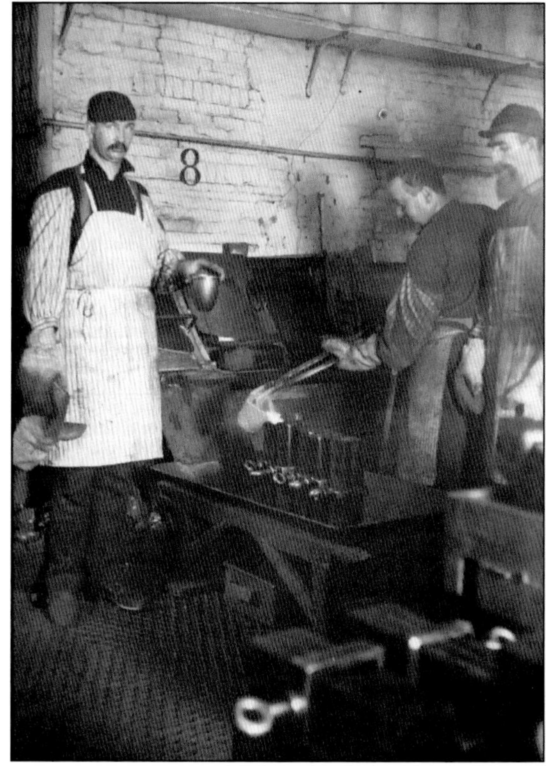

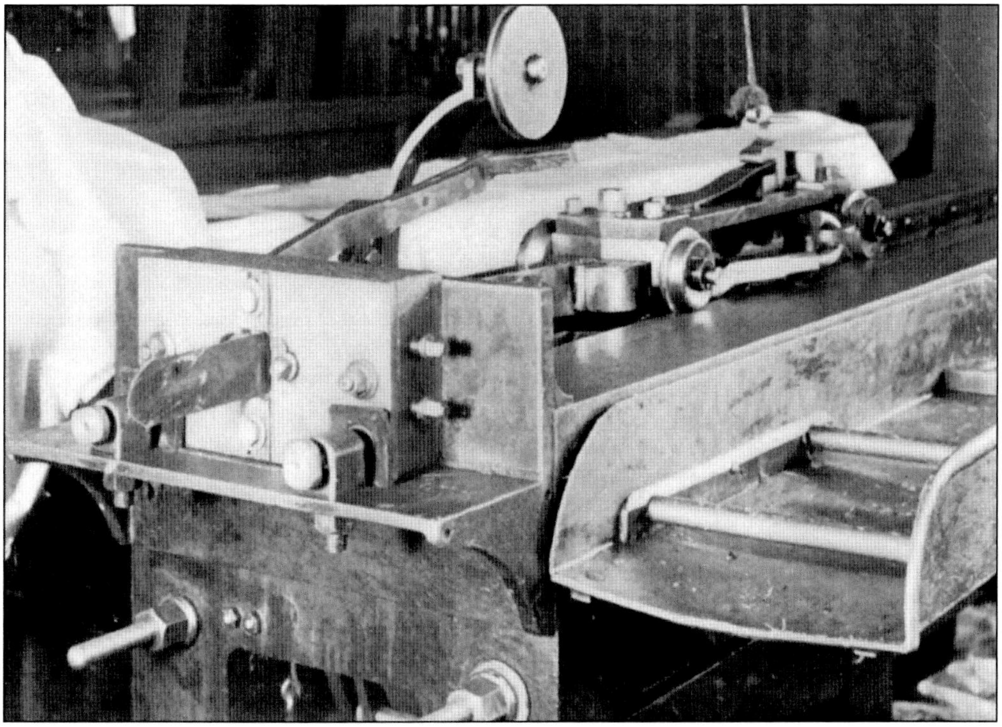

Approved ingots were then sent on to the rolling room, where the thick blocks of metal were rolled through machinery and turned into strips of metal in varying thicknesses, depending on the type of coin being made. The equipment seen in this image is a drawbench, where mint employees passed the strips through cylinders to fine-tune the thickness of the metal. A strip of metal, appearing similar to the end of a large popsicle stick, can be seen popping out of the end of the machine on the left. (Courtesy of the Library of Congress, Francis B. Johnston Photograph Collection.)

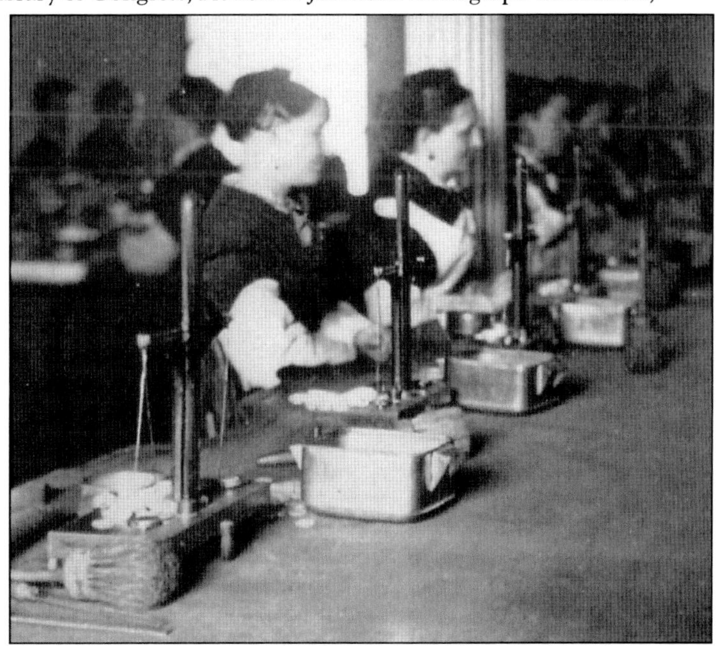

Here is the adjusting room, where coin blanks were weighed and sorted to ensure they were the correct size for striking into coins. Various items sat in an adjuster's workspace, including stacks of blanks, metal sorting boxes, scales, and other devices. (Courtesy of the Library of Congress, Francis B. Johnston Photograph Collection.)

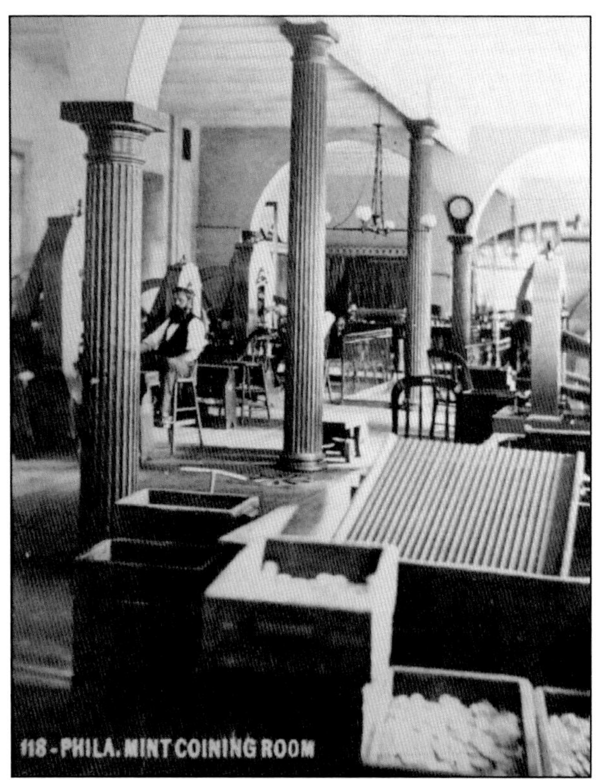

After the rim-upsetting process, which raises a small lip of metal around the edge of the coin, the blanks (or planchets) were then processed into money in the coining room. The coining room of the second Philadelphia Mint is seen here in both images. (Both, courtesy of the Library of Congress, Francis B. Johnston Photograph Collection.)

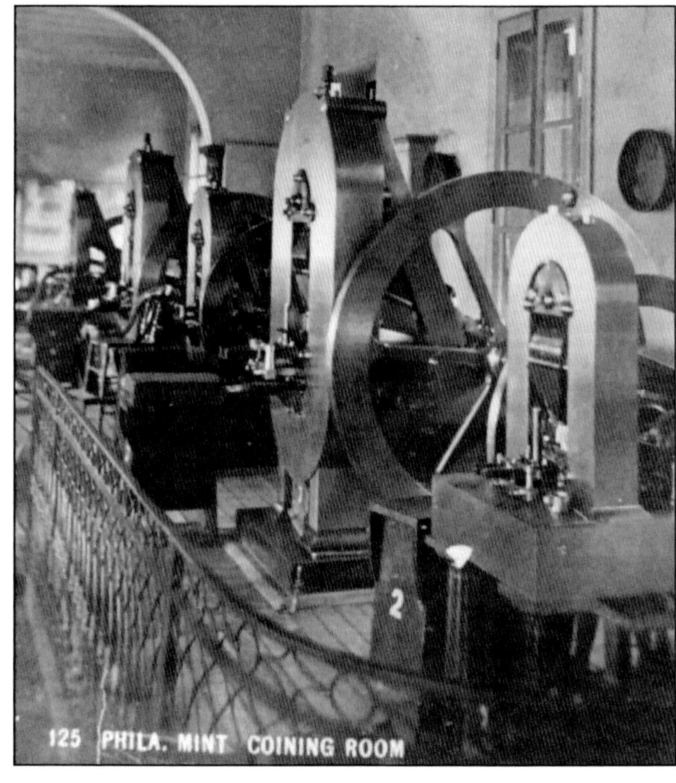

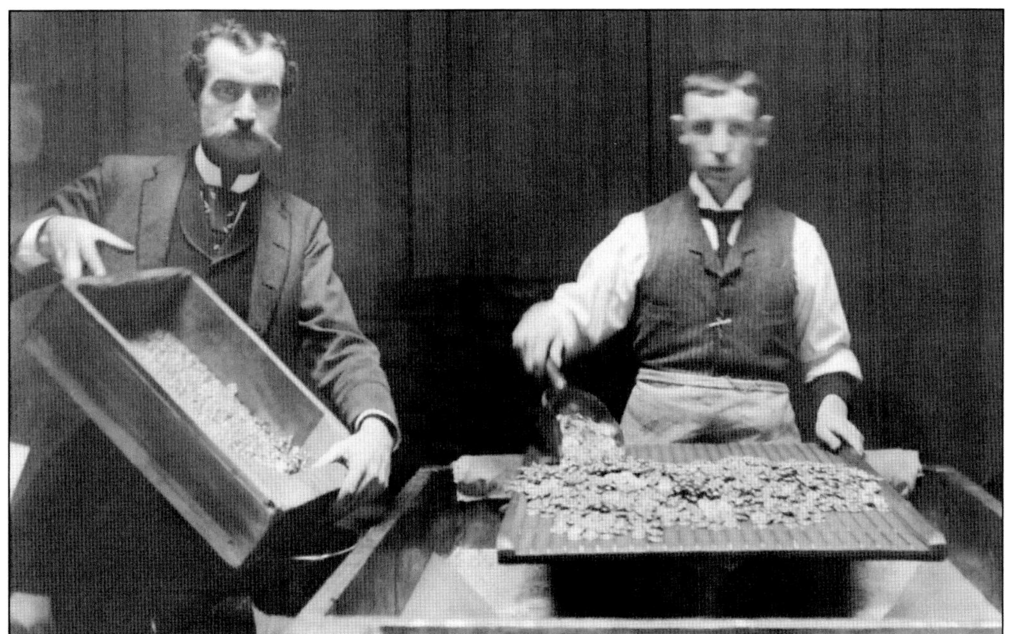

Philadelphia Mint employees Daniel S. Fuller (left) and his assistant James Beale show how small-diameter coins are counted for bagging in 1888. Coins were scooped from a box, such as the one Fuller is holding, and spread across a counting board attached to a rocker atop a bin, which Beale is standing behind. (Courtesy of the Library of Congress, Francis B. Johnston Photograph Collection.)

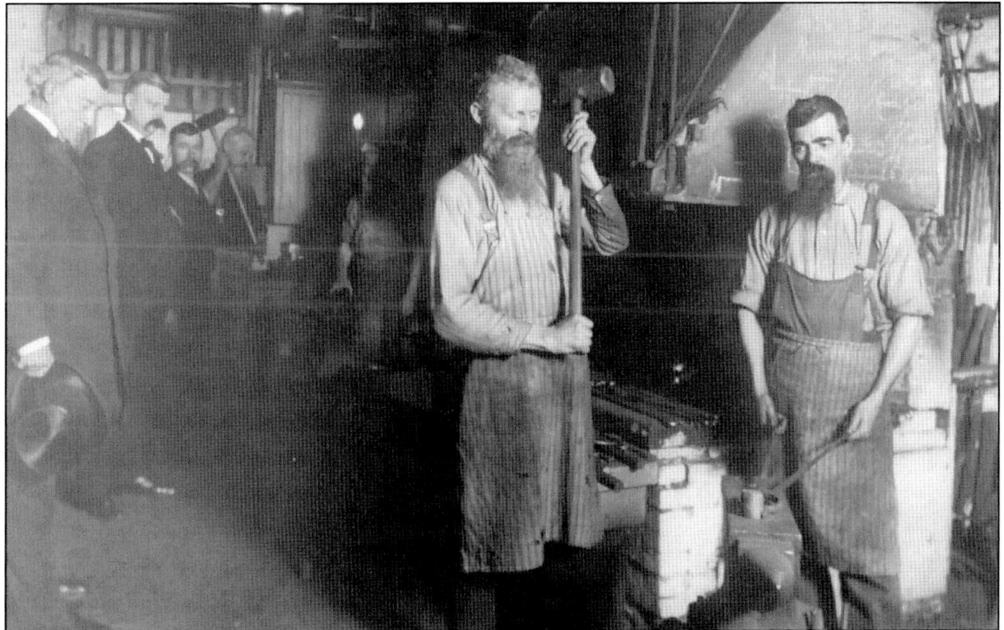

After a die had been exhausted for use, it was destroyed to ensure that it could not be used for any illegitimate purposes, such as striking unauthorized pieces. A die was canceled by first heating it to soften the metal and then striking it with a sledgehammer, decimating the design. In this 1888 image, two blacksmiths are canceling a die, which was witnessed by US Mint employees. (Courtesy of the Library of Congress, Francis B. Johnston Photograph Collection.)

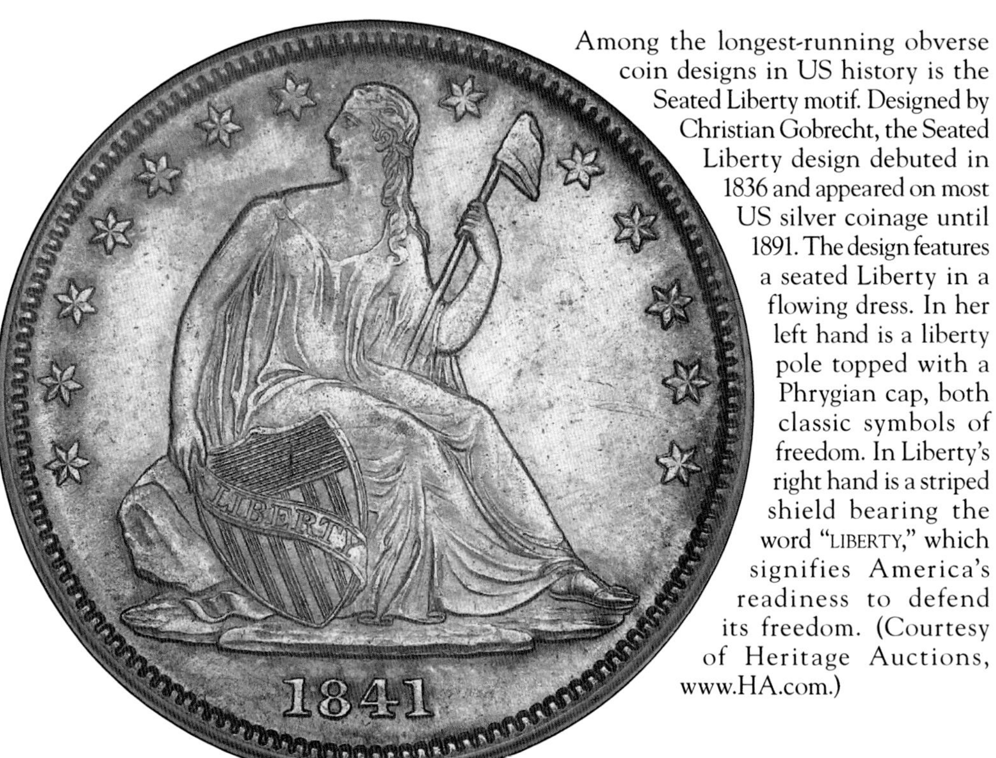

Among the longest-running obverse coin designs in US history is the Seated Liberty motif. Designed by Christian Gobrecht, the Seated Liberty design debuted in 1836 and appeared on most US silver coinage until 1891. The design features a seated Liberty in a flowing dress. In her left hand is a liberty pole topped with a Phrygian cap, both classic symbols of freedom. In Liberty's right hand is a striped shield bearing the word "LIBERTY," which signifies America's readiness to defend its freedom. (Courtesy of Heritage Auctions, www.HA.com.)

Christian Gobrecht was born in Hanover, Pennsylvania, on December 23, 1785. Following the death of Chief of the US Mint William Kneass, Gobrecht served as the third chief engraver from 1840 until his death in Philadelphia on July 23, 1844. Perhaps Gobrecht's most famous numismatic contribution is the Seated Liberty design on the obverses of the half dime, dime, quarter, half-dollar, and dollar coins during much of the 19th century. Variants of the Seated Liberty design also appear on the 20-cent coin (1875–1878), the Trade dollar (1873–1885), and the Gobrecht silver dollar (1836–1839). (Courtesy of John Frost.)

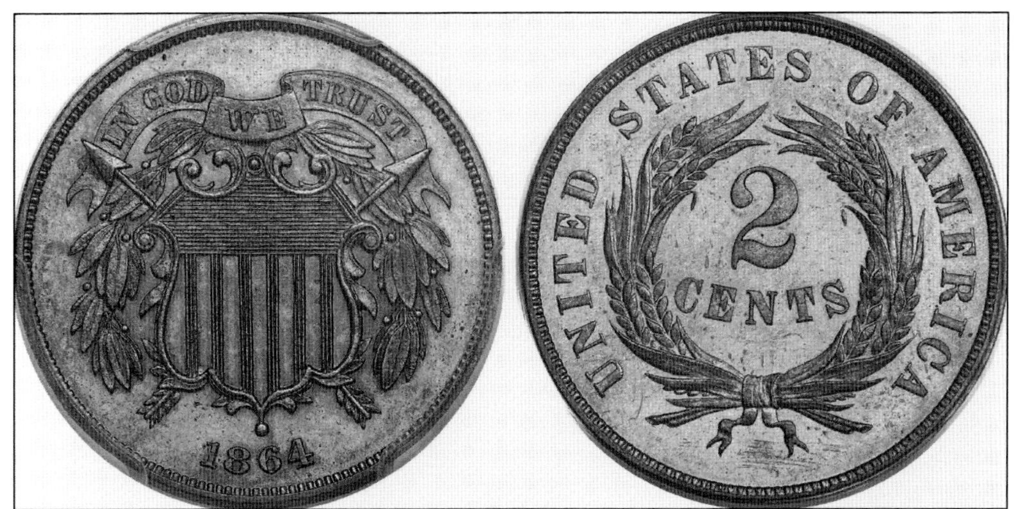

The two-cent coin, designed by chief engraver James B. Longacre and struck from 1864 through 1873, is mostly notable for becoming the first US coin to bear the motto "IN GOD WE TRUST." This bronze coin, which measures 23 millimeters in diameter, filled voids during a major Civil War–era coin shortage. Initially quite popular, the two-cent coin fell out of favor with the public as other small-denomination coinage, such as the three-cent coin and five-cent piece, or "nickel," gained use. (Courtesy of Heritage Auctions, www.HA.com.)

Born in Delaware County, Pennsylvania, on August 11, 1794, James Barton Longacre, seen here in a c. 1855 ambrotype image by Isaac A. Rehn, was a well-known portraitist and engraver. His skills helped him become the fourth chief engraver of the US Mint in 1844, succeeding Christian Gobrecht. Among the list of Longacre's prolific numismatic credits are the two-cent coin, Flying Eagle cent (the nation's first "small-size" cent of modern size), Indian Head cent (1859–1909), Shield nickel (1866–1883), three-cent coinage (1851–1889), and various gold coins of the mid-19th century. (Courtesy of the National Portrait Gallery, Smithsonian Institution.)

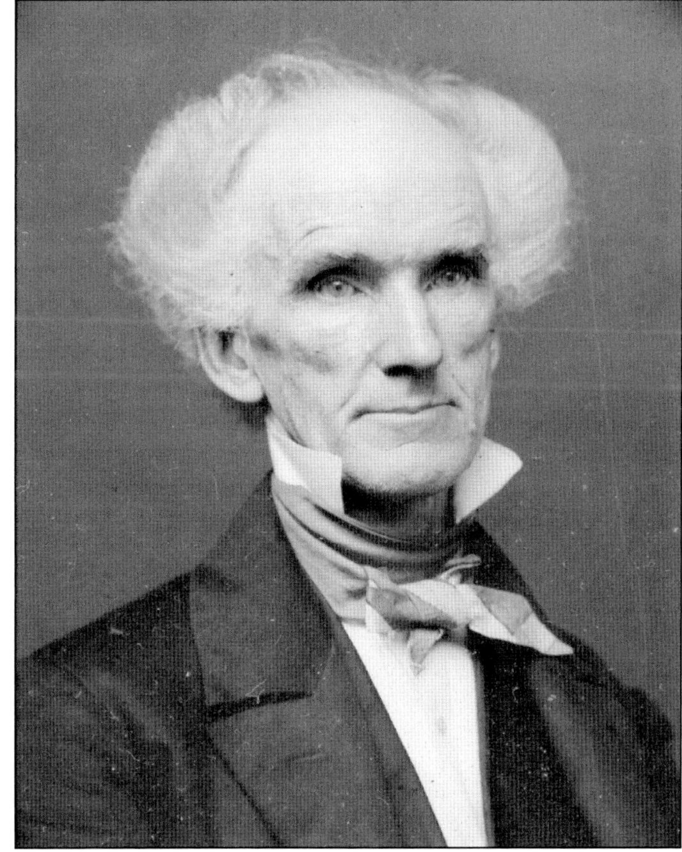

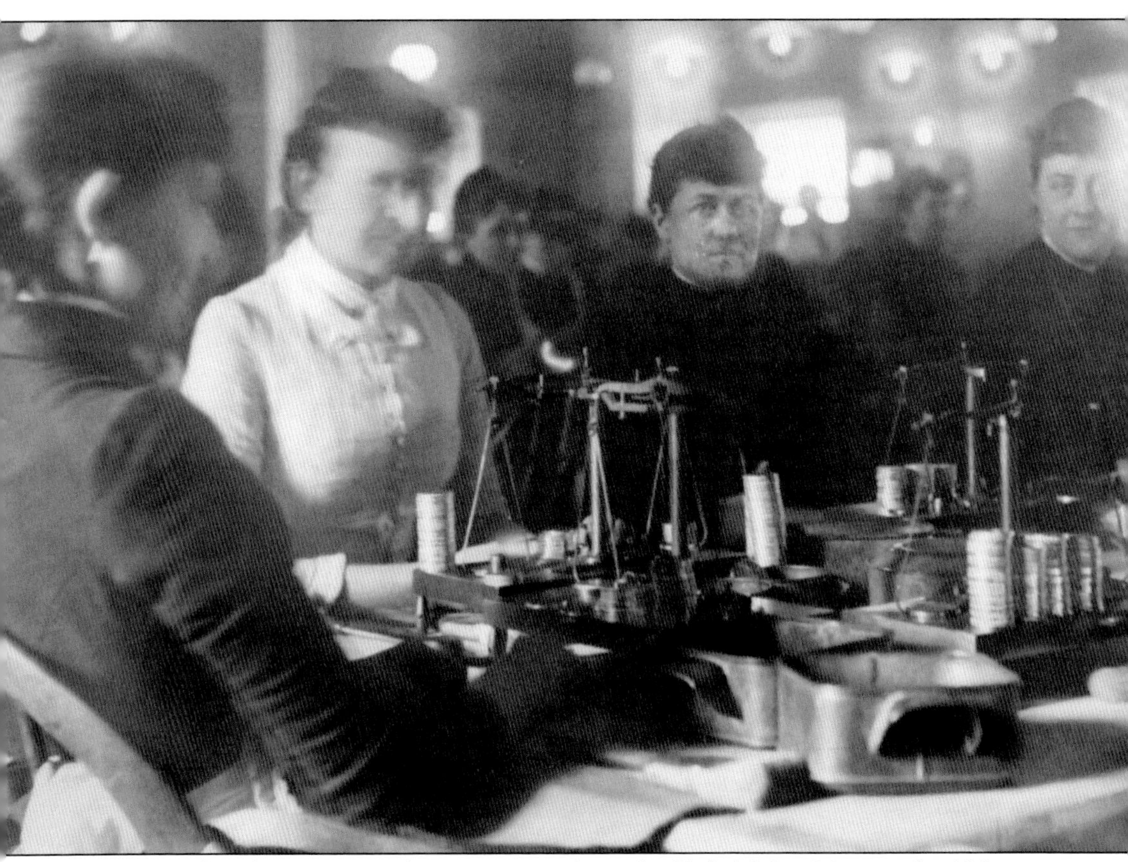

Women played an increasingly prominent role at the Philadelphia Mint in the 19th century. At the time, women were primarily hired for the roles of adjusting coin blanks and operating coin presses. Though serving critical functions as press operators and adjusters in the 1800s, women eventually rose to the highest ranks at the US Mint alongside their male counterparts during the 20th century and beyond. (Courtesy of the Library of Congress, Francis B. Johnston Photograph Collection.)

A woman is seen operating a coin press in 1888. While a typical day for employees at the US Mint involved long hours, work conditions for both men and women were far superior at the mint than in a typical big-city manufacturing facility at the time. (Courtesy of the Library of Congress, Francis B. Johnston Photograph Collection.)

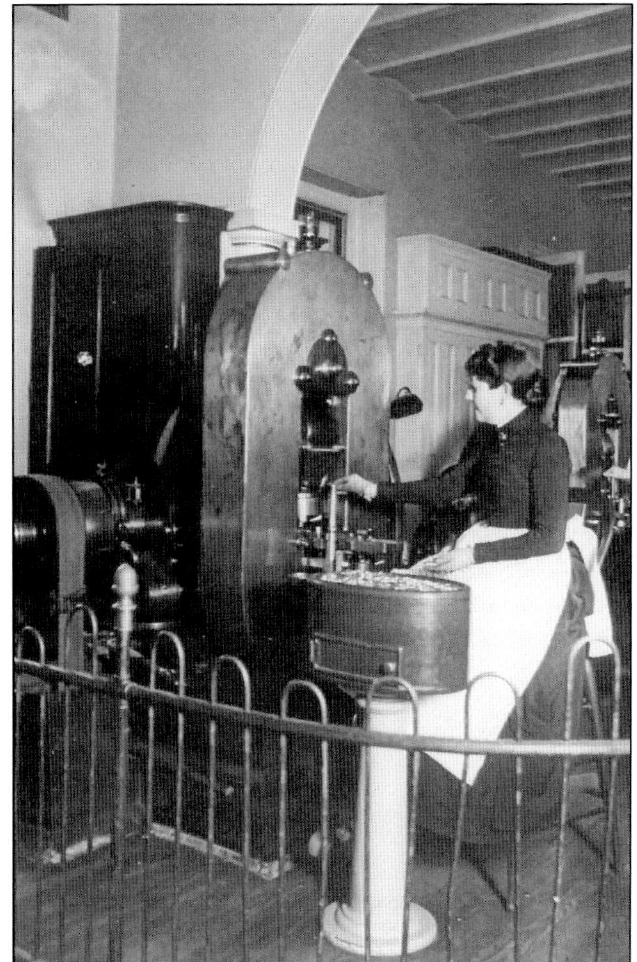

Women employed at the Philadelphia Mint found important camaraderie in working with one another. In this image, female employees are enjoying a few restful moments in the women's dining room between busy shifts. (Courtesy of the Library of Congress, Francis B. Johnston Photograph Collection.)

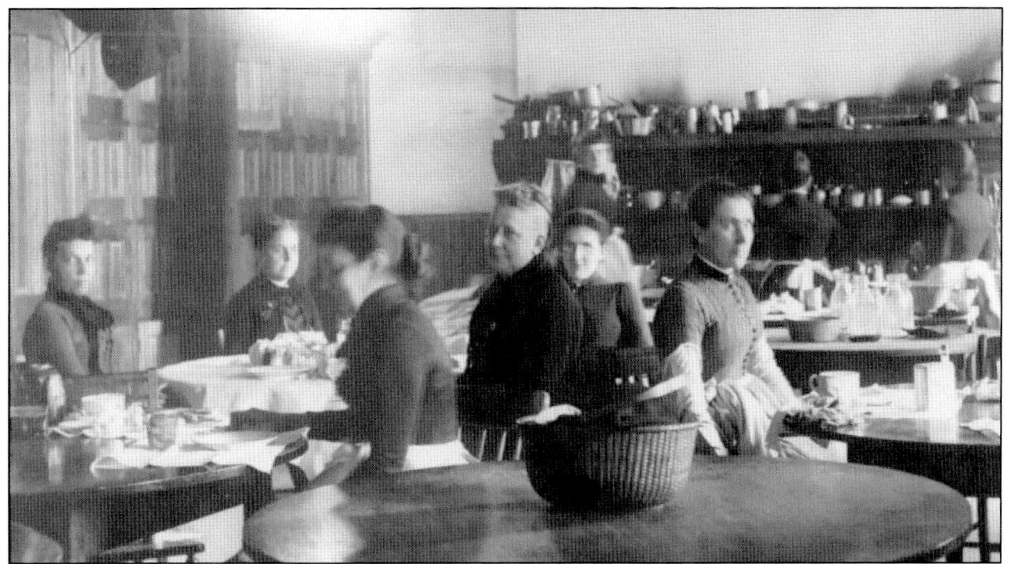

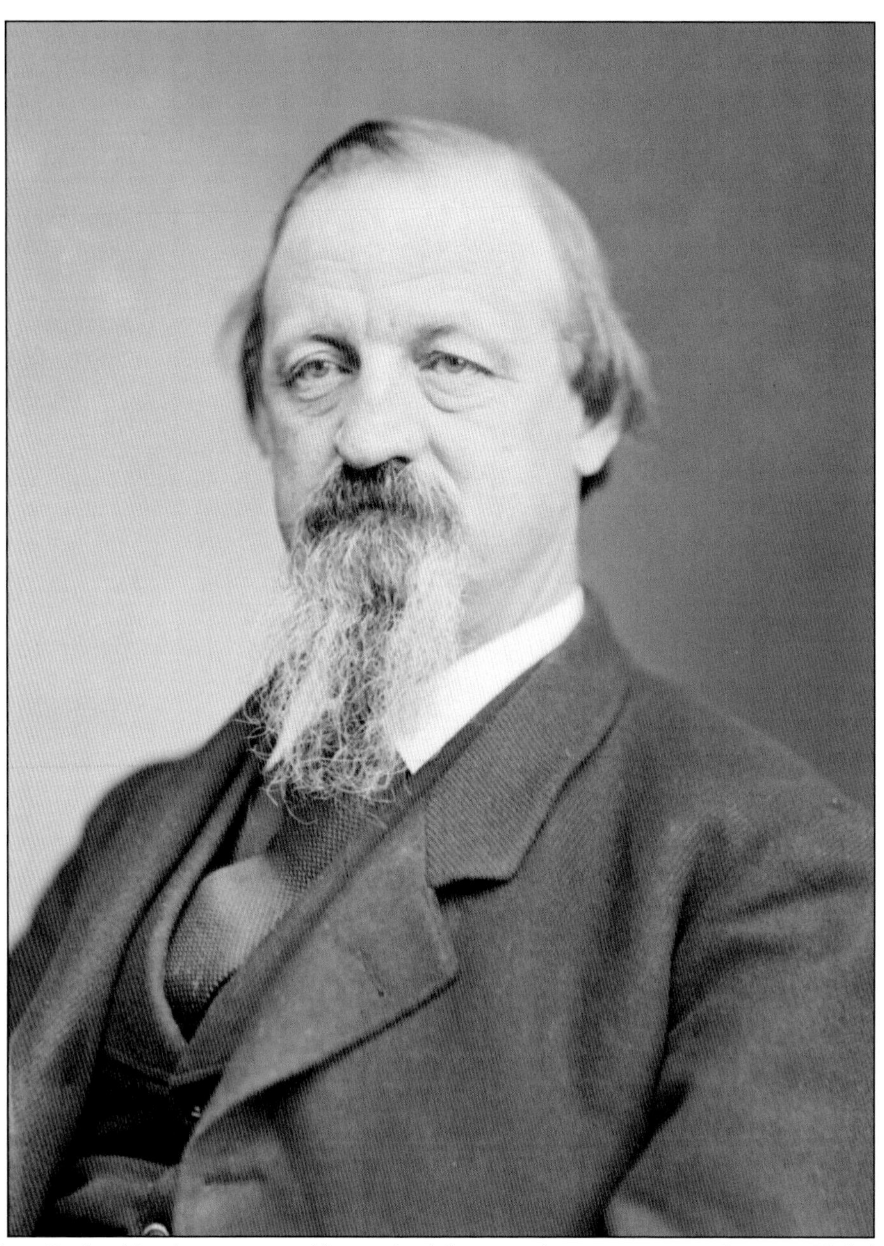

Dr. Henry Richard Linderman earned his medical degree and was a practicing doctor in Philadelphia before becoming a chief clerk with the Philadelphia Mint from 1855 through 1864. He later became a stockbroker but resumed duties with the Philadelphia Mint in 1867, serving as the 12th director of the US Mint until 1869, when the secretary of the treasury reassigned him to monitor operations at the young San Francisco Mint. After touring several European mints, he helped draft the Coinage Act of 1873. Several matters addressed in the legislation include the relocation of the US Mint's central office, which was moved to Washington, DC. Linderman became the first director of the mint under the Coinage Act of 1873 in a role that entailed watching over all of the US Mint facilities around the United States. A new superintendent position for each US Mint facility was assigned by the act. (Courtesy of the Library of Congress, Francis B. Johnston Photograph Collection.)

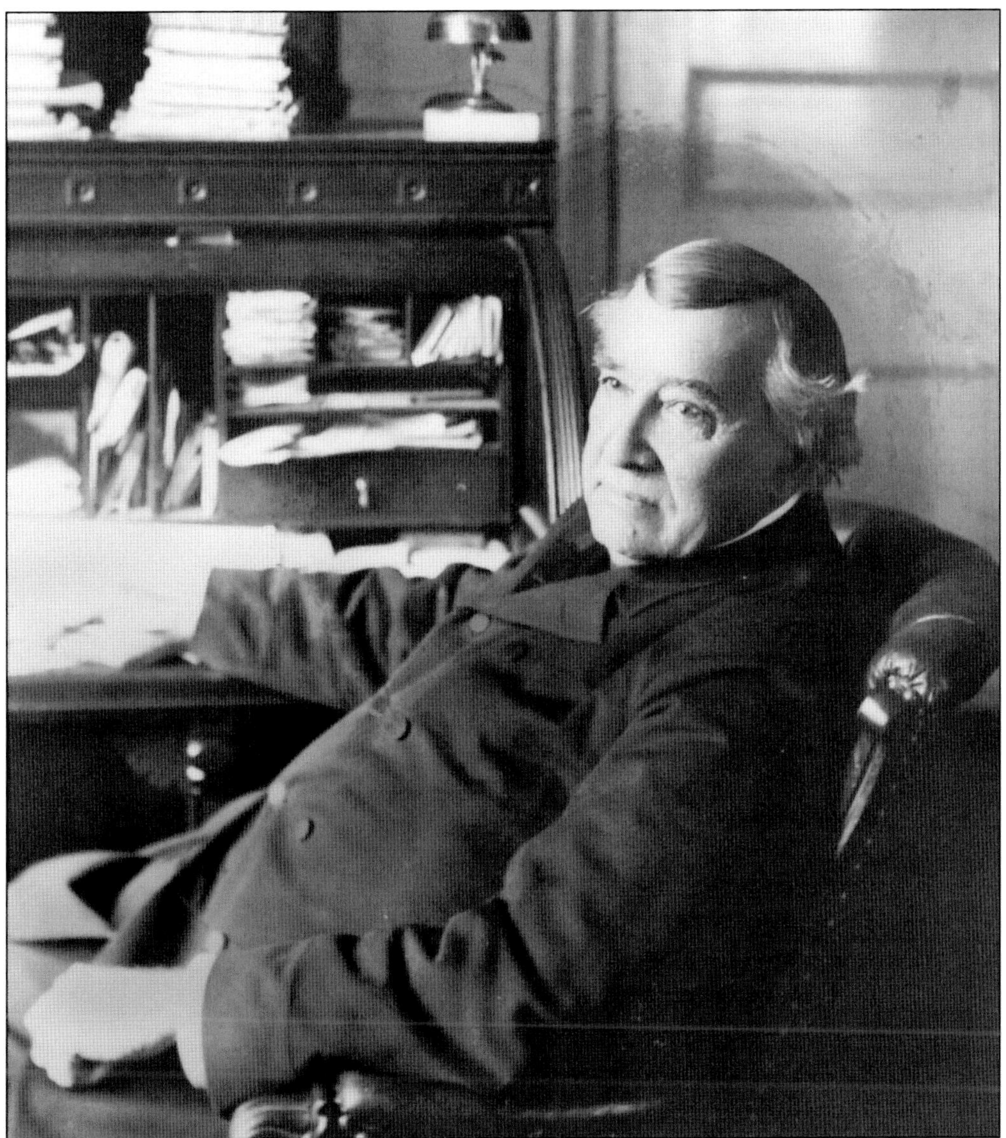

This 1888 image shows Superintendent of the Philadelphia Mint Daniel M. Fox in his office. As superintendent, Fox and others in his position served as a manager of the mint. Minding the mint was no small role, and individuals who were in the running for the high-profile position were subject to a background check by the Secret Service and generally had many social and political connections on a local and federal level. A superintendent was assigned to each US Mint location (of which there were several branch facilities around the nation by the 1880s) and answered to the director of the mint, whose office had moved from Philadelphia to Washington, DC, in 1873. (Courtesy of the Library of Congress, Francis B. Johnston Photograph Collection.)

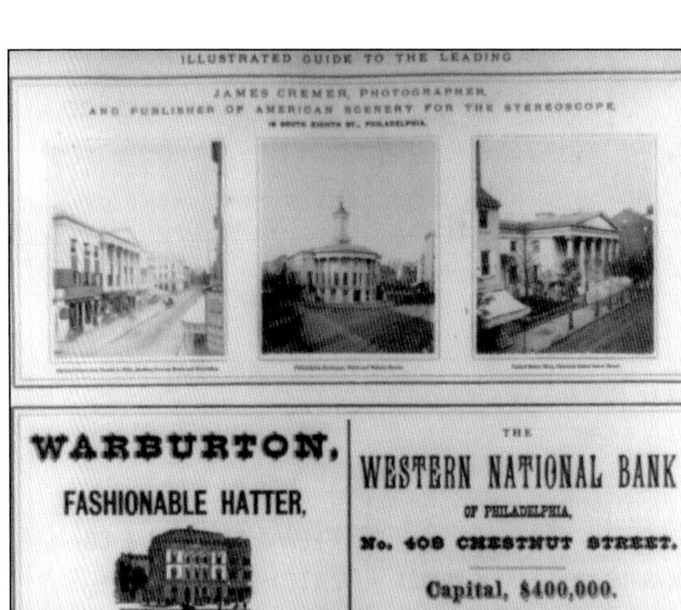

ILLUSTRATED GUIDE TO THE LEADING

JAMES CREMER, PHOTOGRAPHER,
AND PUBLISHER OF AMERICAN SCENERY FOR THE STEREOSCOPE,
18 SOUTH EIGHTH ST., PHILADELPHIA.

WARBURTON,
FASHIONABLE HATTER,
No. 430 Chestnut Street
(NEXT DOOR TO POST-OFFICE.)
PHILADELPHIA.

THE
WESTERN NATIONAL BANK
OF PHILADELPHIA,
No. 408 CHESTNUT STREET.
Capital, $400,000.

PRESIDENT. JOSEPH PATTERSON. CASHIER. C. N. WEYGANDT.

DIRECTORS.
JOSEPH PATTERSON, MORRIS PATTERSON, H. L. CARSON, ISAAC JEANES, WILLIAM MILLER, A. McINTYRE, JOHN J. THOMPSON, R. S. JANNEY, Jr. LEVI KNOWLES.

THE
MECHANICS' NATIONAL BANK
OF PHILADELPHIA.
Nos. 22 & 24 South Third Street.
CAPITAL, $800,000. SURPLUS, $390,000.

PRESIDENT. JOS. G. MITCHELL. CASHIER. J. WIEGAND, Jr.

DIRECTORS.
JOSEPH G. MITCHELL, BENJAMIN W. TINGLEY, GEORGE H. STUART, GUSTAVUS ENGLISH, FRANCIS E. REEVES, JOHN C. DAVIS, WILLIAM A. BROWN, GEORGE H. BOKER, JOHN ROMMEL, Jr.

THE
UNION BANKING COMPANY,
(STATE BANK.)
N. E. Corner FOURTH and CHESTNUT Streets, Philadelphia.
CAPITAL, $200,400.
ACCOUNTS AND CORRESPONDENCE SOLICITED.
INTEREST ALLOWED ON DEPOSITS
CERTIFICATES OF DEPOSITS ISSUED, PAYABLE WITH FIVE DAYS' NOTICE, BEARING 5 PER CENT. INTEREST.
COLLECTIONS MADE EVERYWHERE.
JAS. A. HILL, Cashier. N. C. MUSSELMAN, President.

The US Mint is seen in the upper-right corner of this page of advertisements in a c. 1871 edition of the *Illustrated Guide to the Leading Wholesale and Retail Business Houses of Philadelphia*. The mint is included among a trio of images that also includes the custom house and post office (left) and Philadelphia Exchange (center), as captured by stereoscopic photographer James Cremer. The image below shows an example of a stereoscope photograph of the second Philadelphia Mint. The images required a costly dual-lens camera to capture, and those who saw these photographs in stereo viewers enjoyed a three-dimensional viewing experience. (Left, courtesy of the Library of Congress; below, courtesy of Roger Burdette.)

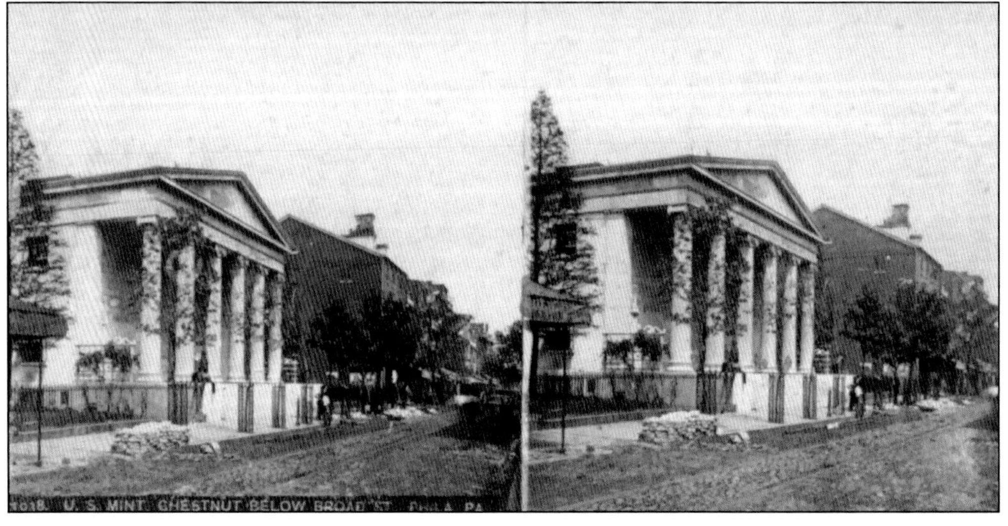

The operations of the US Mint have long been a curiosity to the public, and mint officials have indulged Americans with tours of the various mint facilities and other glimpses of their inner workings for many decades. In this photograph is the US Mint exhibit at the 1864 Great Central Sanitary Fair in Philadelphia. A coining press is seen here under a banner declaring, "For sale. Tokens coined by this engine press! For silver, 50¢ each. Copper 10¢." (Courtesy of Leonard Augsburger and Joel Orosz.)

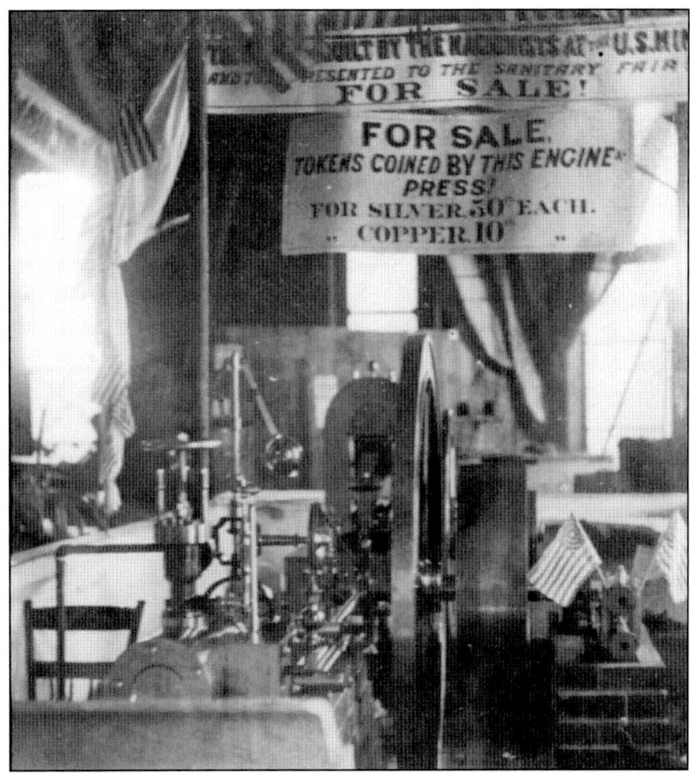

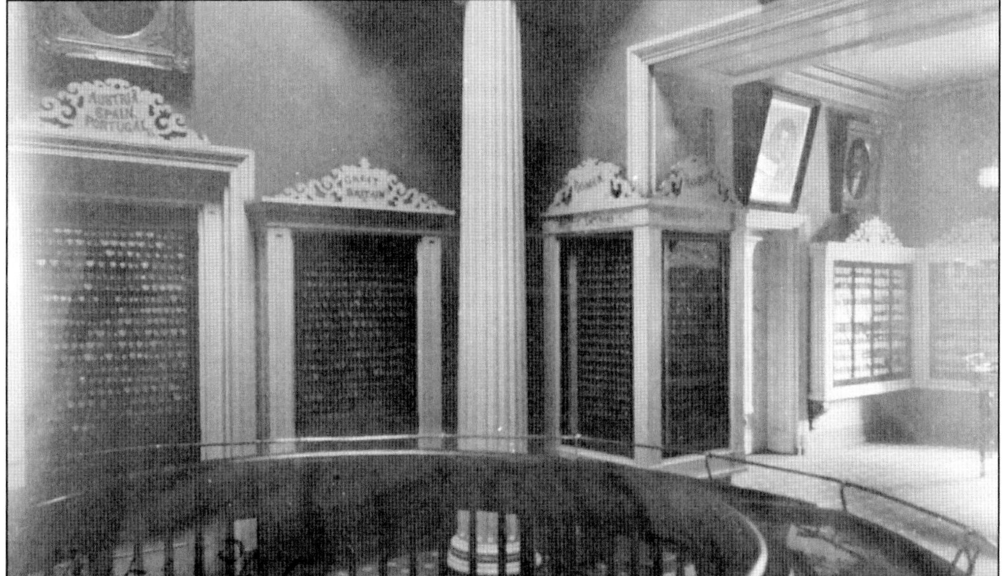

Those visiting the Philadelphia Mint could tour its coin collection in this gallery, seen in 1888. Those wishing to learn more about the collection could purchase a pamphlet, while those who wanted to build their own collections had the opportunity to purchase proof collector coinage. Proof coins are struck multiple times by specially prepared dies on polished planchets, producing coins of quality superior to typical business-strike coins made for circulation. (Courtesy of the Library of Congress, Francis B. Johnston Photograph Collection.)

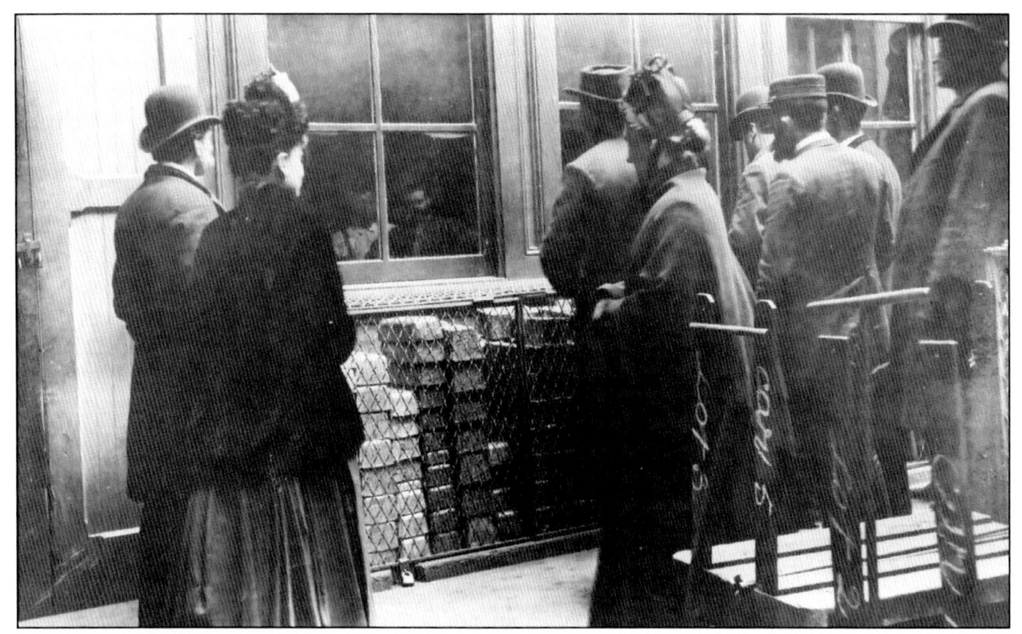

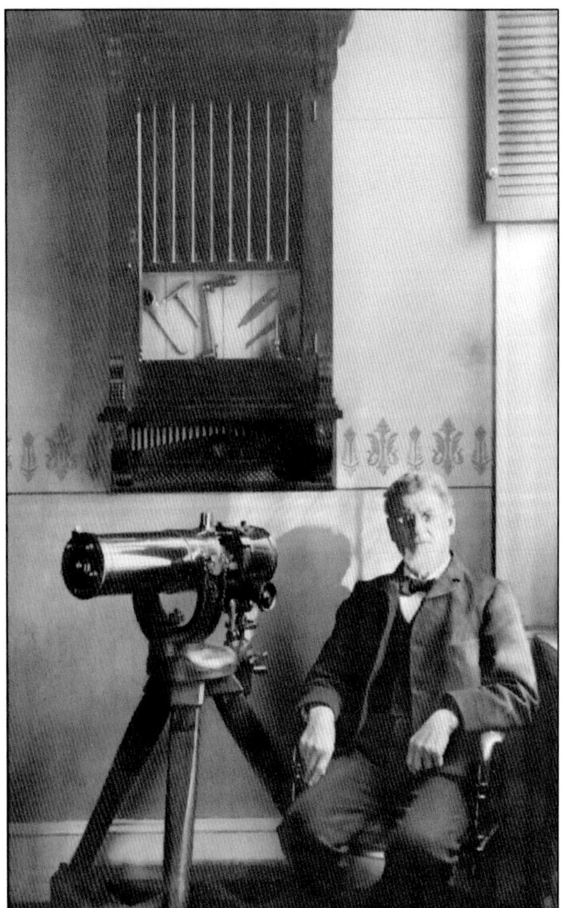

The second Philadelphia Mint had become cramped in its later years, with even vault space becoming premium real estate. This is evidenced in the 1888 photograph above, as guests touring the mint view stacks of silver bars locked up outdoors in the facility's interior, open-air courtyard. (Courtesy of the Library of Congress, Francis B. Johnston Photograph Collection.)

George W. Brown, seated here beside a Gatling gun, was among the security team at the second Philadelphia Mint. The security force at the US Mint during the mid-19th century included a captain of the night watch and about a dozen privates. Weaponry included two Gatling guns positioned at either end of the main hall and an arsenal of handguns and rifles. (Courtesy of the Library of Congress, Francis B. Johnston Photograph Collection.)

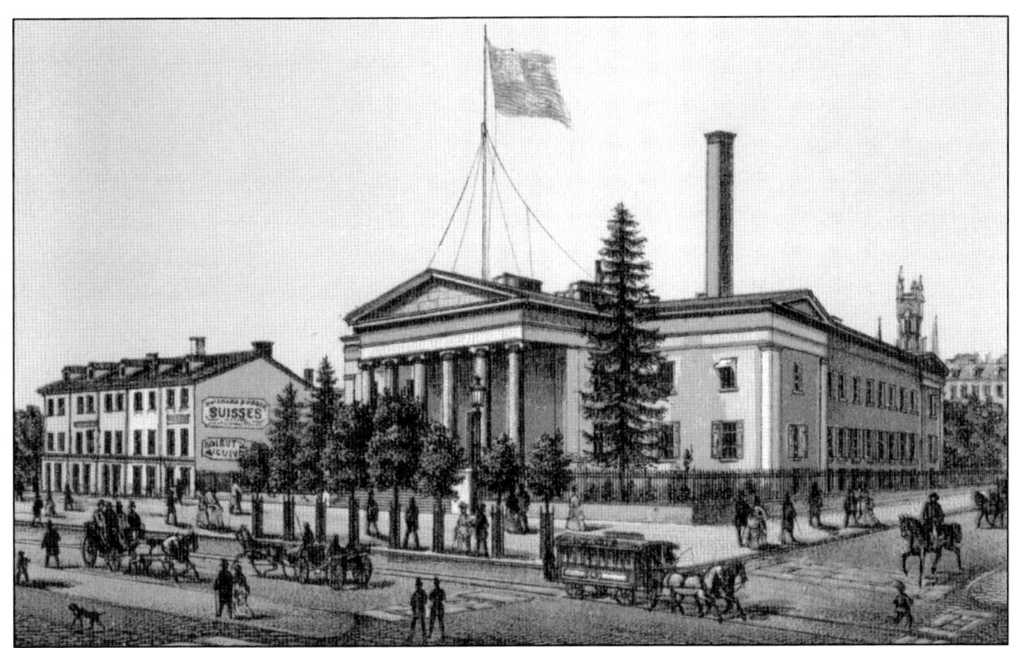

The second Philadelphia Mint is seen here in two images depicting the facility about two decades apart. In the image above, sketched in 1876, the building sports a towering chimney that was constructed in 1835 to help ventilate acid fumes and smoke from burning coal. Also notable is an American flag atop a mast, foreshadowing the patriotic bunting seen in the c. 1895 image below. (Both, courtesy of the Library Company of Philadelphia.)

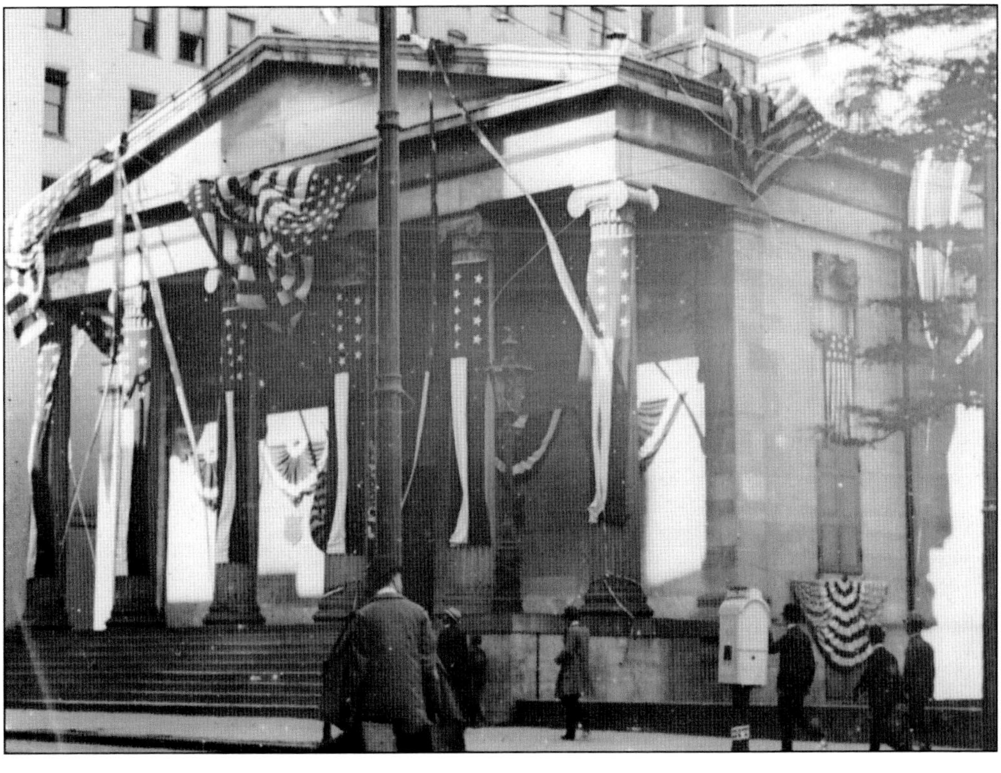

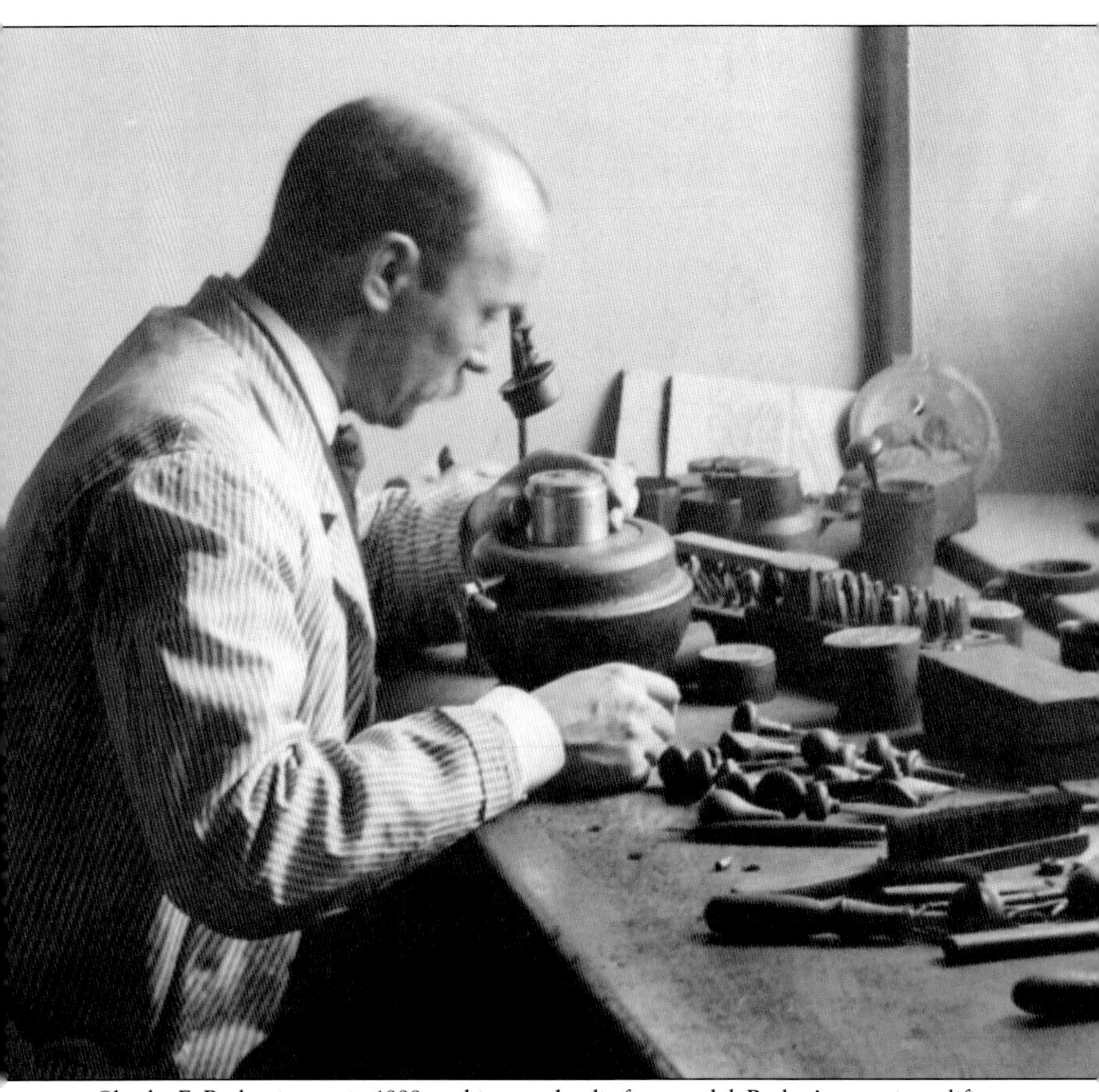

Charles E. Barber is seen in 1888 working on the die for a medal. Barber's name is prolific among late 19th- and early 20th-century coinage. His father, William Barber, succeeded James Barton Longacre and served as the fifth chief engraver of the US Mint for a decade, from 1869 until his death at the age of 72 in 1879. The younger Barber then succeeded his father in 1879 and continued as the sixth chief engraver of the US Mint until his own passing at the age of 76 in 1917. The Barbers originally hailed from England and settled in Boston before relocating to Philadelphia. While William Barber's coinage credits notably include the Trade dollar and 20-cent piece, it was his son Charles whose name became ubiquitous in numismatics. Charles Barber's designer initial "B" can be found on a variety of coins, including the Liberty Head nickel (officially struck from 1883 through 1912, though five pieces were made in 1913 and are now extremely rare); the Liberty Head, or "Barber," dime and quarter (1892–1916); and the Liberty Head, or Barber, half-dollar (1892–1915). He also designed several commemorative coins. (Courtesy of Roger Burdette.)

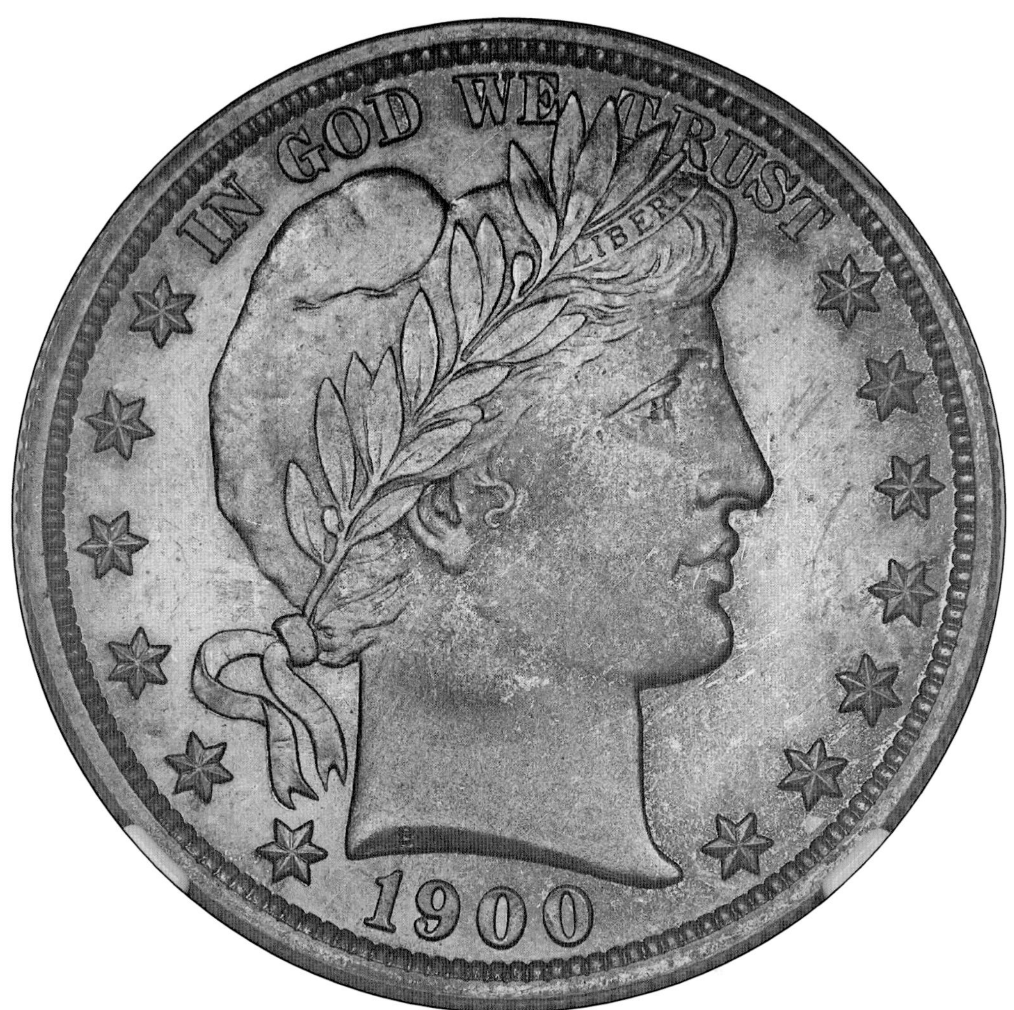

This is an example of a Liberty Head half-dollar. Virtually identical obverse designs appear on the similar Liberty Head dime and quarter from the same period and replaced the Seated Liberty design that debuted in the 1830s. The right-facing Liberty Head depicted on the trio of "Barber" silver coins shows the goddess Liberty wearing a crown of olive leaves bearing the word "LIBERTY." Artistically, the Liberty bust depicted on these particular Barber coins combines classical influences, Roman stylization, and direct inspiration from certain French silver coins of the late 19th century. While the Barber dime, quarter, and half-dollar received lukewarm critical reception from the artistic community and the public at large, the design endured until 1915 on the half-dollar and 1916 on the dime and quarter. Today, Barber coinage is highly collectible, and many issues are considerably rare. (Courtesy of Heritage Auctions, www.HA.com.)

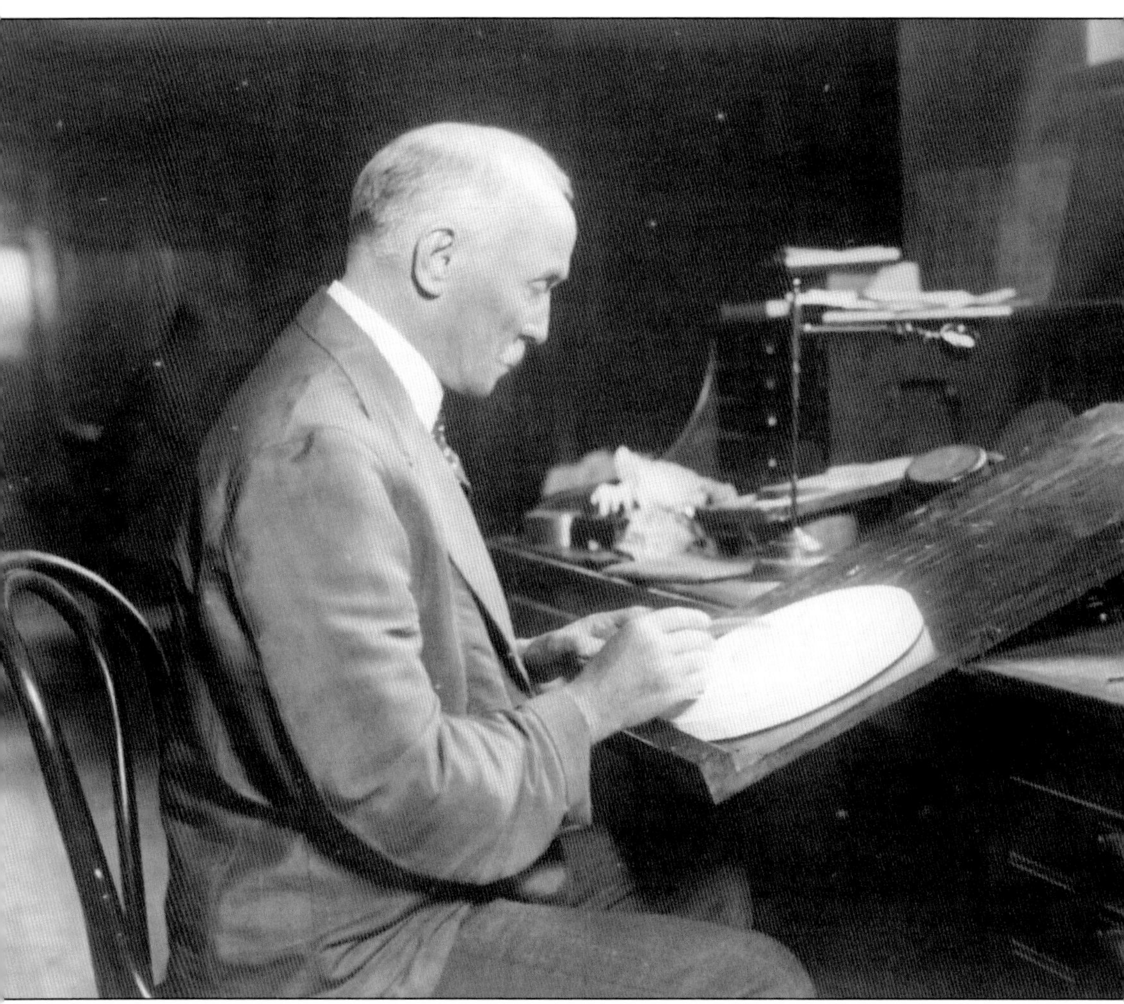

Engraver George T. Morgan, who served for years as an assistant to Charles E. Barber, is a numismatic icon in his own right. Morgan, a United Kingdom transplant akin to the Barbers, was a native of Birmingham, England, and moved to the United States in 1876. In October of that year, he was hired by Director of the US Mint Henry Richard Linderman and worked on a variety of pattern coins (those bearing prototype designs), most notably the $100 Gold Union, which was never released. While he shares credit with Charles E. Barber on the Columbian commemorative half-dollar (1892–1893), his most famous work by far is the Liberty Head, or "Morgan," silver dollar. The Morgan dollar was struck from 1878 through 1904 and once more in 1921 and is now one of the most widely collected US coins of all time. Following the death of Charles E. Barber in 1917, Morgan became the seventh chief engraver and served in that role until his own passing in 1925. (Courtesy of Alex Doty.)

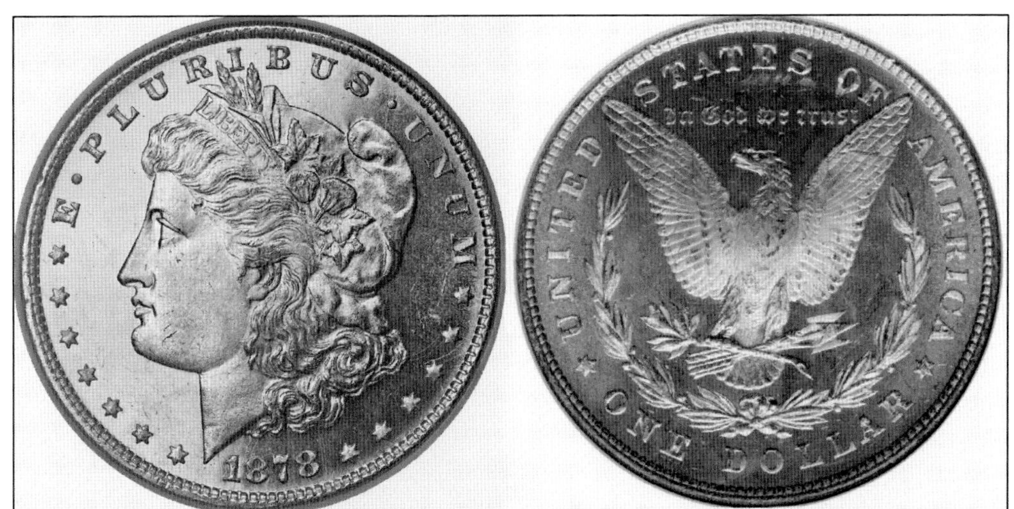

The Morgan dollar is familiar to both coin collectors and many noncollectors. Hundreds of millions were struck from 1878 through 1921, and they circulated widely around the United States, though they were most frequently used on the western frontier. For that reason, many people attach romantic notions of the Old West to Morgan dollars, and the large silver coins are often referenced in classic Western films and television shows. (Courtesy of Heritage Auctions, www.HA.com.)

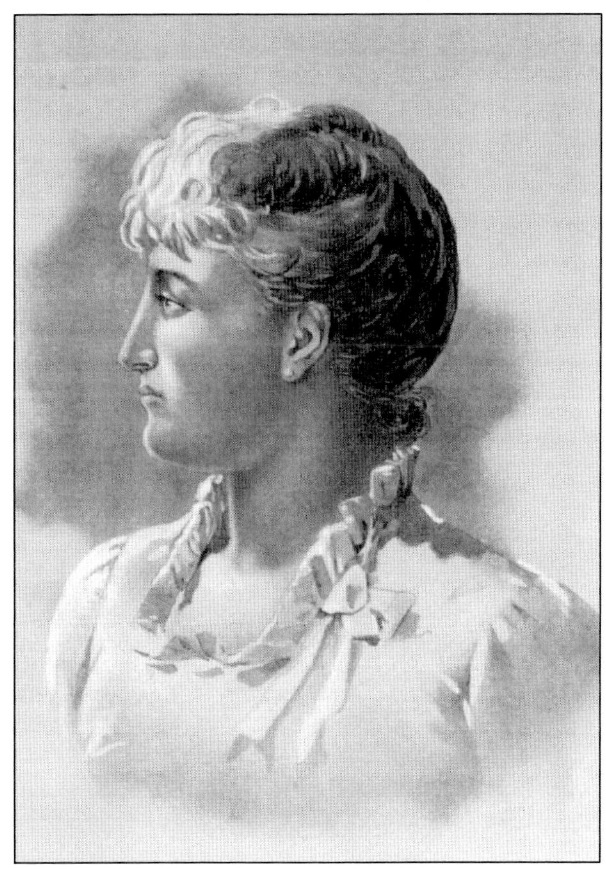

When director Henry Richard Linderman assigned George T. Morgan to design a new dollar coin, the engraver wanted an American woman to serve as his model for Liberty. Numismatic lore says Morgan, upon the suggestion of Philadelphia artist Thomas Eakins, hired young Philadelphia schoolteacher Anna Willess Williams, depicted here, as his model in 1876. The first Liberty Head, or "Morgan," dollars were struck in 1878. Williams, who reportedly became famous for her connection with the Morgan dollar, never desired the limelight and rejected offers for acting roles. She retired as a teacher in 1924 and passed away two years later. (Author's collection.)

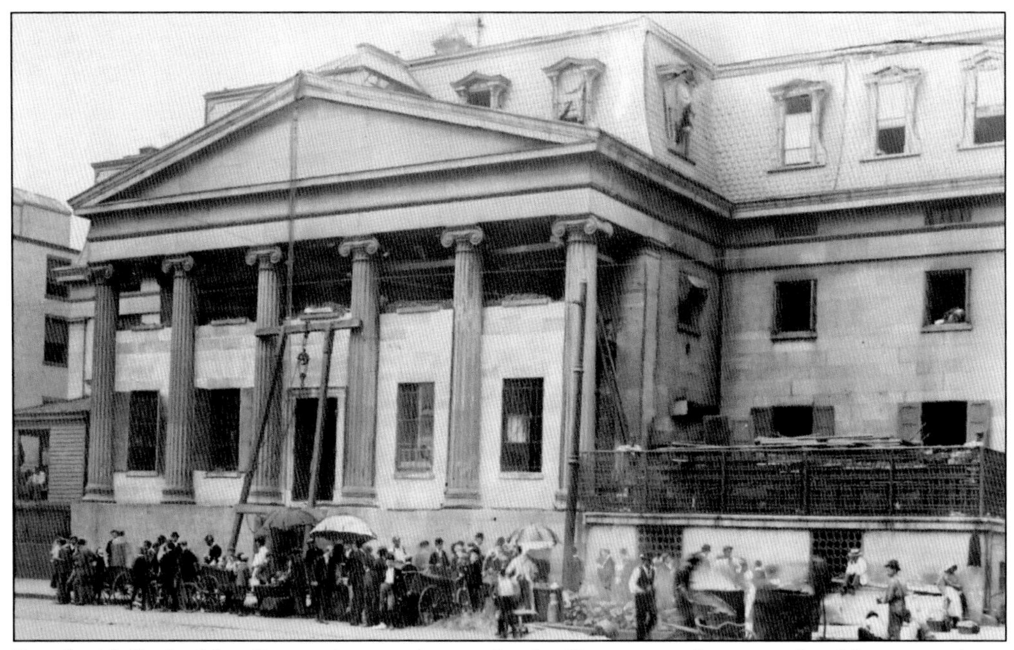

Faced with limited funding options and no action by Congress to buy more land for expansions, Superintendent of the Philadelphia Mint Daniel M. Fox ordered the addition of a temporary mansard roof to vertically add space at the increasingly cramped minting quarters. The bright-red mansard on the ionic Grecian Temple spurred editorial staff at Philadelphia's *The Times* to dub the mint the "first and only sample of Franco-Grecian architecture in the country," adding "there is certainly nothing else like it in Philadelphia." Fox sarcastically replied, "You will perhaps remember that no temple to Juno ever had a high brick chimney sticking up out of it." (Courtesy of the Special Collections Research Center, Temple University Libraries, Philadelphia, PA.)

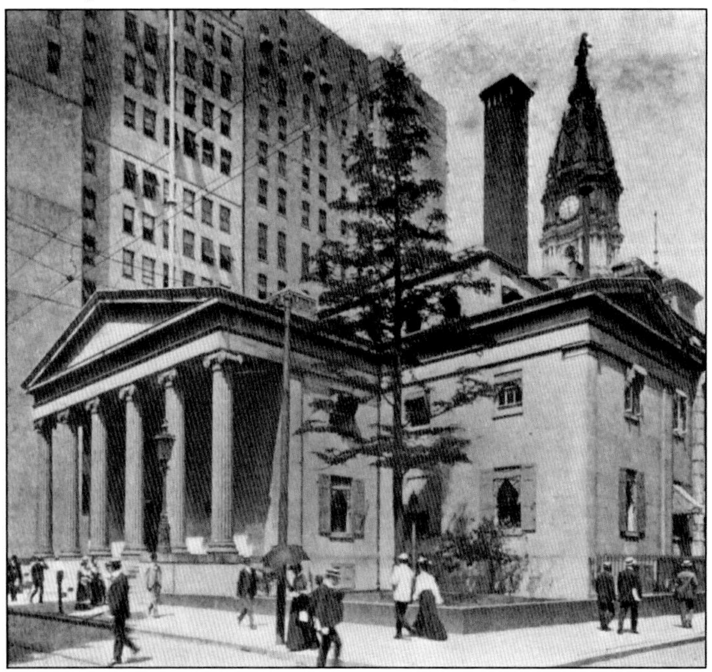

The second Philadelphia Mint is seen during the late 1890s with Philadelphia City Hall and its imposing tower soaring into the skyline. City hall was completed in 1901 and stands 548 feet tall, which includes its iconic 37-foot-tall statue of Pennsylvania's founder, William Penn. City hall was the tallest habitable building in the world from 1894 through 1908 and remained the tallest building in Philadelphia until One Liberty Place surpassed it in 1987. (Courtesy of the Library of Congress.)

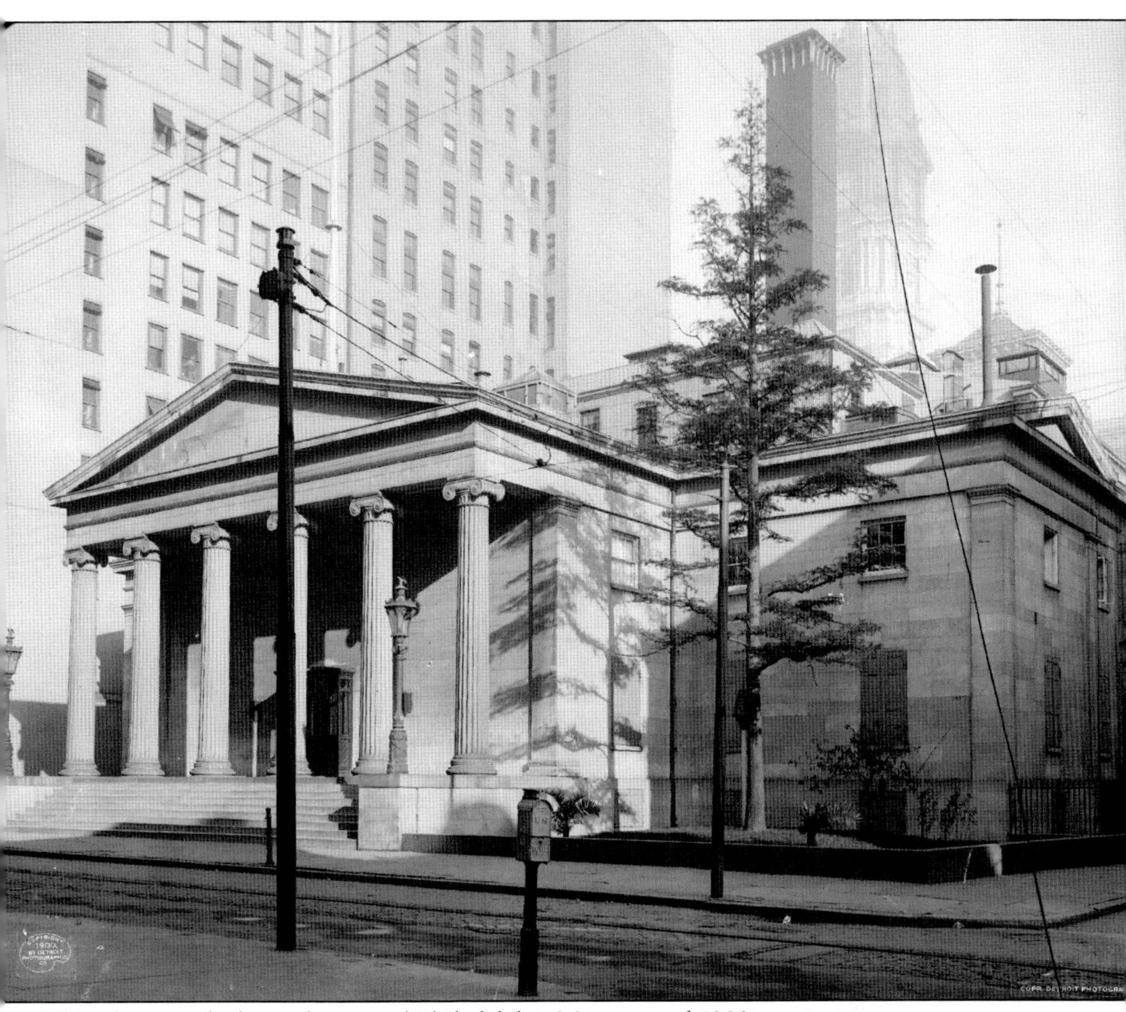

This photograph shows the second Philadelphia Mint around 1900 as minting operations were in the process of being transferred to the newly constructed Philadelphia Mint located at 1700 Spring Garden Street in Center City. Several additions had been made to the 1833-vintage structure over the years with the intent of expanding the building's usable space. Still, the second Philadelphia Mint had become obsolete by the turn of the 20th century. The Grecian Temple, hardly resembling its former glory following various architecturally incongruent additions and years of poor maintenance, was demolished around 1902 soon after the property was sold. The site was redeveloped over the following decade, and emerging from the property was the Widener Building. Opened in 1914, the Widener Building, at 1339 Chestnut Street (1 South Penn Square), underwent a series of renovations that have helped it evolve with the ever-changing Center City landscape. (Courtesy of the Library of Congress.)

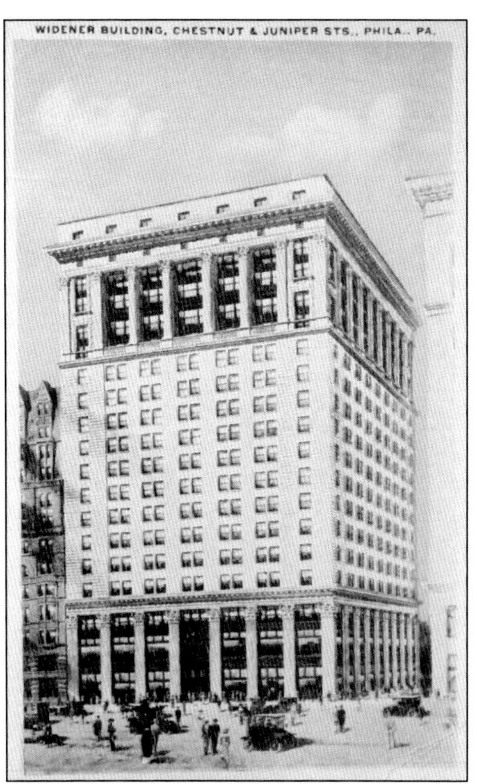

The 18-story Widener Building, standing on the site of the second Philadelphia Mint, was designed by Philadelphia architect Horace Trumbauer, who was involved with designing the Philadelphia Museum of Art and central building of the Free Library of Philadelphia. The Widener Building, standing 260 feet tall, lost many of its original touches when the structure was brutally altered in the 1960s. Later renovations painstakingly recreated or restored many of the elements lost during the remodel, including the Chestnut Street facade and a magnificent three-story arcade inside the building. (Author's collection.)

In 1904, the six ionic marble columns that stood sentry at the front of the mint for some seven decades were donated to Jewish Hospital in Philadelphia (renamed Albert Einstein Medical Center in 1952). The arrangement of the 24-foot-tall columns is seen in the 1913 photograph at the entrance of the hospital. They were temporarily removed in November 2000 when the entrance to Einstein Medical Center on Old York Road was renovated, but they were reinstalled in April 2013 and remain there today. (Courtesy of the Library Company of Philadelphia.)

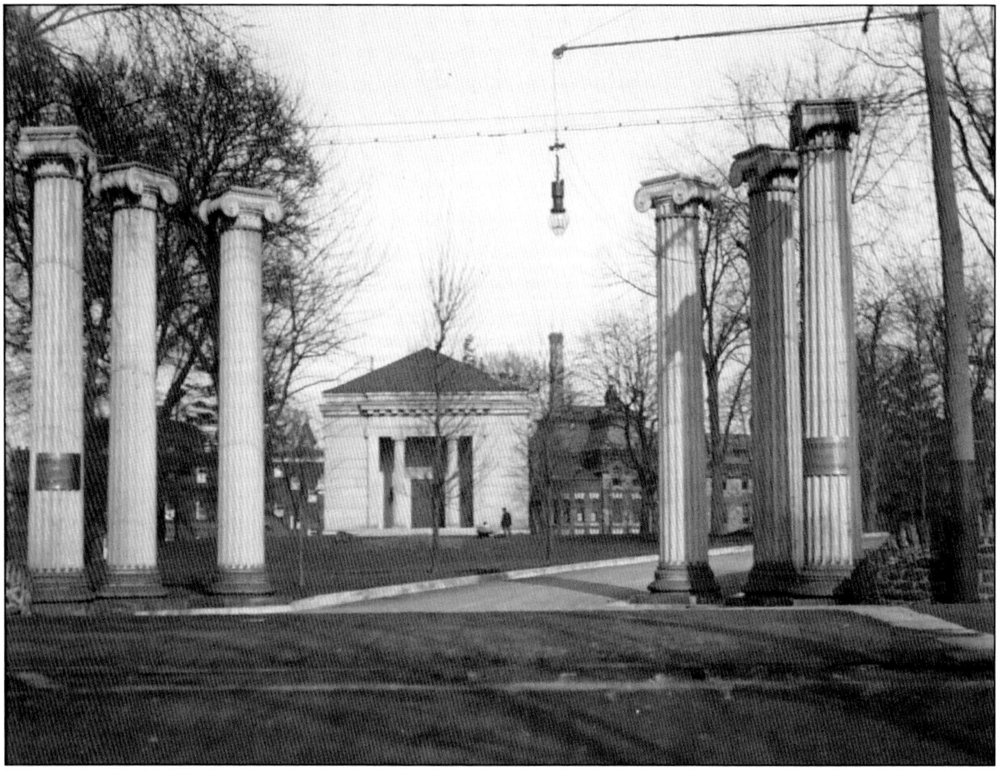

Four

The Third Philadelphia Mint

In Operation from 1901 to 1969

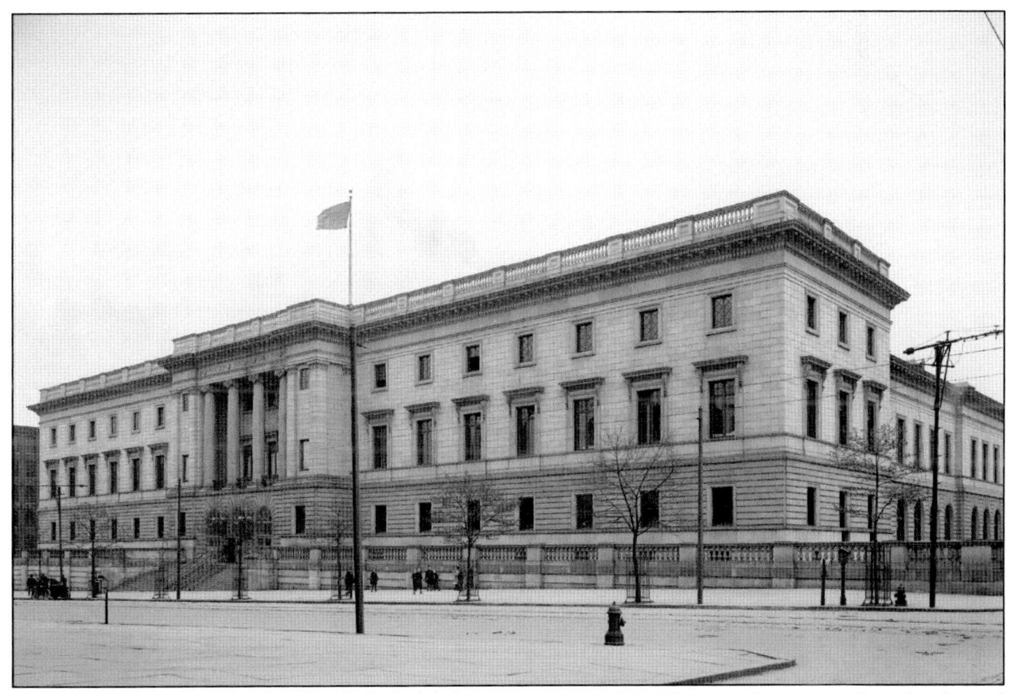

This photograph shows the third Philadelphia Mint around 1905, just a few years after the formal opening ceremony was held on June 13, 1901. The impressive Beaux-Arts building, reaching 395 feet long and consuming an entire city block on Spring Garden Street, was designed by US Mint supervisory architect William Aiken and constructed under Aiken's successor, John Taylor Knox. The land, the building, and the minting equipment within the new structure cost a grand total of $3 million. The land on which the mint building stands formerly belonged to a 1,830-acre manor owned by William Penn, which he named "Springettsbury" for his wife, Gulielma Springett. (Courtesy of the Library of Congress.)

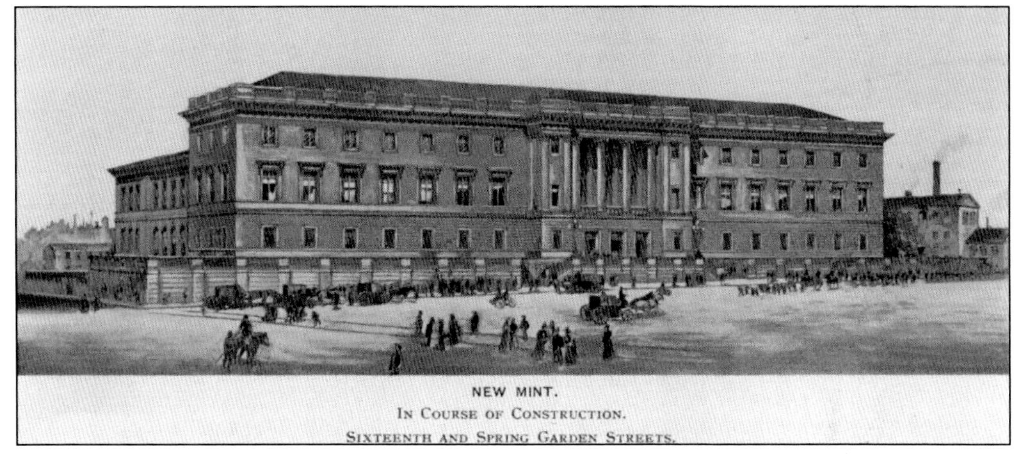

This c. 1898 concept for the third Philadelphia Mint shows a sprawling facility that in every way proved a tremendous step forward for the US Mint, which had long since outgrown its previous building. Planning for the third building began in the late 1880s, eventually laying the groundwork for what became an 81,575-square-foot facility with the latest electrical equipment and state-of-the-art coining equipment. (Courtesy of the National Archives and Records Administration.)

Buttonwood Street.
Rolling and Cutting Room.
Whitening Room.
Melting Room
Coining Room
East Court Yard
Annealing Room
West Court Yard
Book Keepers
Toilet
Counting Room
Chief Clerk
Supt.
Cashier
16th Street
17th Street
Spring Garden Street.
·U·S·MINT.(NEW)·
PHILADELPHIA, PA.
Drawing No 420.
·FIRST·FLOOR·ASSIGNMENT·PLAN·
Scale 3/32 inch = One Foot.

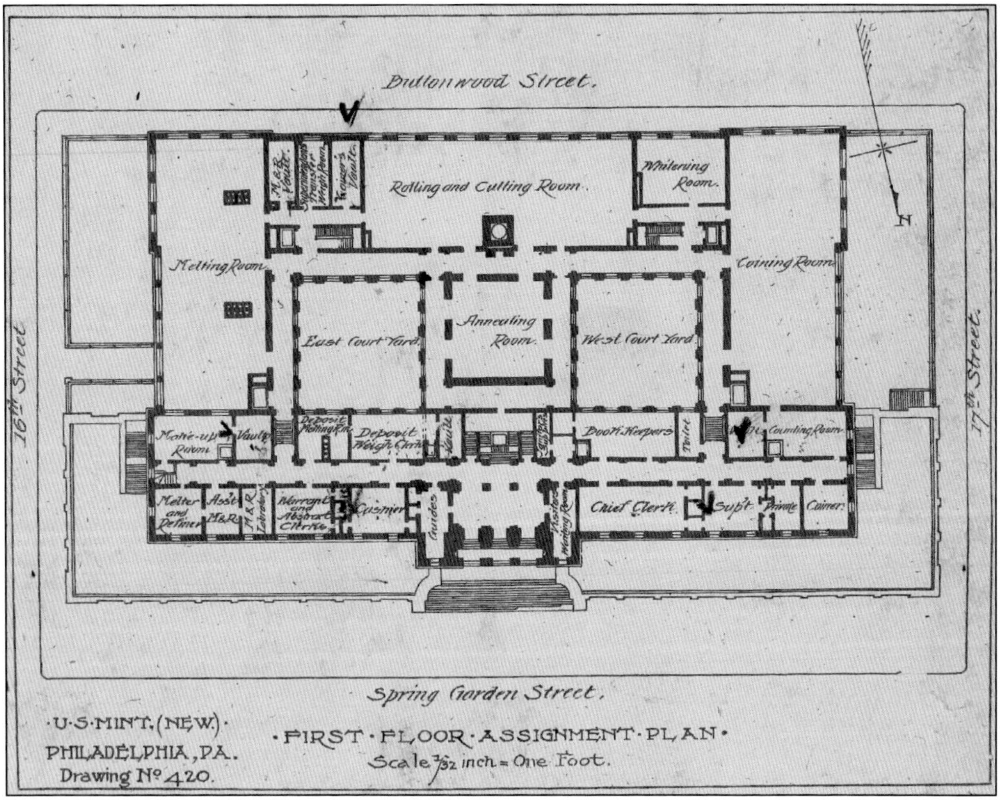

This image shows one of several floor plans designed for the third Philadelphia Mint. In this photograph is the layout of the new mint's first floor, which includes rooms designated for rolling, cutting, and coining operations as well as offices for bookkeepers and the chief clerk, a waiting area for visitors, and restroom facilities. (Courtesy of the National Archives and Records Administration.)

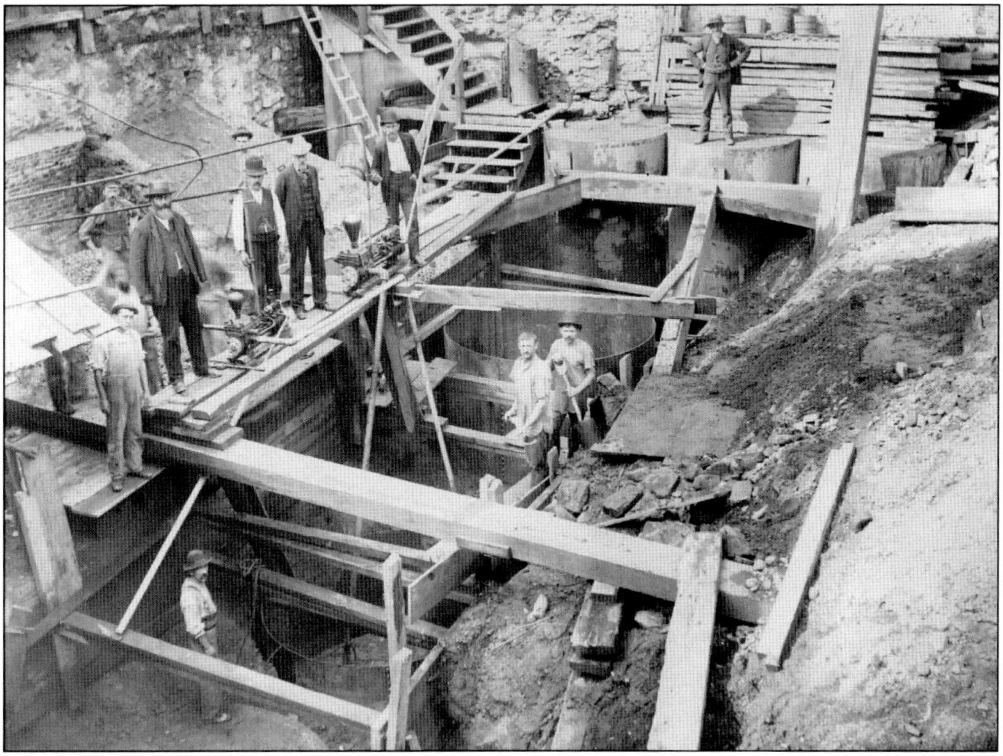

Above, construction workers build caissons, or deep shafts, that will be filled with concrete to help support the foundation for the new mint building. The image below, taken on December 31, 1897, from the southeast corner of the property, shows the entire site early in the preparation stages. Several Philadelphia landmarks are clearly visible, including the former Philadelphia High School for Girls (built in 1876 and replaced in 1933 by a newer building, now named Julia R. Masterman School), located at center at the intersection of Seventeenth and Spring Garden Streets. (Both, courtesy of the National Archives and Records Administration.)

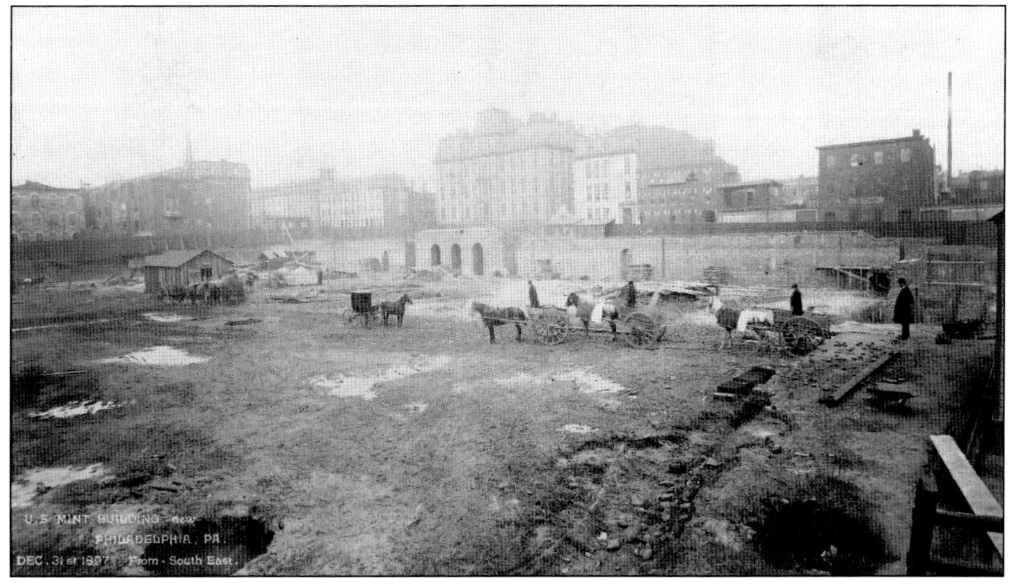

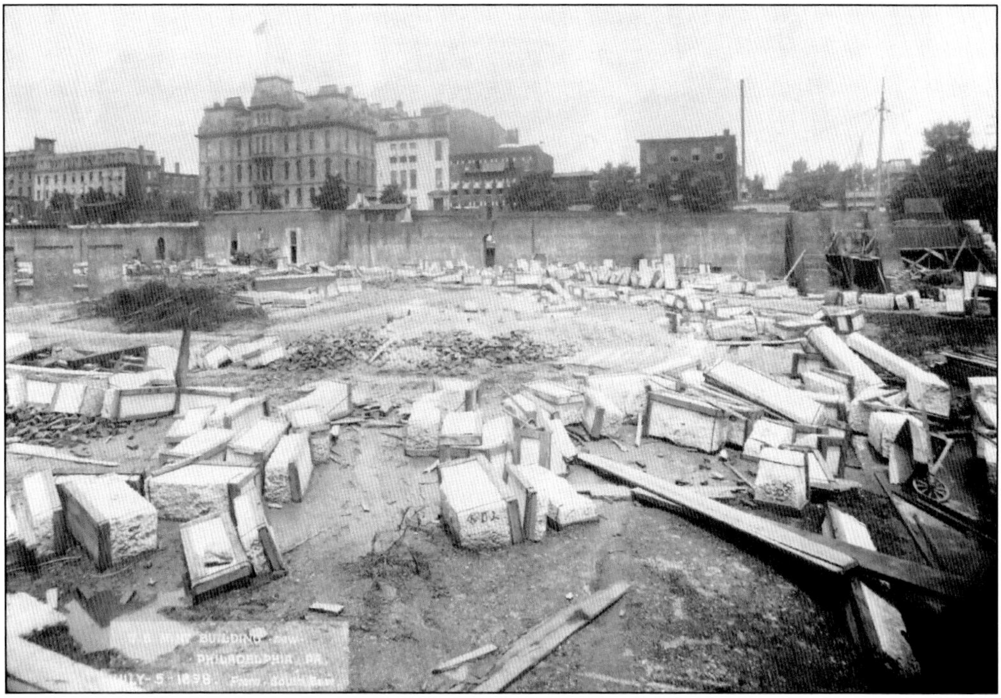

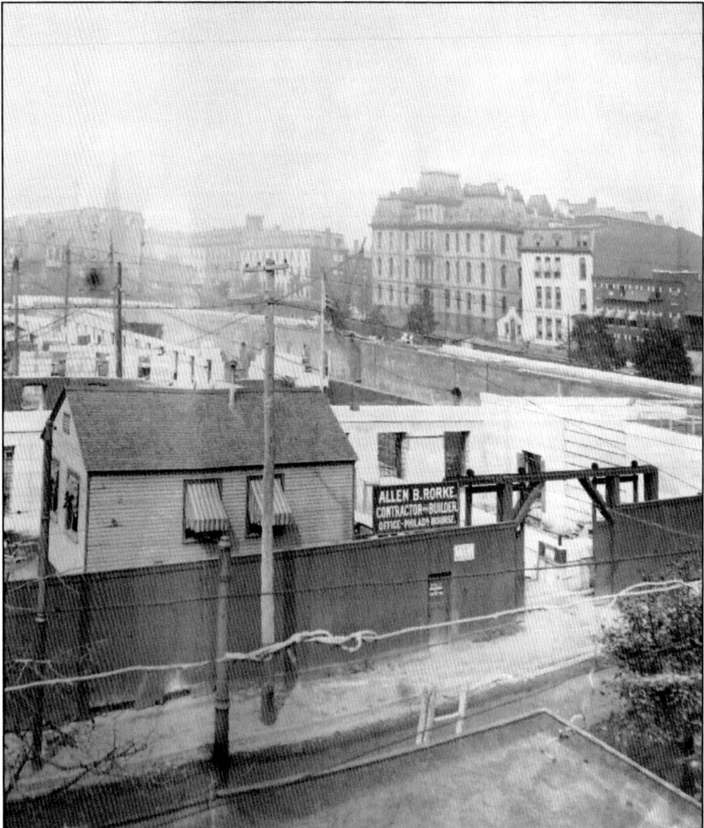

In the photograph above, taken on July 5, 1898, stone segments lay waiting for the walls and other foundational components of the new building. The image at left, from October 1, 1898, shows the lower walls have taken shape. (Both, courtesy of the National Archives and Records Administration.)

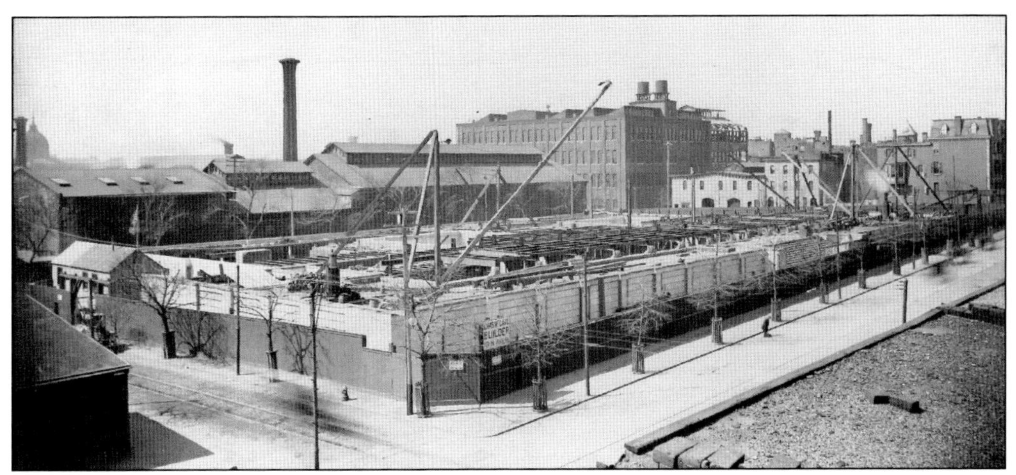

These images, taken from the northeast corner of the new mint site, show dramatic progress on the building's construction. The photograph above was taken on March 31, 1899, and reveals the completion of the first-floor facade, with beams in place for the second floor. The September 30, 1899, image below shows work crews well on their way to completing the third floor. (Both, courtesy of the National Archives and Records Administration.)

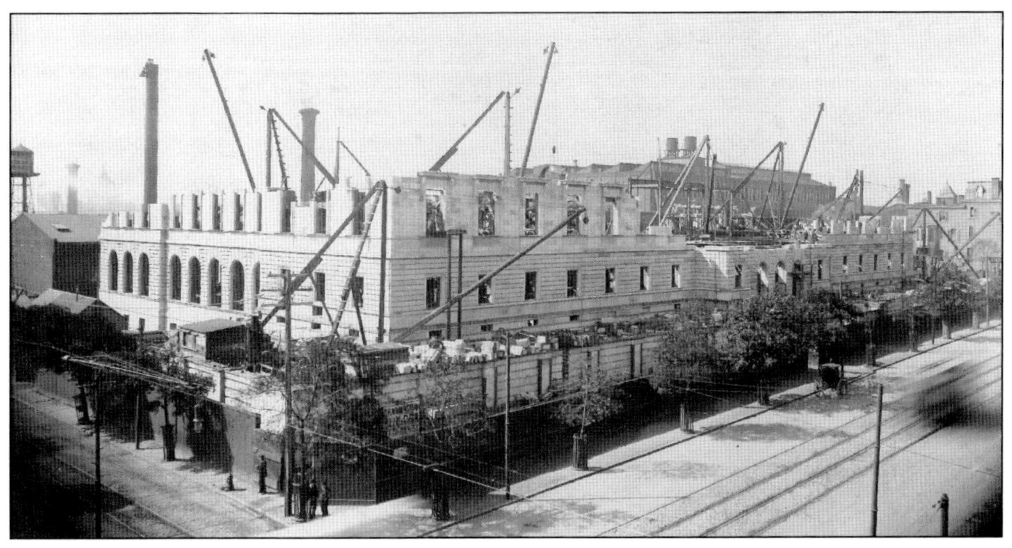

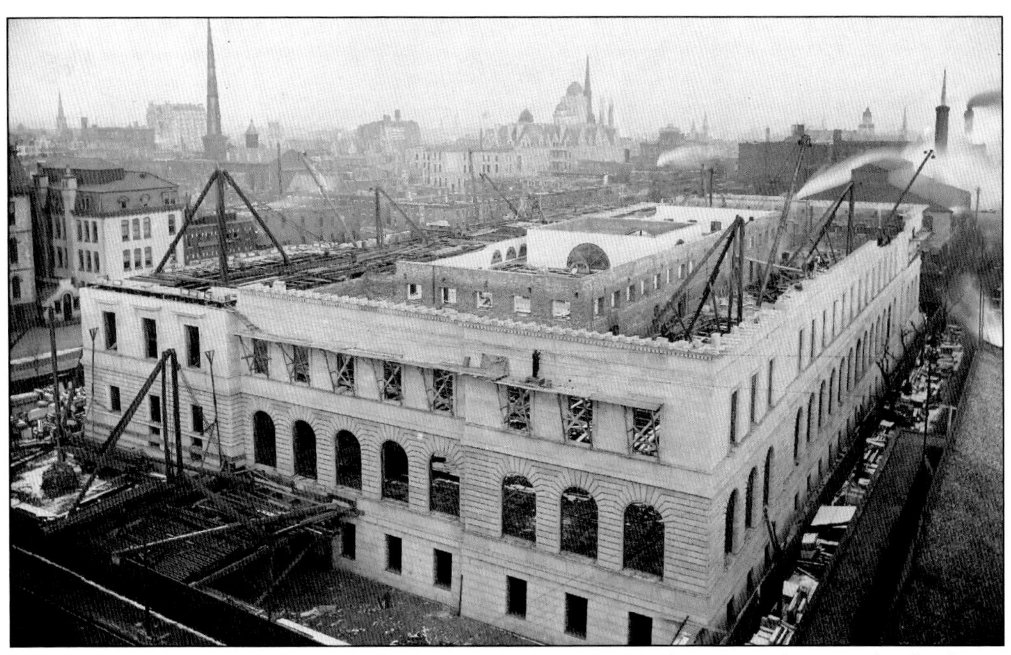

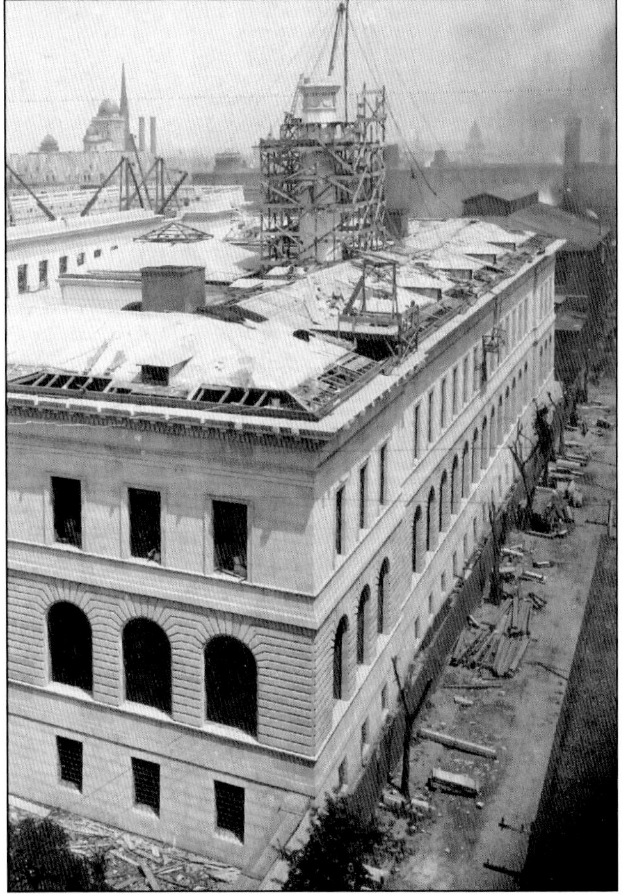

These two photographs, both taken from the southwest side of the site, show progress on the construction on the third Philadelphia Mint as the 1890s close and the 1900s begin. The image above, taken on December 30, 1899, shows the building topping out and primary internal structural elements taking shape. In the June 30, 1900, photograph at left, roofing has been installed and chimneys rise above the roofline. (Both, courtesy of the National Archives and Records Administration.)

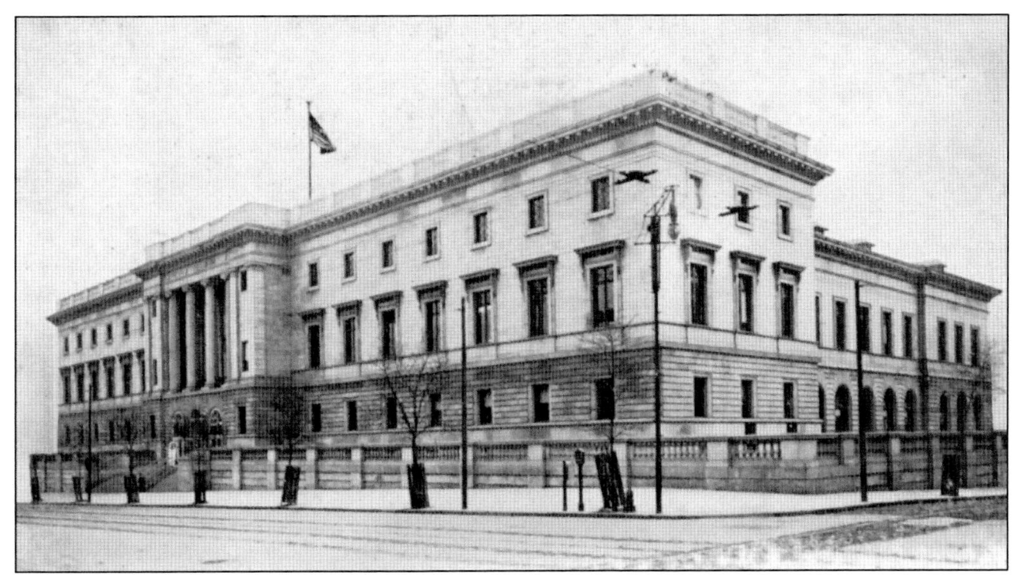

Once completed, this was the exterior appearance of the Philadelphia Mint on the side of its main entrance, which faces the south side of Spring Garden Street between North Sixteenth and Seventeenth Streets. The image above shows a postcard dated from approximately 1905, while the photograph below was taken some 70 years later, after the Philadelphia Mint moved to its current facility located at 151 North Independence Mall East in 1969. The Community College of Philadelphia took over the former mint building in 1971 and has transformed it into the school's main campus. (Above, author's collection; below, courtesy of the Community College of Philadelphia.)

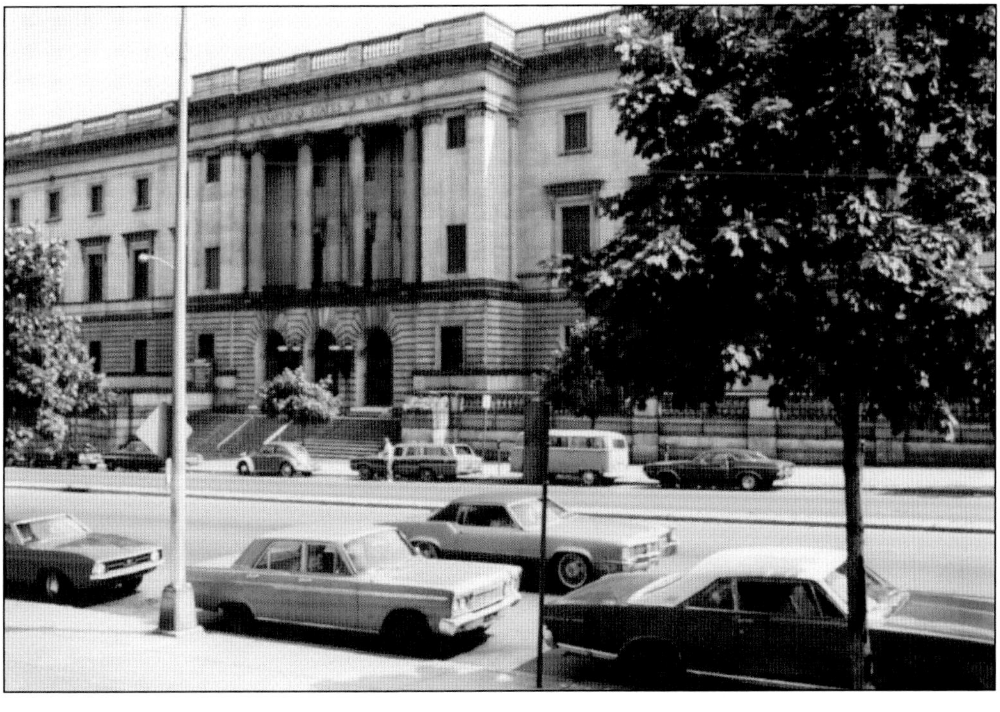

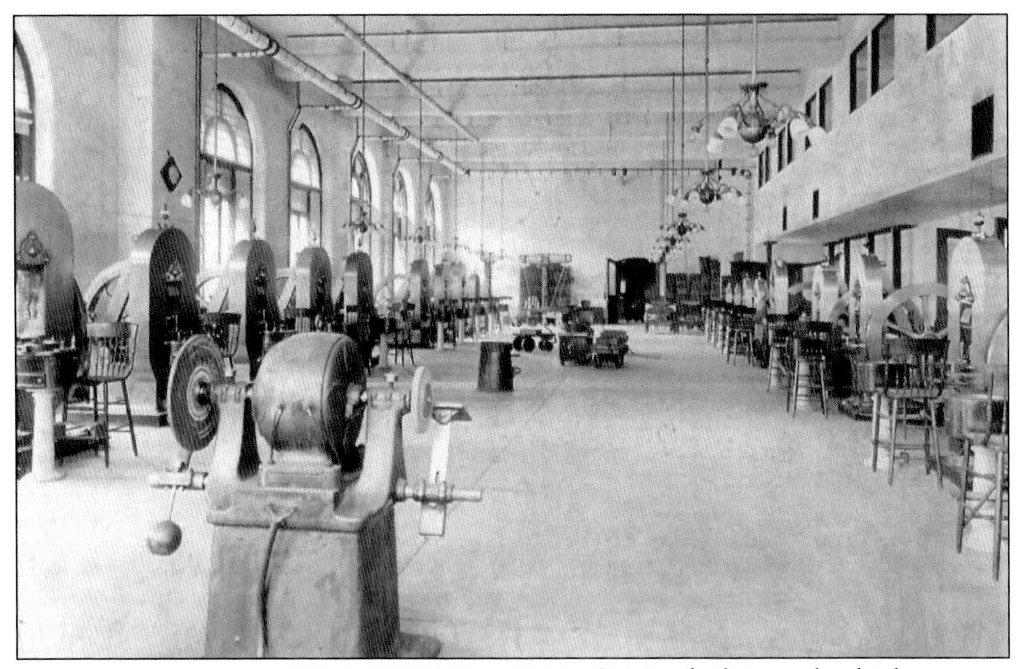

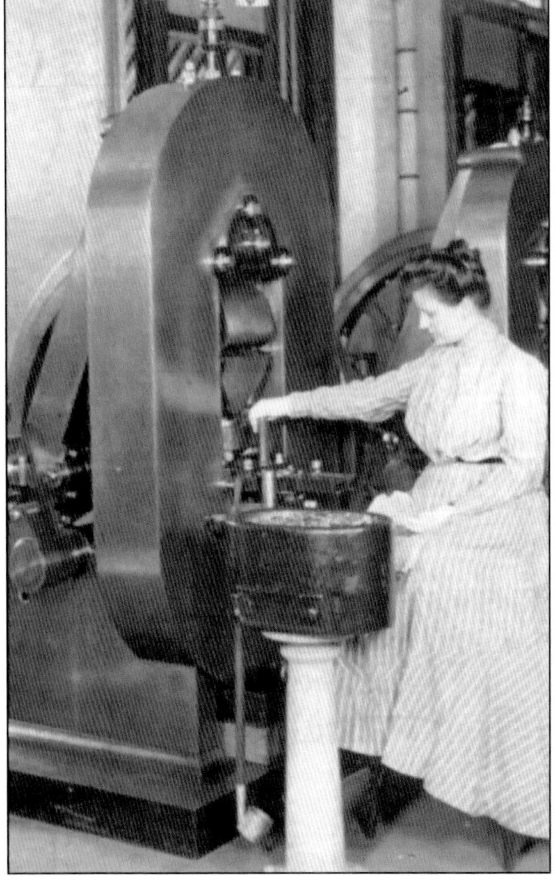

Coining facilities at the third Philadelphia Mint were significantly improved in size and efficiency compared to the tighter quarters at the previous building. Seen here are numerous coin presses primed for a busy day of coin production. This photograph was taken in 1903, which is the year the Philadelphia Mint struck more than 200 million coins, including US business-strike and collector coinage; territorial coinage for the Philippines; and foreign coinage for Costa Rica and Venezuela. (Courtesy of Roger Burdette.)

Sunlight spills in on the coin presses at the mint building, which featured spacious equipment rooms and many tall windows in all principal work areas. This 1903 photograph shows a mint employee in the bright, airy coining room operating a press, which could strike approximately 90 coins per minute. (Courtesy of Roger Burdette.)

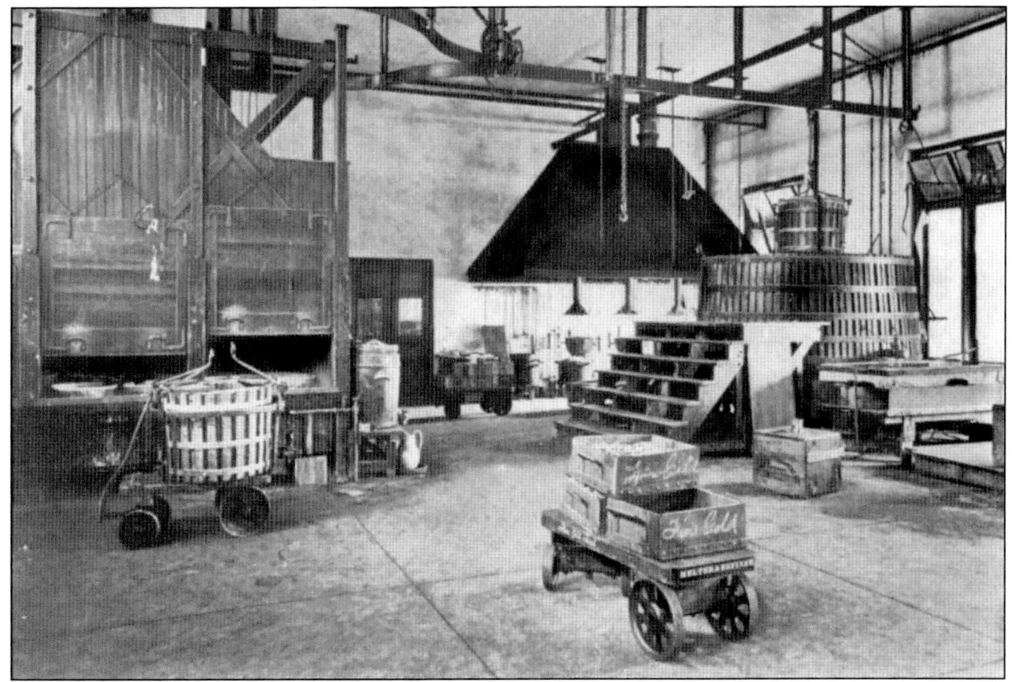

The refining room bustled with activity as mint crews melted and refined precious metals to make new coins. The refining process involves melting raw metal, processing it to a specific degree of purity with the use of acids, and casting the molten metal into bars or ingots that are later transformed into blanks. (Courtesy of Roger Burdette.)

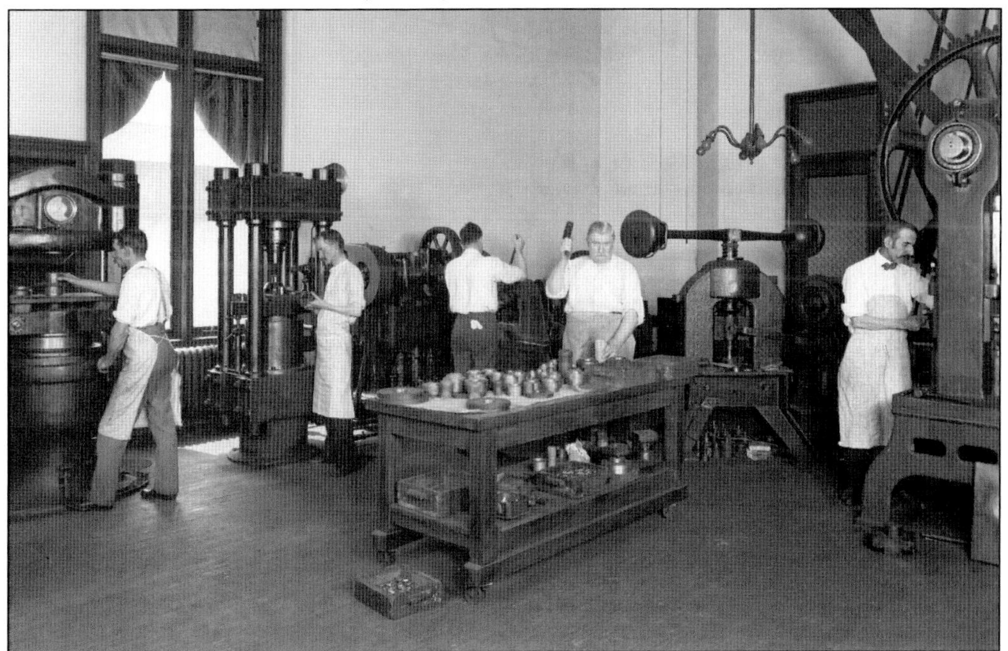

Mint employees work in the Philadelphia Mint's medal room in 1903. These men are using a variety of equipment to create medal dies and strike medals. Note the large screw press in the background. (Courtesy of Roger Burdette.)

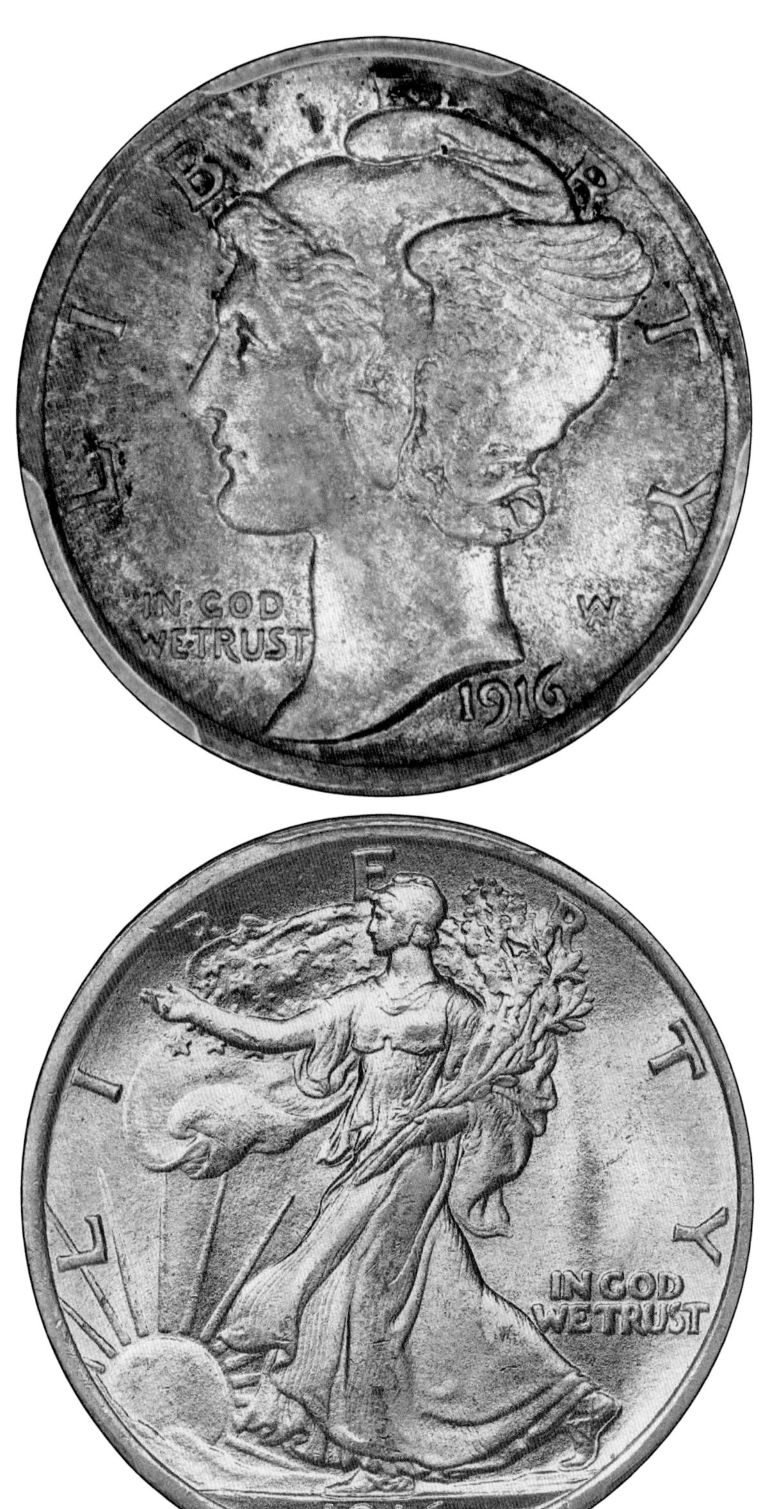

American coinage was experiencing an artistic renaissance in the early 1900s. It was a movement that stems from a note written around 1905 by Pres. Theodore Roosevelt, who desired new designs for all circulating American coinage. It was during this time that several now-familiar coins, such as the Lincoln cent, Buffalo nickel, Standing Liberty quarter, Peace silver dollar, and several classic gold coin designs were born. Among these new coins were the Winged Liberty Head ("Mercury") dime (top) and the Walking Liberty half-dollar (bottom), both of which debuted in 1916. Both designs, by Adolph A. Weinman, have reappeared on US bullion coinage since 1986. (Both, courtesy of Heritage Auctions, www.HA.com.)

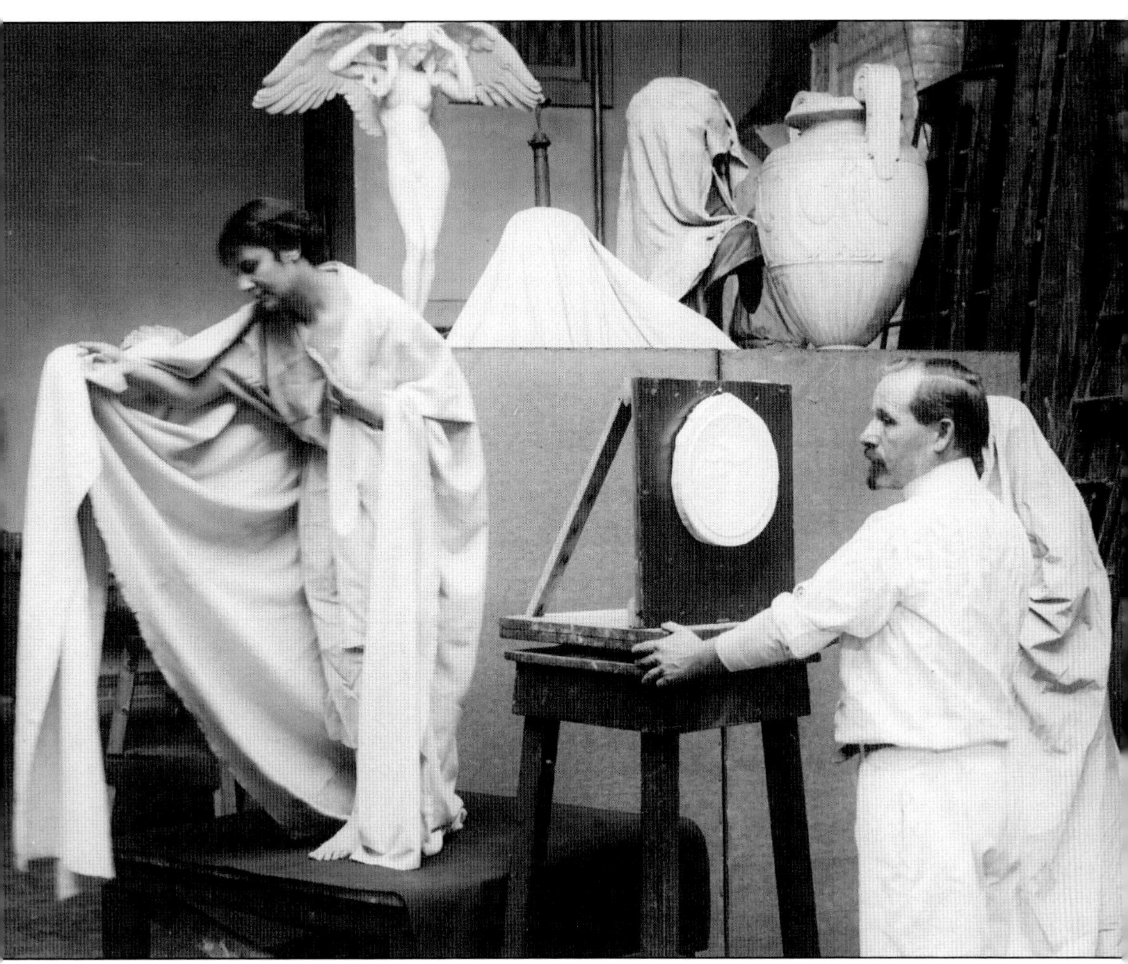

The Mercury dime and Walking Liberty half-dollar designs by Adolph A. Weinman were chosen in a limited competition coordinated by the US Mint, US Treasury, and Commission of Fine Arts in 1916. Weinman, seen here working with a model in his studio, was born in Germany in 1870. He came to the United States at the age of 14 and studied at The Cooper Union for the Advancement of Science in Art in New York City. Eventually studying under sculptor Augustus Saint-Gaudens and others, Weinman opened a studio in 1904. He earned acclaim as a sculptor and was already well known by the time his designs first appeared on US coinage. Among his many non-numismatic works are a statue of Pennsylvania Railroad president Alexander Johnston Cassatt that was originally erected at Pennsylvania Station in New York City but now resides at the Railroad Museum of Pennsylvania in Strasburg. Weinman passed away in 1952, leaving an indelible legacy in numismatics and in the greater art world alike. (Courtesy of the Smithsonian Institution.)

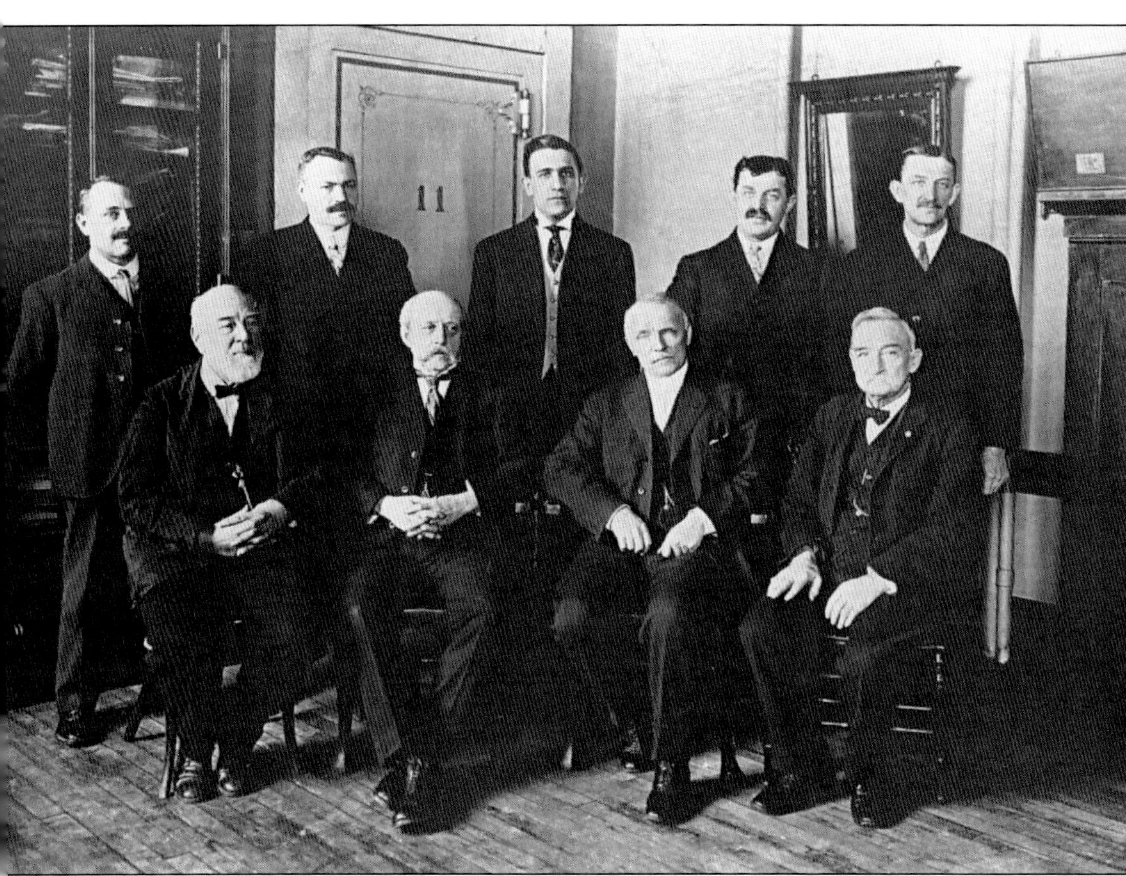

While several sculptors and artists outside the Philadelphia Mint were competing in and winning coin design competitions held by the US government during the early decades of the 1900s, that does not mean the US Mint's sculptors and engravers were waiting around for work. They were still quite busy handling many other coin design projects and engraving duties. This 1902 photograph shows several key members of the early 20th-century engraving team. Seated are, from left to right, William Key, Charles E. Barber, George T. Morgan, and George B. Soley. The men standing are unidentified but are likely members of the die preparation staff. The first two decades of the 20th century witnessed many drastic design changes on US coinage. The artistic revival, initiated by Pres. Theodore Roosevelt and sculptor Augustus Saint-Gaudens around 1905, is often referred to as the "Renaissance of American Coinage." (Courtesy of Robert W. Julian.)

Among the most beautiful coin designs in the world is a gold double eagle (pictured) designed by famous sculptor Augustus Saint-Gaudens. The Saint-Gaudens $20 gold coin, struck from 1907 through 1933, depicts Liberty striding from the horizon with the rising sun behind her. Theodore Roosevelt hoped Saint-Gaudens could redesign several US coins, but the ailing American sculptor managed to produce final designs for just two denominations before passing away, including the $10 gold eagle. (Courtesy of Heritage Auctions, www.HA.com.)

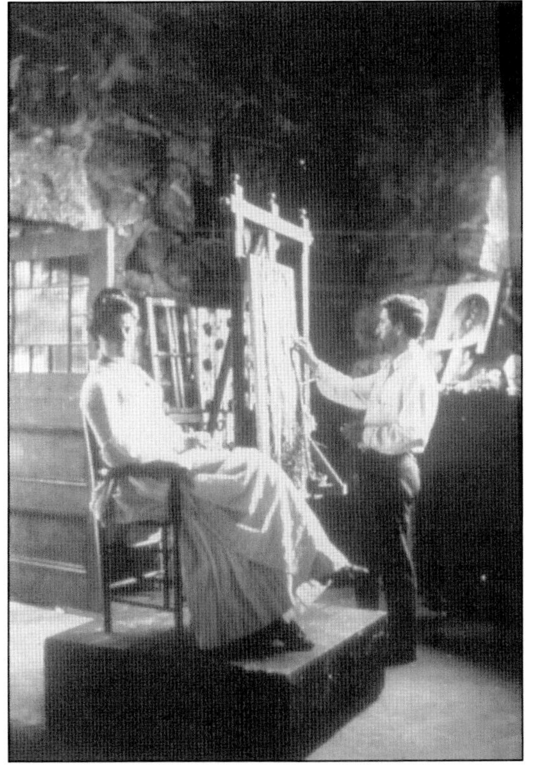

Born in Dublin, Ireland, on March 1, 1848, Augustus Saint-Gaudens rose to fame as a Beaux-Arts sculptor. Seen here working with a model in his studio, Saint-Gaudens produced many famous works, including several that have been on display at the Philadelphia Museum of Art and Delaware Art Museum in Wilmington. One of his most famous works, "Diana" (1892–1893), resides at the Philadelphia Museum of Art. While the legendary sculptor died at the age of 59 in 1907, his work resonates through the generations, and his coin designs still represent the pinnacle of numismatic art. (Courtesy of Saint-Gaudens National Historic Site, Cornish, New Hampshire.)

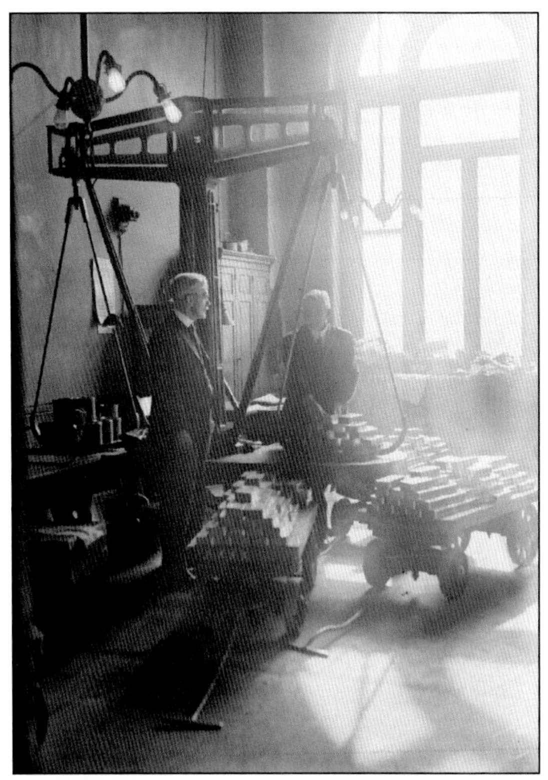

Even back when a $20 gold coin was really worth only its face value of $20, the yellow metal was nonetheless still considered precious and was carefully handled at all stages of processing at the Philadelphia Mint. In this February 1917 photograph, personnel use a massive scale to weigh gold bricks from a recent shipment of ingots from Europe. (Courtesy of the Library of Congress.)

On April 5, 1933, during the depths of the Great Depression, Pres. Franklin Delano Roosevelt issued Executive Order 6102, forbidding the hoarding of gold coinage, gold bullion, and gold certificates. Minting of gold coins stopped soon after, and millions of circulating gold coins were redeemed by the government and melted. In this 1937 photograph, Philadelphia Mint employees pour liquid gold into molds to create gold bars that will be shipped for storage in a bullion depository until future use. (Courtesy of the Historical Society of Pennsylvania.)

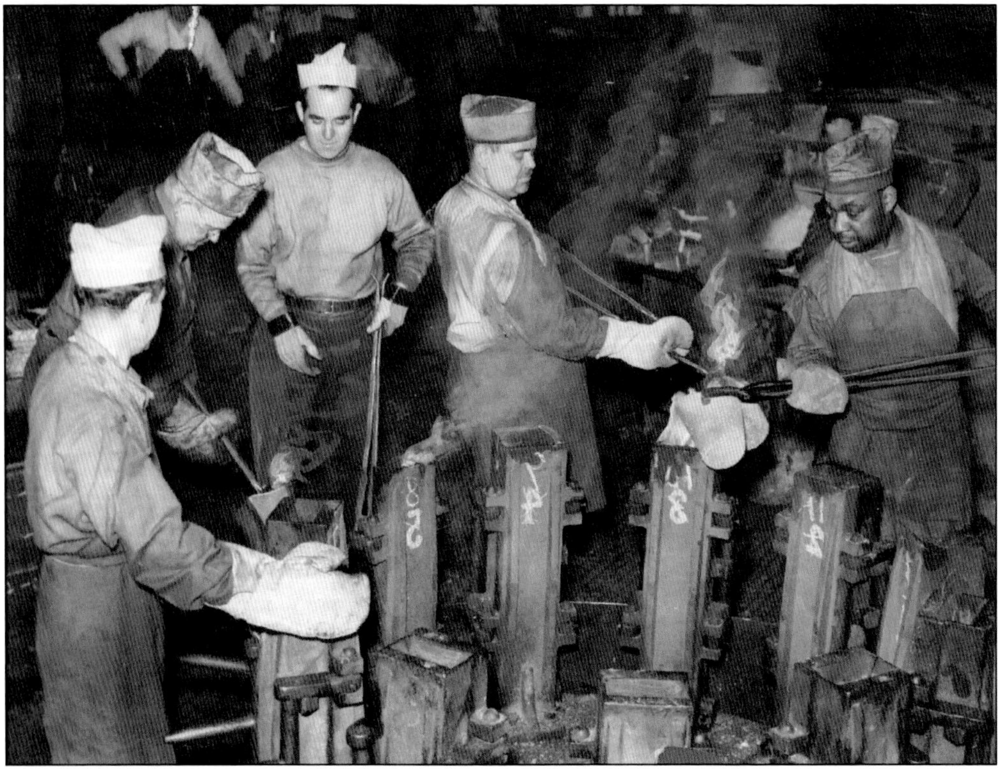

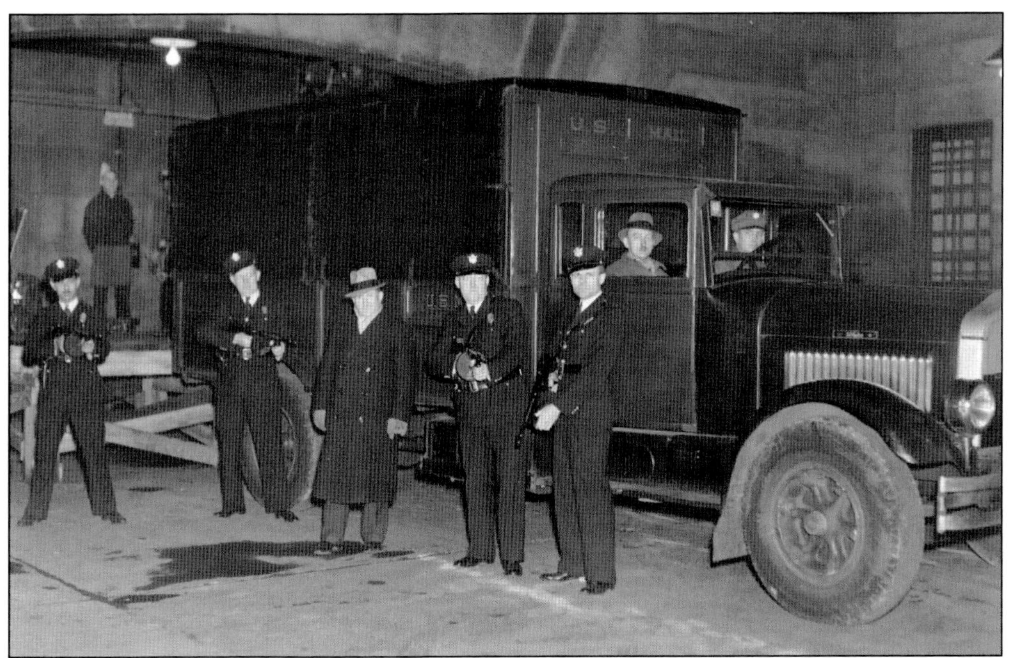

Following the signing of Executive Order 6102 in 1933, production of US legal-tender gold coins swiftly ended and did not resume for some 50 years. In this 1937 photograph, Philadelphia Mint guards wield submachine guns to protect a $1 million shipment of gold bars bound for the US Bullion Depository at Fort Knox, which just began taking gold shipments earlier that year to store reclaimed gold. (Courtesy of the Historical Society of Pennsylvania.)

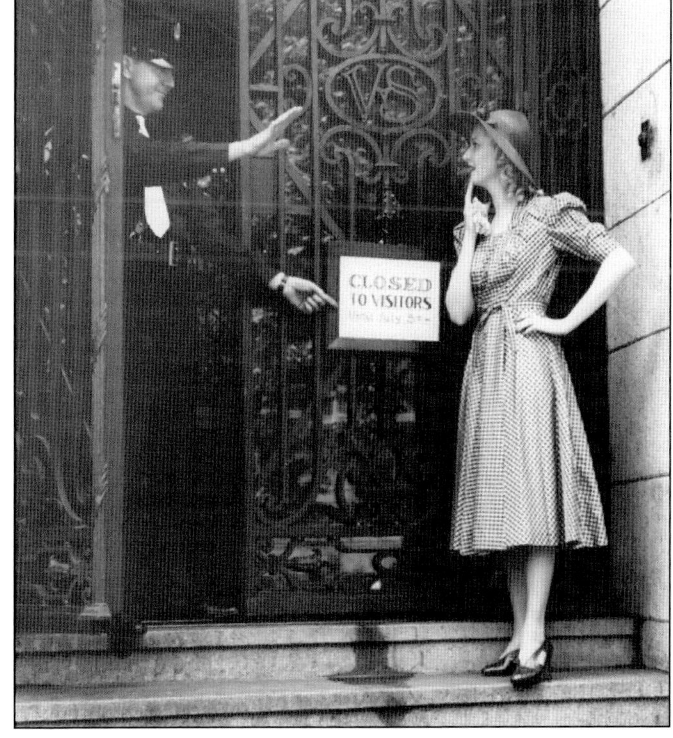

"Halt, no gold diggers allowed in the Philadelphia Mint!" or so the guard seems to be telling the young woman in this staged scene. The photograph actually captures starlet Ethelreda Leopold, who had a role in the 1938 romantic-comedy film *Gold Diggers in Paris*. The film's other stars include several names familiar to audiences of the day, like Rudy Vallee, Rosemary Lane, and Hugh Herbert. Leopold starred in more than 60 other films between 1934 and 1972, including a variety of productions with the comedy duo Bud Abbott and Lou Costello, as well as the iconic Three Stooges slapstick and farce team. (Courtesy of the Historical Society of Pennsylvania.)

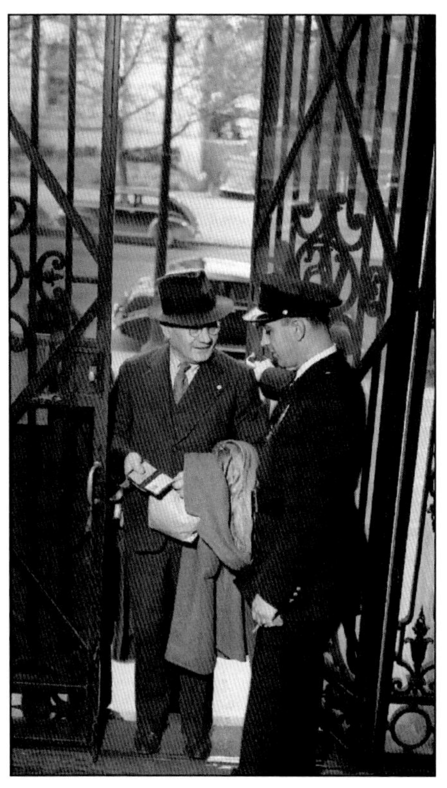

While the Philadelphia Mint guard stopping "gold digger" Ethelreda Leopold may have been acting in jest, minding the mint is no laughing matter. This guard is checking the credentials of an employee entering the Philadelphia Mint in 1941. The US Mint Police was founded in 1792 and is among the nation's oldest federal law enforcement agencies. The mint's police and security force have grown from a handful of guards and a police dog named Nero in the early 1790s to some 300 officers who help protect more than 1,800 employees, tens of thousands of visitors, and billions of dollars in coinage and other assets. (Courtesy of the Historical Society of Pennsylvania.)

Following the lean years of the Great Depression, which caused nationwide unemployment rates to surpass 20 percent in 1933 and reduced the need for new coinage throughout the early 1930s, US coin production began increasing in the mid-1930s. In 1936, construction began on an addition that was completed around 1937 to help expand space for minting operations. This is a view looking northeast from North Seventeenth Street toward the west wall of the mint building. (Courtesy of the National Archives and Records Administration.)

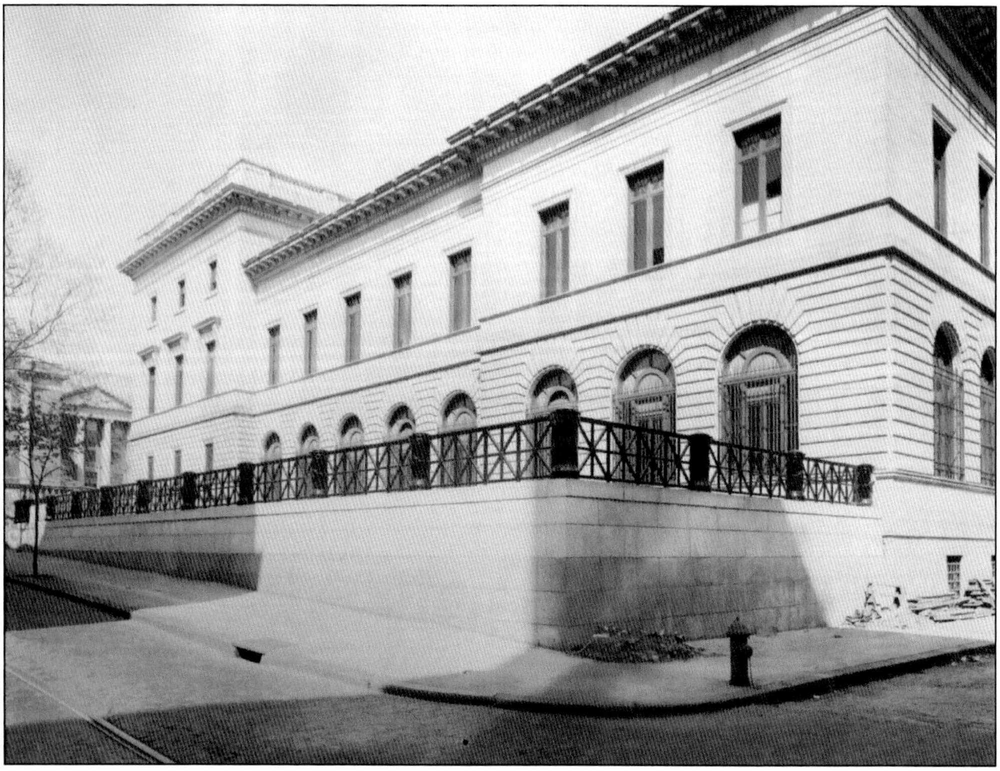

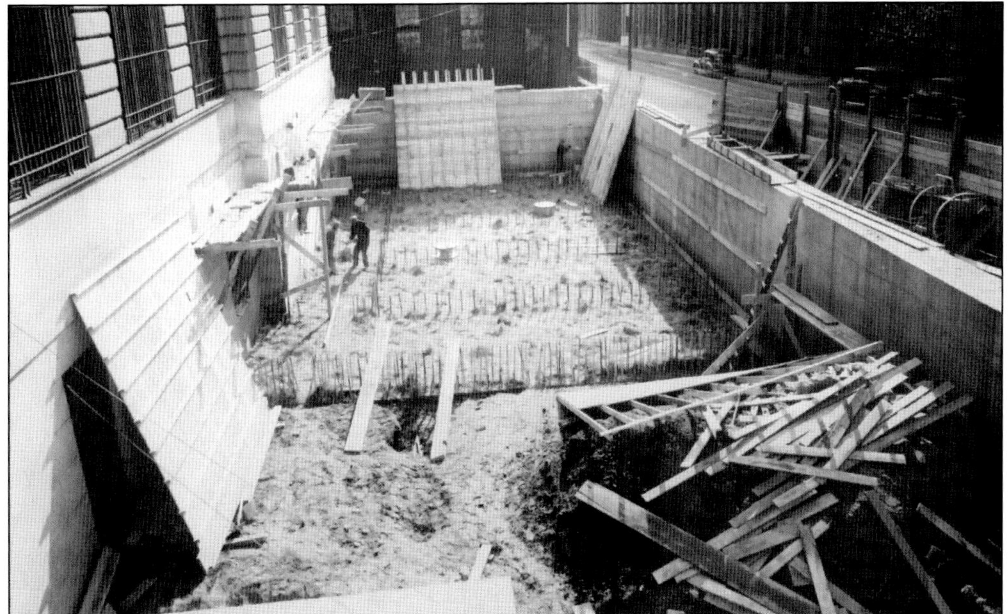

Foundational work for the expansion is under preparation in this c. 1937 southward view. While construction crews were busy adding space at the Philadelphia landmark, the work outside hardly slowed down coining operations inside the mint. More than 525 million coins were made at the Philadelphia Mint in 1937, including some 475 million for domestic use and coin collectors and another 51 million for foreign nations, including territorial coinage for the Philippines. (Courtesy of the National Archives and Records Administration.)

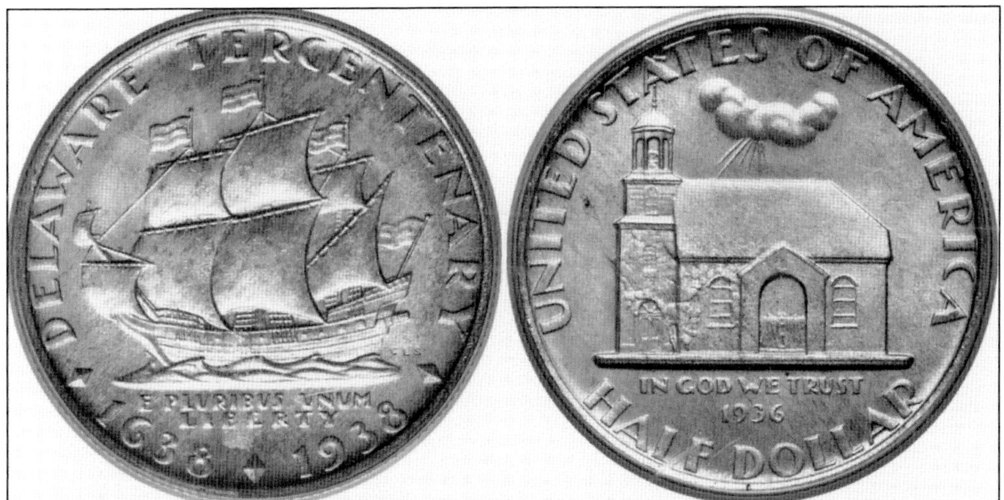

Among the expanded duties at the Philadelphia Mint in the 1930s was the production of many collector coins, such as special-finish proof collector coins and a variety of commemorative coins. Many commemorative half-dollars were struck during this period, including this 1936-dated commemorative half-dollar honoring the 300th anniversary of Delaware's founding in 1638. Struck at the Philadelphia Mint in 1937, the 1936 Delaware half-dollar features Old Swedes Church in Wilmington on its obverse and on the reverse a depiction of the Dutch-built merchant ship *Kalmar Nyckel*, which carried Swedish settlers to North America, where they established the colony of New Sweden in 1638. (Courtesy of Heritage Auctions, www.HA.com.)

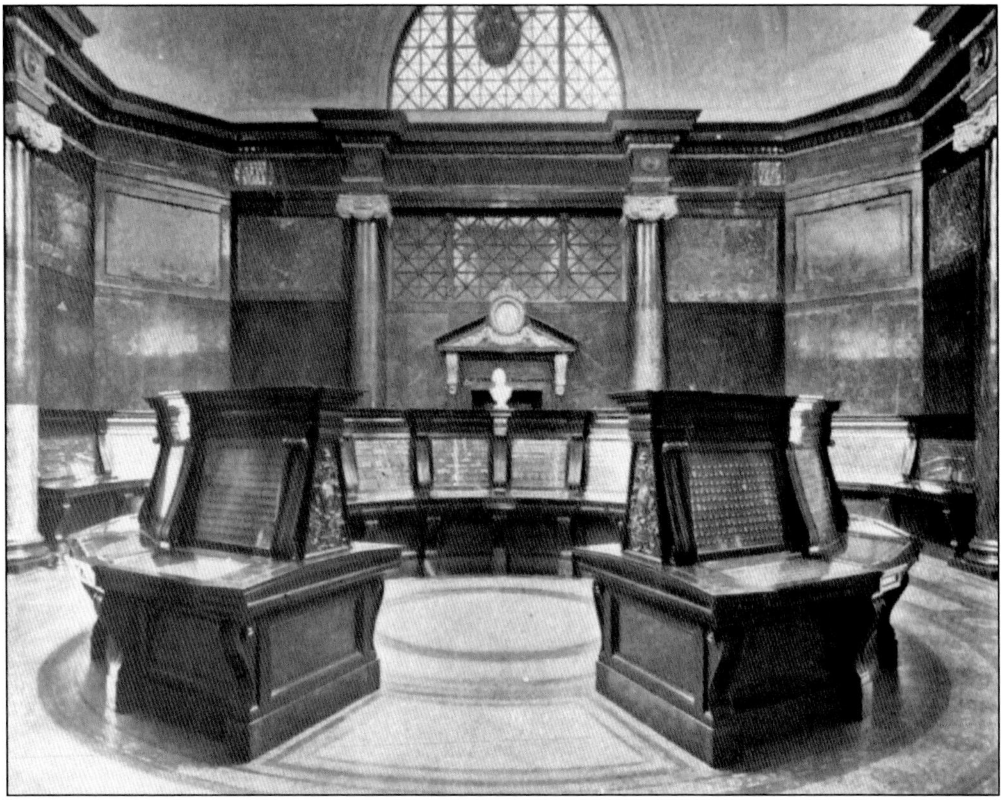

Those visiting the third Philadelphia Mint could view the mint's massive coin and medal collection in a beautiful rotunda. The mint's numismatic collection was larger and broader in scope than just about any other collection on public display and was a favorite stop for the thousands of people who visited the Philadelphia Mint each year. The collection was exhibited in the mint's mezzanine area, which was also where a viewing gallery was located for guided tours of the Philadelphia Mint. The collection was transferred to the Smithsonian Institution in 1923. (Courtesy of Roger Burdette.)

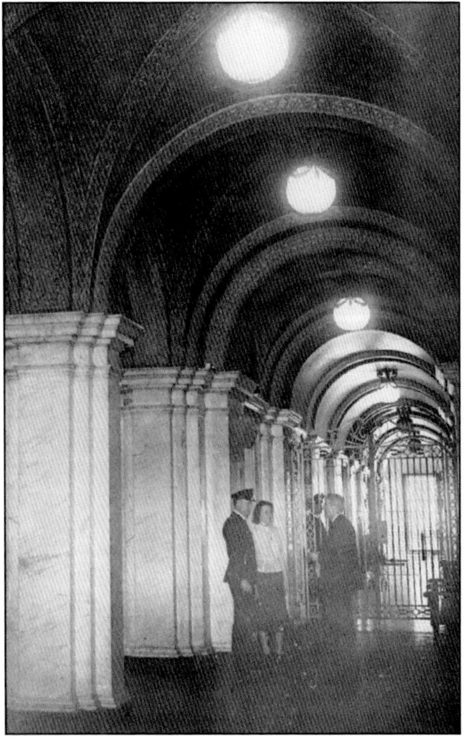

Visitors at the US Mint were not only treated to a close encounter with its extensive numismatic collection and views of the coining operations, but they also had the opportunity to see this Philadelphia architectural masterpiece from the inside. This long corridor with marble columns and impressive arches was among the many fascinating sights welcoming guests at the third Philadelphia Mint. (Courtesy of the Pennsylvania Historical and Museum Commission, Pennsylvania State Archives.)

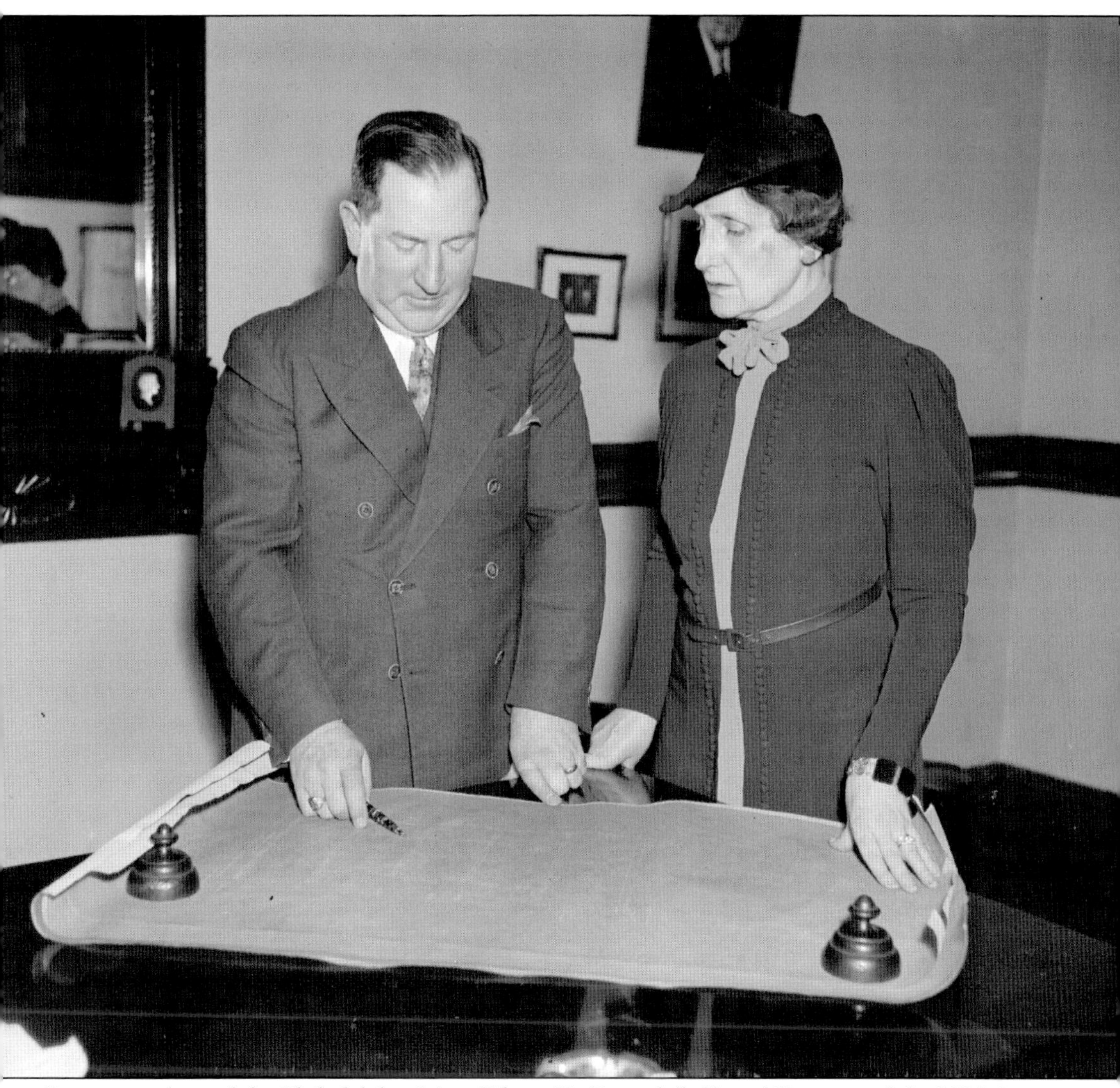

Superintendent of the Philadelphia Mint Edwin H. Dressel (left) and Director of the US Mint Nellie Tayloe Ross discuss plans for transferring gold to Fort Knox in 1937. Ross, who was born in 1876, broke many barriers at a time when women had only recently gained the right to vote in the United States. In 1925, just five years after the ratification of the Nineteenth Amendment that gave American women the right to vote, Ross became the first female to be sworn in as the governor of any state (Wyoming). In 1933, she became the first woman to serve as director of the US Mint, a position she held for five terms until retiring in 1953. After her retirement, she wrote articles for a variety of women's magazines. When she died in 1977 at the age of 101, she was the nation's oldest ex-governor. (Courtesy of the Library of Congress.)

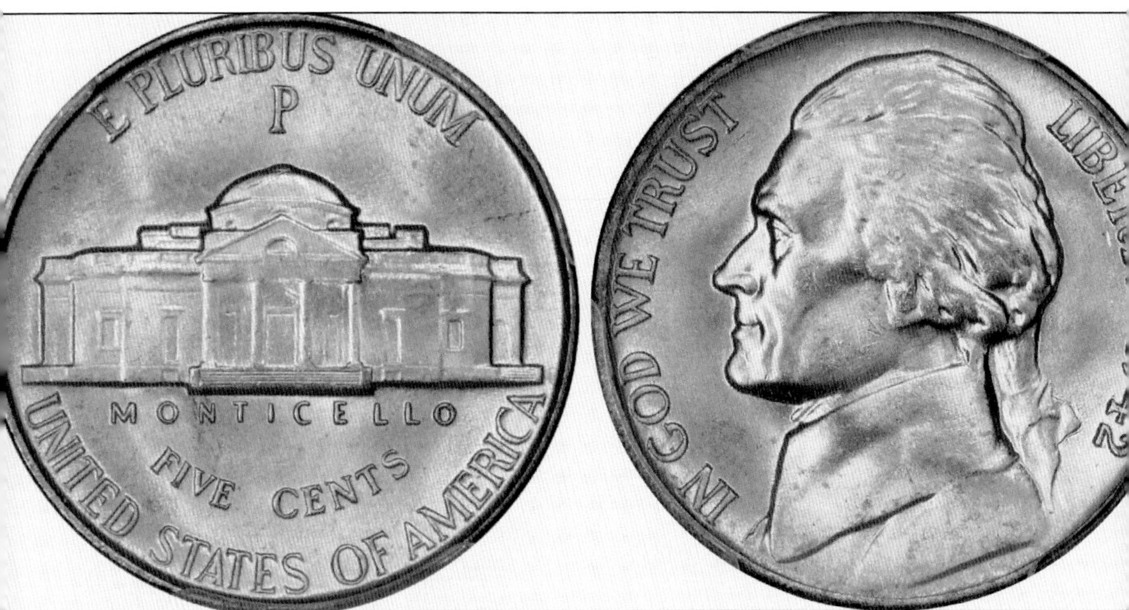

America's full involvement in World War II in 1941 necessitated rationing of certain materials. Nickel was integral for armor plating, and thus, the US government ordered the removal of nickel from five-cent coins, which are ordinarily made from a composition of 75 percent copper and 25 percent nickel. In late 1942, the US Mint began producing five-cent coins composed of a 35-percent silver alloy (the balance containing copper and manganese). These so-called "war nickels" are distinguished from "regular" nickels with the placement of a large mintmark over the dome of Monticello on the coin's reverse. This led to the first-ever appearance of a "P" mintmark signifying coins made at the Philadelphia Mint. (Courtesy of Heritage Auctions, www.HA.com.)

Wartime metal rations also affected the one-cent coin, which in 1943 was made from steel to save copper for the war effort. However, many people did not like using the 1943-dated steel cents because they tended to rust and were often confused with the dime. Responding to the outcry, the US Mint began making one-cent coins from recovered copper cartridge casings in 1944, a practice continued through 1946. Pictured in 1944, Philadelphia Mint employee Charles Donahue is scooping ammunition casings in preparation for striking so-called "shell case cents." (Courtesy of the Historical Society of Pennsylvania.)

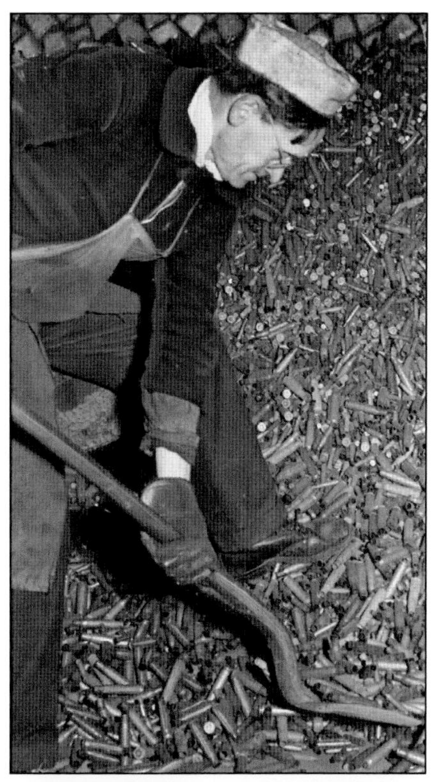

Even with improved technology during the middle of the 20th century, producing coinage of the highest quality still required the human touch. In this 1942 photograph, Assistant Superintendent of the Philadelphia Mint Helen C. Moore inspects newly minted coins to ensure they appear as they should before they enter circulation. Even today, US Mint employees examine samples of coinage to inspect their quality and appearance before they reach public hands. (Courtesy of the Historical Society of Pennsylvania.)

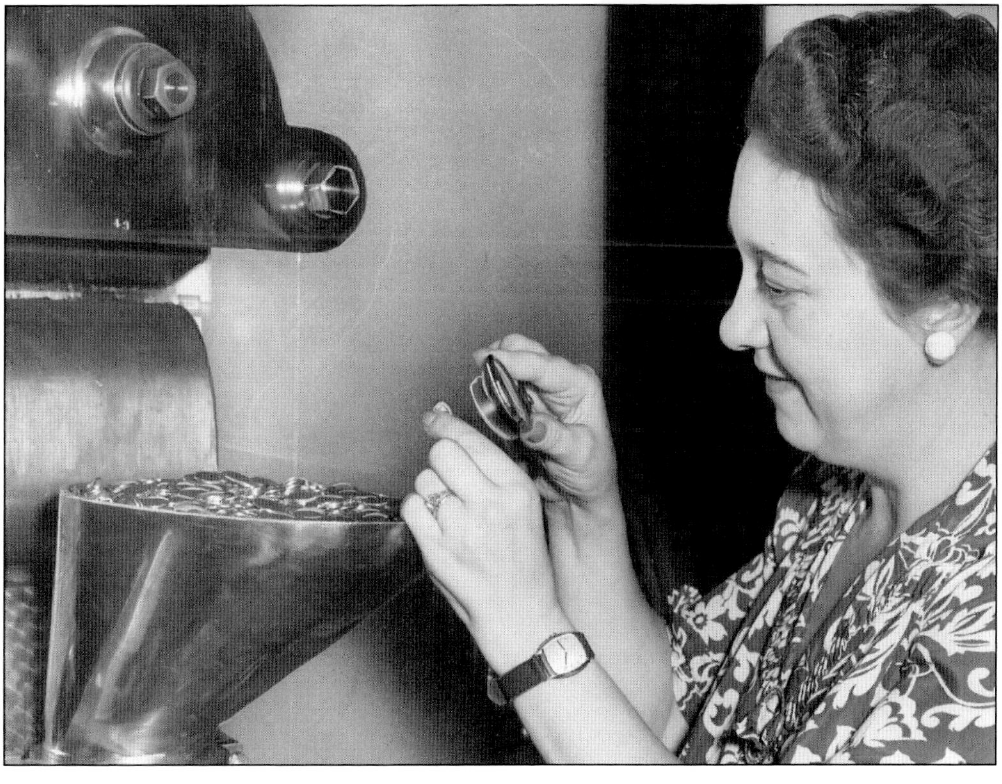

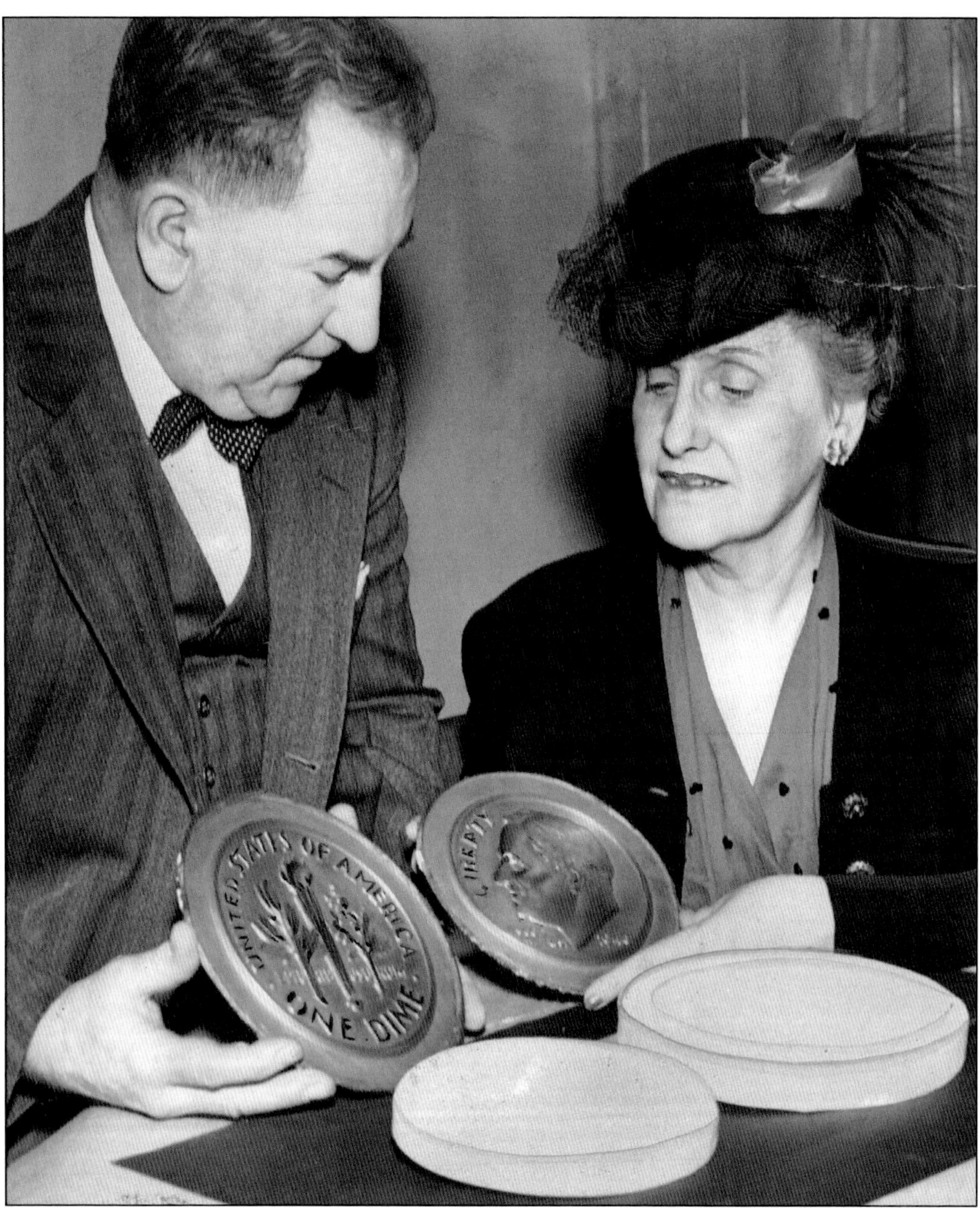

Franklin Delano Roosevelt was not only a popular president, but he also helped bring awareness to polio, a paralytic disease with which he was diagnosed at the age of 39. In 1938, he founded a nonprofit organization originally called the National Foundation for Infantile Paralysis to combat polio. The campaign encouraged Americans to send in dimes to support the cause and led to the organization's eventual renaming as the March of Dimes. When Roosevelt died on April 12, 1945, at the age of 63, it was thought appropriate to honor the fallen president on the dime. John R. Sinnock, who served as the eighth chief engraver from 1925 through 1947, designed the Roosevelt dime. This January 1946 photograph shows models of the new dime being held by Philadelphia Mint superintendent Edwin H. Dressel (left) and US Mint director Nellie Tayloe Ross. The first Roosevelt dimes were released in early 1946, replacing the Winged Liberty Head, or "Mercury," dime. (Courtesy of the Historical Society of Pennsylvania.)

Roosevelt dimes and Washington quarters, the latter introduced in 1932 to honor the 200th anniversary of George Washington's birth, were workhorse coins in US commerce during the 1950s and 1960s, as they are today. In 1965, when silver prices were skyrocketing, the US Mint changed the composition of both the dime and quarter from 90 percent silver and 10 percent copper to the current copper-nickel clad. In the photograph at right, a mint employee is seen inspecting examples of the new copper-nickel clad Roosevelt dimes, and below, press operators examine new copper-nickel clad Washington quarters. (Both, courtesy of the Lawrence S. Williams Inc. Collection, the Athenaeum of Philadelphia.)

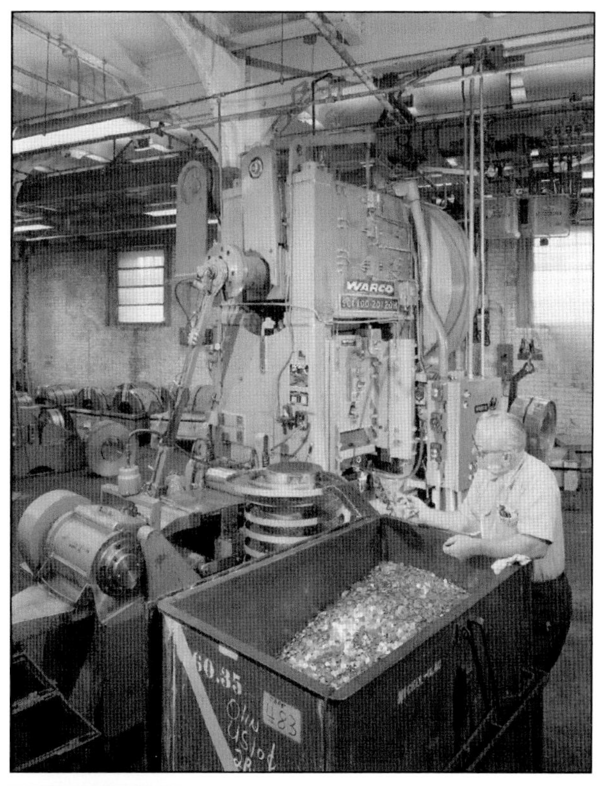

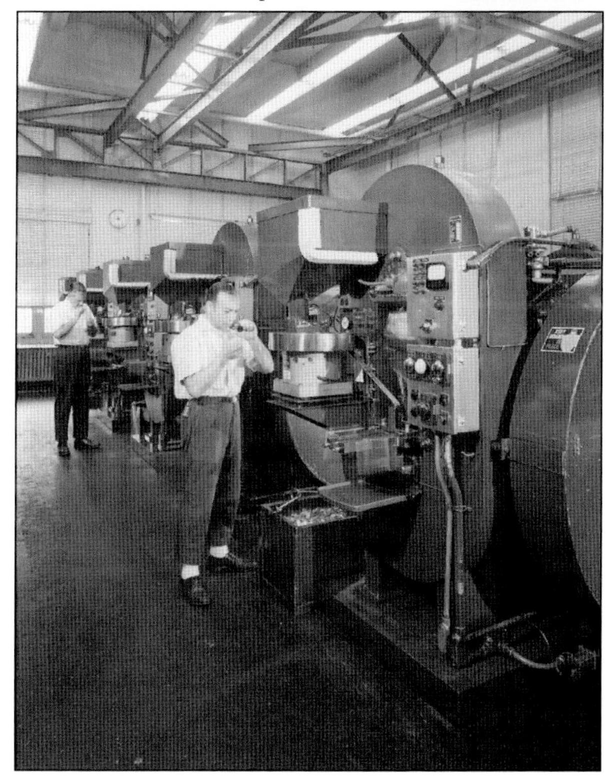

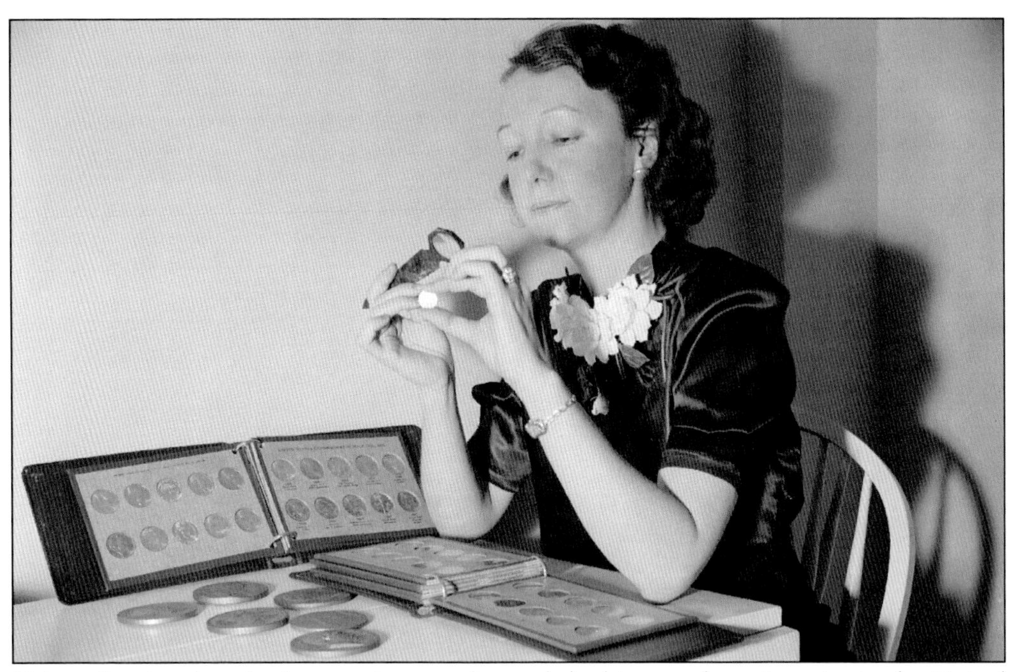

Coin collecting dates back to ancient royalty, and the history of numismatics in the United States traces back to the nation's earliest days. However, the hobby became increasingly popular in the United States during the middle of the 20th century in large part due to the introduction of albums and boards that made it easy for Americans to pick coins from circulation and neatly organize them in attractive displays. Coin collector Edness Wilkins, secretary of mint director Nellie Tayloe Ross, is proudly inspecting her collection of US coins in this 1938 photograph. (Courtesy of the Library of Congress.)

The 1950s was an exciting period in American numismatics, which was growing unlike ever before. Part of the popularity was driven by the discovery of the coin pictured. It is a 1955 Lincoln cent that was made at the Philadelphia Mint with a major mistake—it was struck by a die with a doubled design (note the doubling of the obverse lettering and date). This so-called "doubled die," caused inadvertently in the hubbing process when two identical images were distinctly impressed on the die at slightly offset angles, remains one of the most famous coin oddities. Numismatic experts believe only about 20,000 were made, and each of these legendary coins is now worth about $1,000 or more. (Courtesy of Heritage Auctions, www.HA.com.)

The US Mint has been offering coins and coin products specifically for collectors since the 19th century. Among the most popular items are uncirculated sets. In this photograph, Assistant Superintendent of the Denver Mint Marshall Reddish holds up a 1962 US Mint uncirculated set. On the left is one half of the set containing examples of a Lincoln cent, Jefferson nickel, Roosevelt dime, Washington quarter, and Franklin half-dollar from his branch facility. On the right is the other half of the 1962 uncirculated set with uncirculated examples of the same coins struck at the Philadelphia Mint. (Courtesy of the Denver Public Library.)

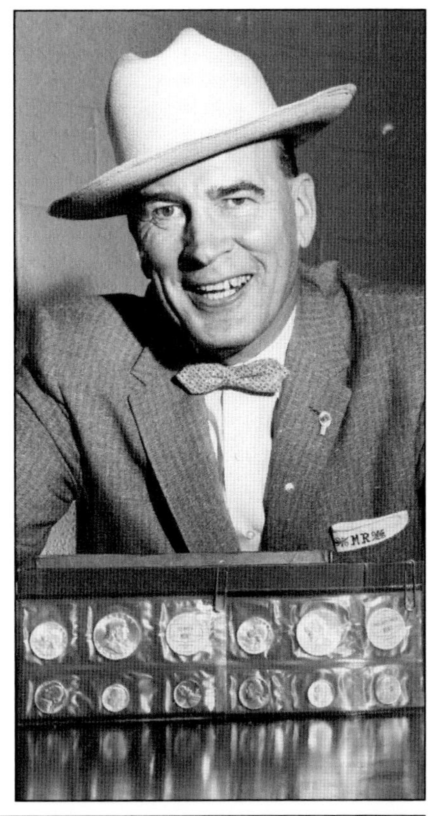

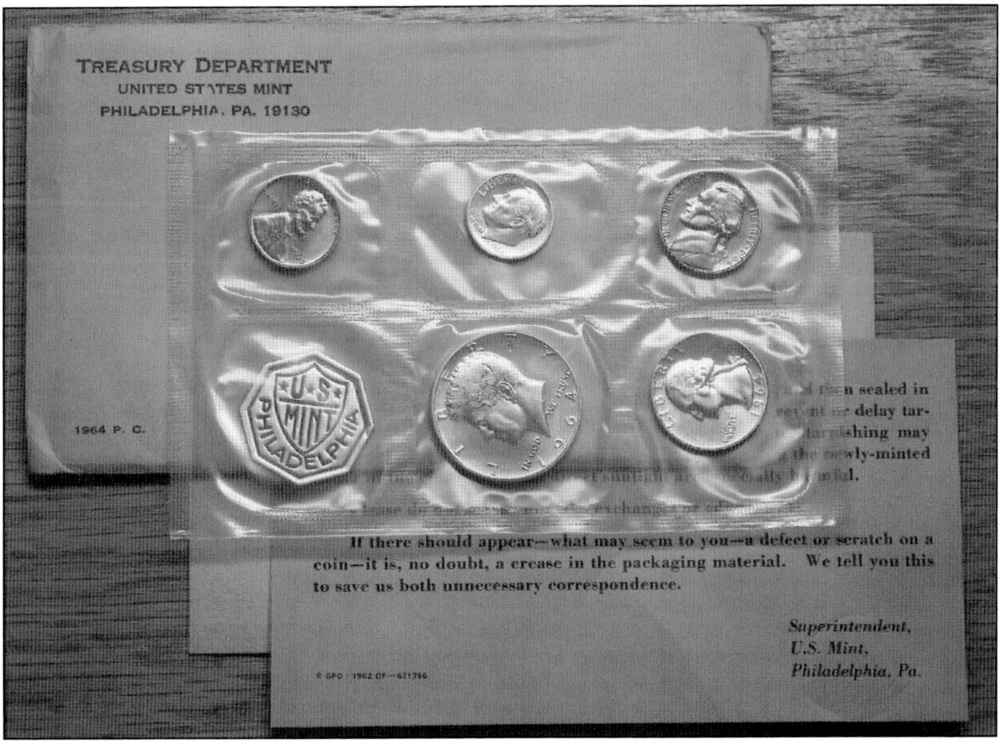

The US Mint has struck proof coins since the 1800s, and historically, they were made at the Philadelphia Mint. A proof coin is made with polished blanks, or planchets, and is struck multiple times by specially prepared dies to bring up even the most minute design details. Therefore, "proof" describes not the condition of a coin, but rather its method of manufacture. This photograph shows a 1964 proof set from the Philadelphia Mint containing proof examples of each circulating coin made that year, including the Lincoln cent, Jefferson nickel, Roosevelt dime, Washington quarter, and Kennedy half-dollar. (Author's collection.)

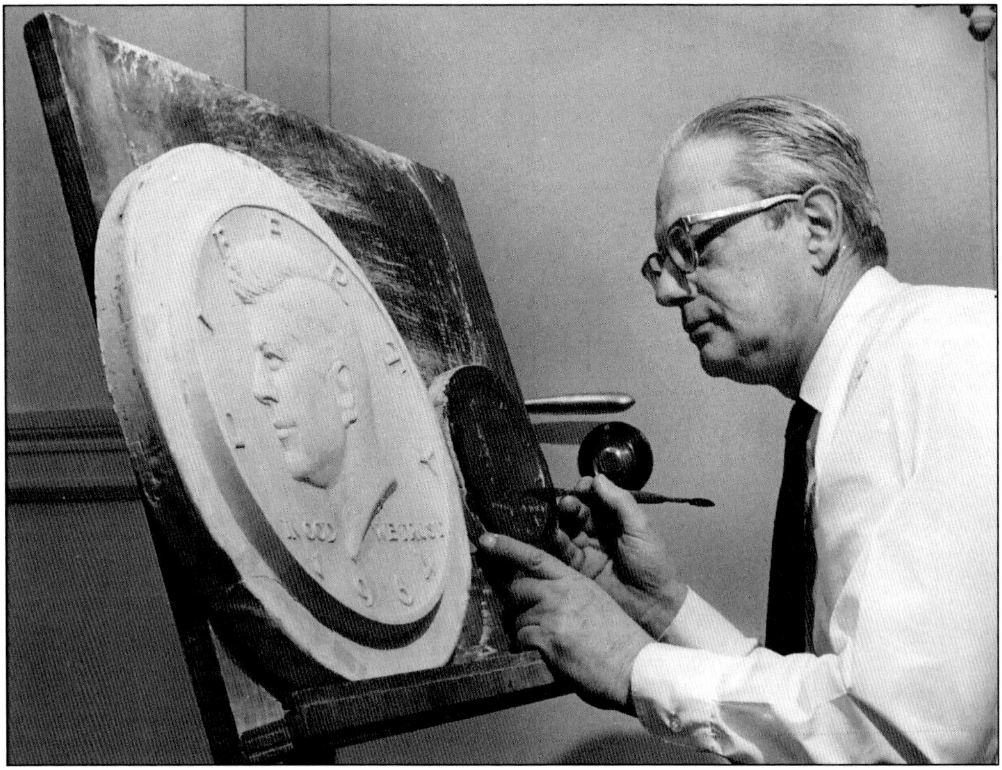

The nation was in mourning after the November 22, 1963, assassination of Pres. John F. Kennedy. Within days, mint director Eva Adams was discussing plans with chief engraver Gilroy Roberts (above) to redesign a silver coin in Kennedy's honor. Congress moved expeditiously on the matter, and on December 30, 1963, Pres. Lyndon B. Johnson signed legislation authorizing a half-dollar design with Kennedy's likeness. (Courtesy of *Coin World*.)

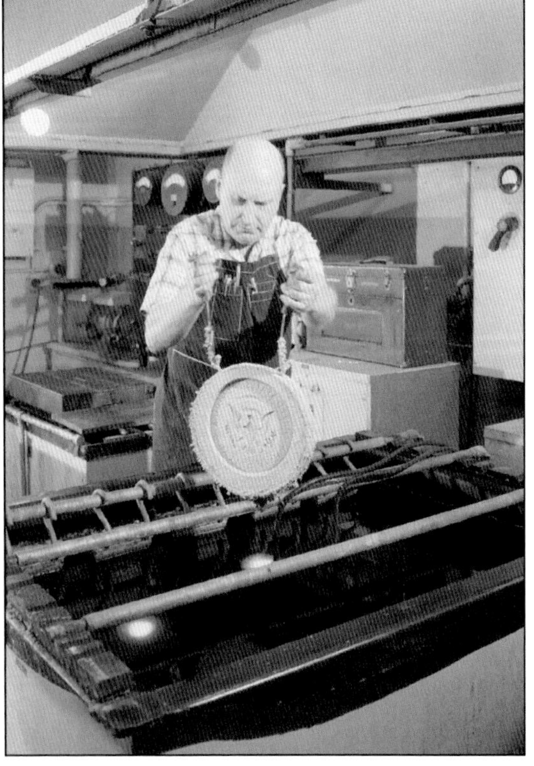

This photograph shows preparation of a model bearing the reverse design of the Kennedy half-dollar depicting the Seal of the President, the iconic symbol of the US presidency. The crest shows an eagle under an arc of 13 clouds and a constellation of 13 stars symbolizing the nation's 13 original colonies. In the eagle's left claw are 13 arrows symbolizing the nation's preparedness to defend freedom, and in its right claw is an olive branch as a symbol of peace. (Courtesy of the Lawrence S. Williams Inc. Collection, the Athenaeum of Philadelphia.)

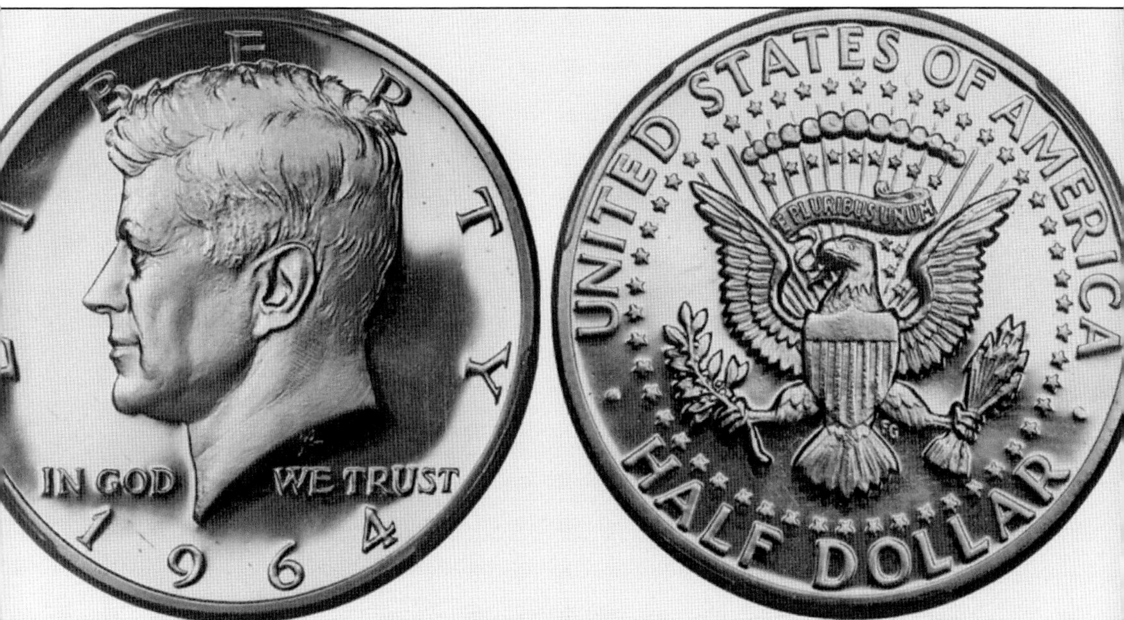

The obverse (left) of the Kennedy half-dollar was designed by Gilroy Roberts, who was then serving as the US Mint's ninth chief engraver. On the reverse of the coin (right) is the presidential seal as prepared on the coin by US Mint engraver Frank Gasparro. The first Kennedy half-dollars were struck in early 1964 and proved massively popular with the public. Kennedy half-dollars virtually disappeared from circulation by the early 1970s as more people saved, rather than spent, the coins. In 2002, the US Mint stopped issuing half-dollars for circulation, though legal-tender Kennedy half-dollars are still made for collectors. (Courtesy of Heritage Auctions, www.HA.com.)

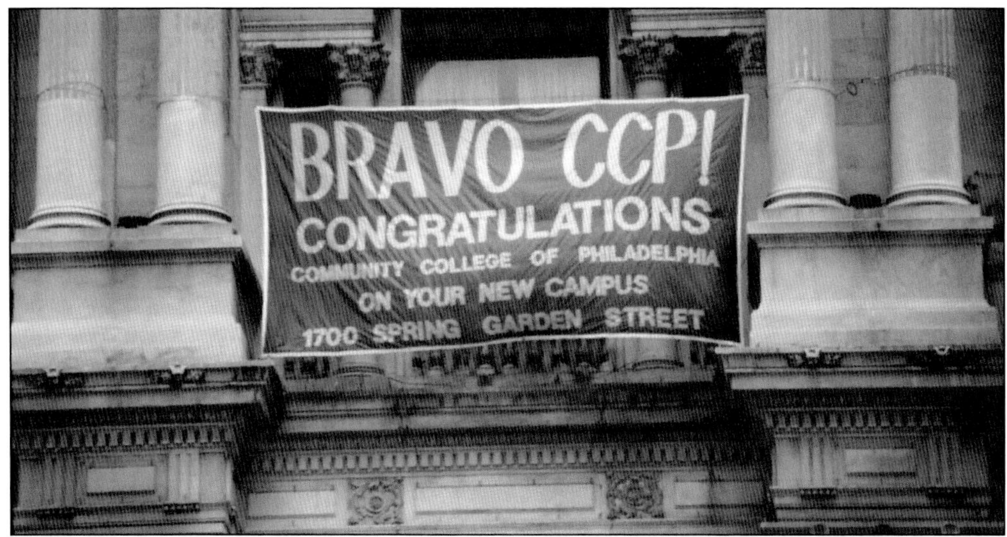

While the third Philadelphia Mint was state of the art when it opened in 1901, expanding operations eventually outgrew the space at 1700 Spring Garden Street. In 1969, the US Mint formally moved to its current location at 151 North Independence Mall East after years of planning for a new building. The former third Philadelphia Mint property did not remain vacant long. The Community College of Philadelphia, which opened its doors on September 23, 1965, in the former Snellenberg Building at 34 South Eleventh Street, took possession of the Spring Garden Street landmark in 1971 as its main campus and soon began holding classes there. (Courtesy of the Community College of Philadelphia.)

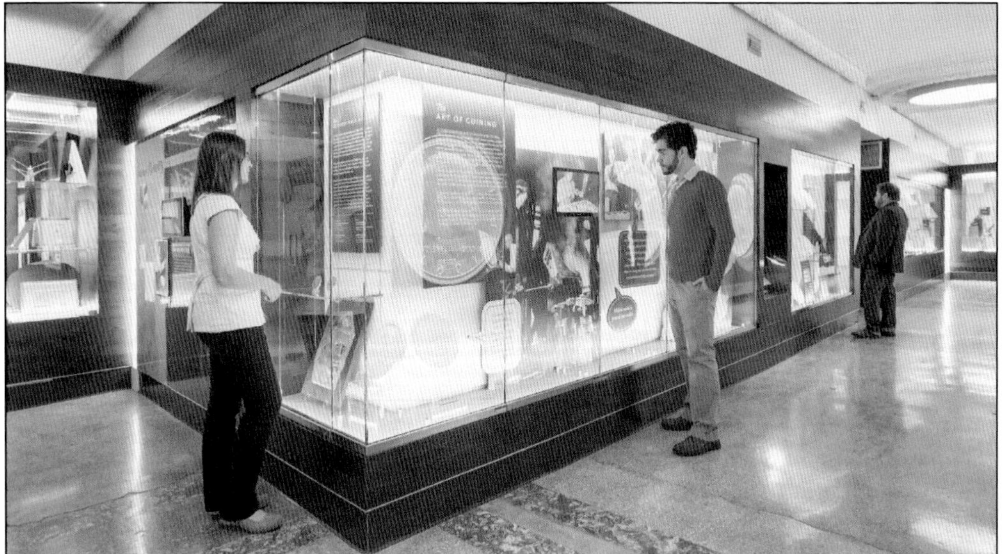

The Community College of Philadelphia has significantly modified the property surrounding the former Philadelphia Mint building but keeps most of the original exterior architecture and many interior details beautifully intact. The school also pays homage to the building's past with its Gilroy Roberts Gallery, where students and others can explore US Mint history. There, they can also learn about the man who spent nearly 20 years in the building as chief engraver and helped immortalize Pres. John F. Kennedy on the half-dollar. (Courtesy of the Community College of Philadelphia.)

Five

The Fourth Philadelphia Mint

In Operation from 1969 to Today

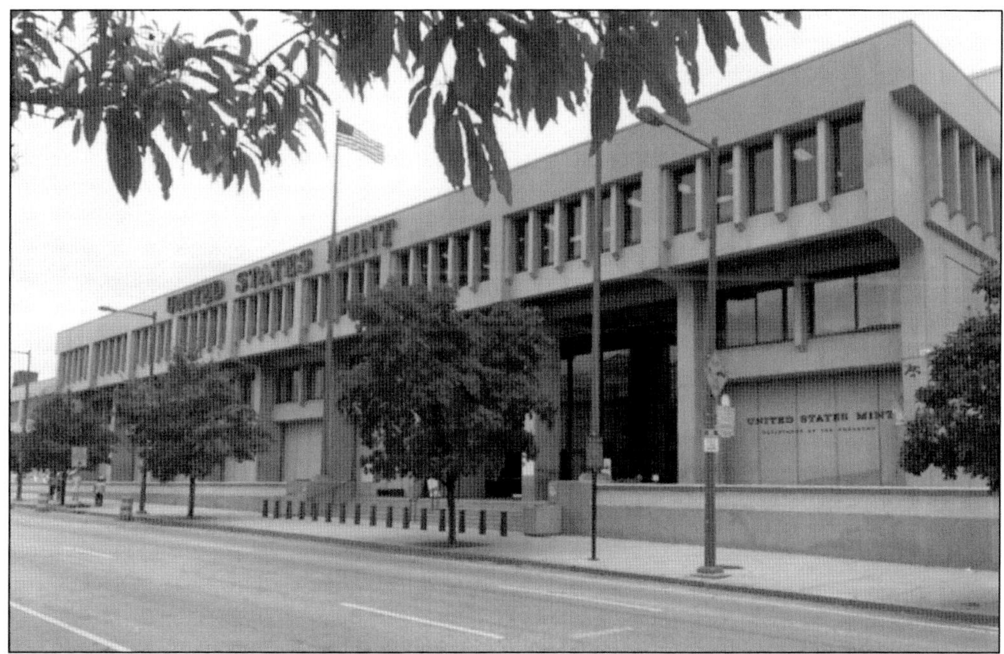

The current US Mint building in Philadelphia was ceremonially unveiled in 1969 following several years of planning and construction. When it opened, the fourth Philadelphia Mint was the largest coin-minting facility in the world. The Philadelphia Mint can produce 1.8 million coins per hour, or more than 32 million coins per day. In total, production capacity at the Philadelphia Mint surpasses 13 billion coins per year. (Author's collection.)

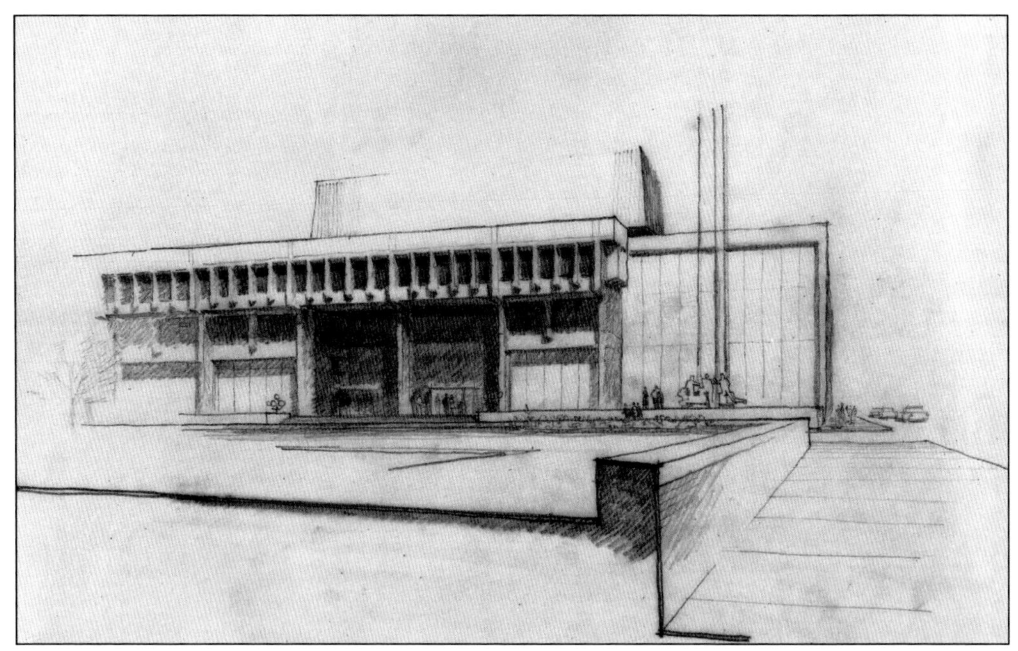

These preliminary sketches of the fourth Philadelphia Mint show architectural planning for the new facility in different stages of development. The draft above was made in 1965 and shows a basic (though very detailed) concept for the exterior appearance of the building. The 1966 rendering below provides a more realistic view of what the new Philadelphia Mint would look like upon its completion. (Above, courtesy of the Lawrence S. Williams Inc. Collection, the Athenaeum of Philadelphia; below, courtesy of the National Archives and Records Administration.)

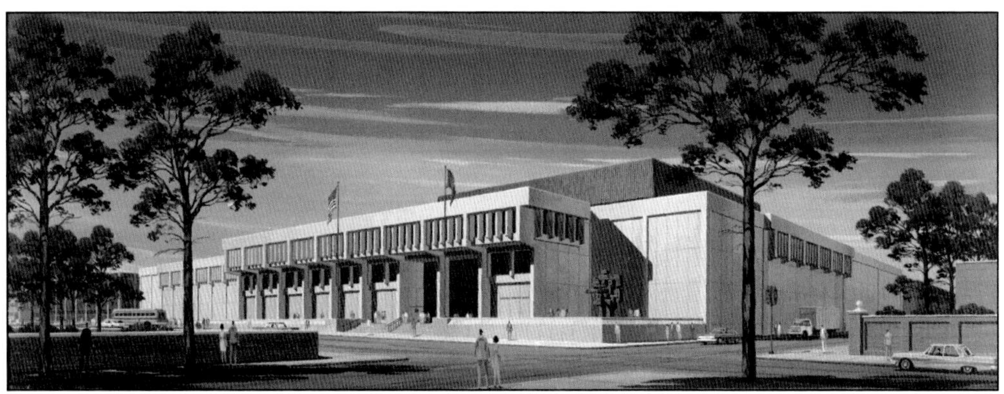

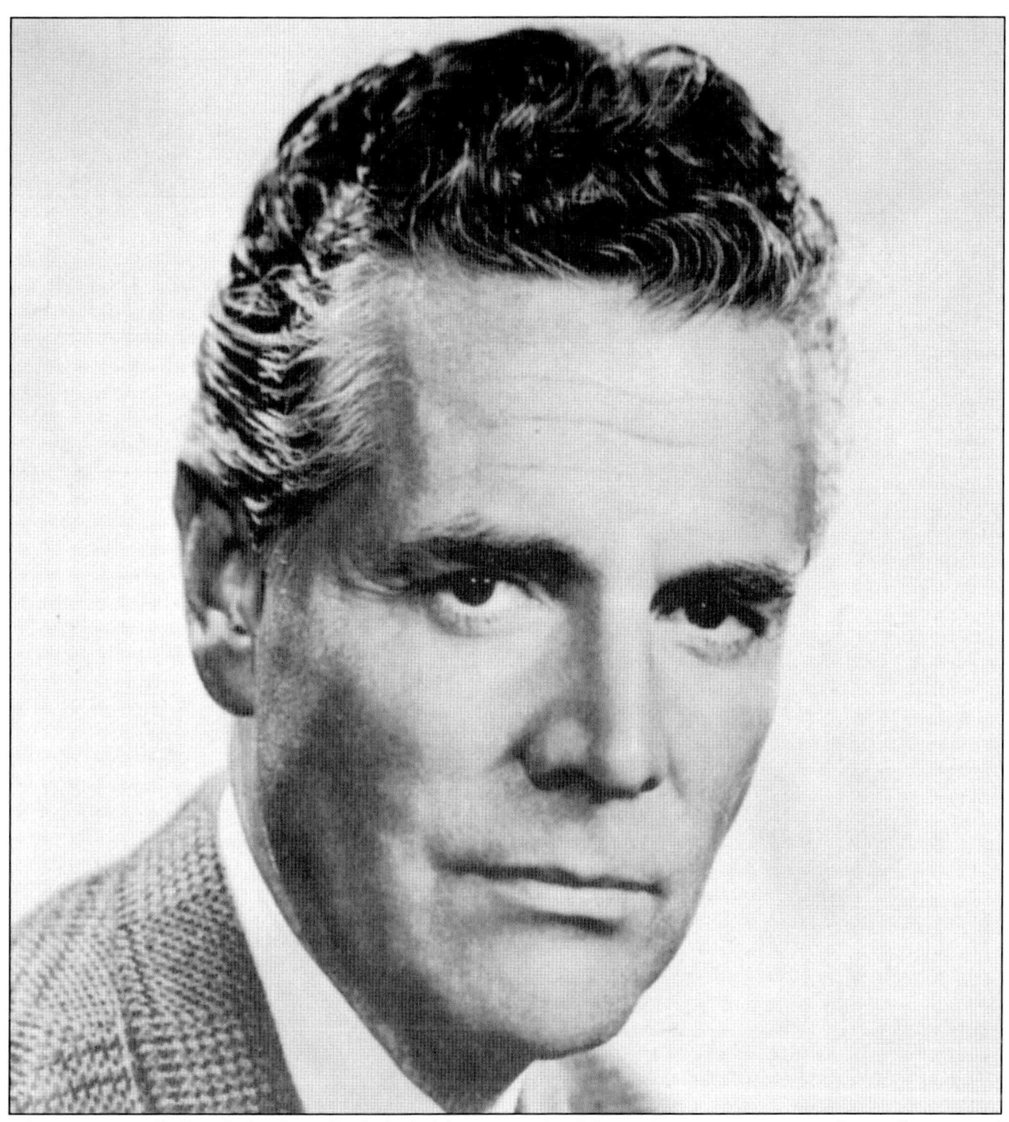

The visionary behind the fourth Philadelphia Mint building was no stranger to the architectural scene in Philadelphia. Vincent G. Kling, the architect who designed the current US Mint facility in Philadelphia, contributed many landmarks to the City of Brotherly Love. Kling, born in East Orange, New Jersey, in 1916, attended Cornell University and the Massachusetts Institute of Technology. Following his service in the Navy during World War II, Kling joined Skidmore, Owings & Merrill, a famous architectural firm in New York. In 1946, he left for Philadelphia to establish his own architectural firm. In addition to the US Mint, Kling designed Penn Center, the Annenberg Center for the Performing Arts, Lankenau Hospital, and John F. Kennedy Plaza ("Love Park"), among many other notable buildings and attractions. By the early 1970s, Kling's firm had grown to more than 400 employees. Meanwhile, he was bestowed with many prestigious accolades, including the John Frederick Harbeson Award from the American Institute of Architects in Philadelphia. Kling, whose illustrious life spanned nearly a century, died at the age of 97 on November 23, 2013. (Courtesy of the Athenaeum of Philadelphia.)

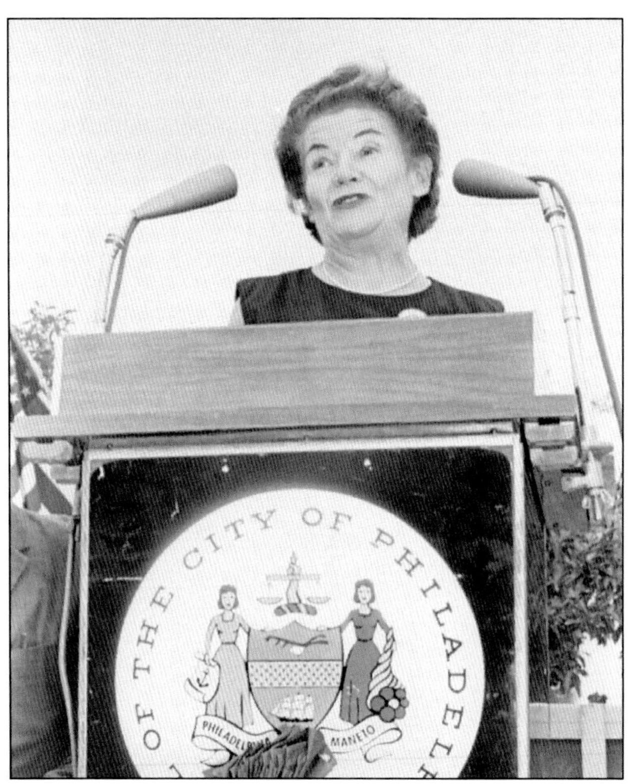

A ground-breaking ceremony for the new Philadelphia Mint building was held at Fifth and Arch Streets on September 17, 1965. At left, mint director Eva B. Adams addresses the crowds at a podium. Below, Adams and others come together to turn the first ceremonial shovelful of dirt to symbolically begin construction on the new Philadelphia Mint. Holding the unique, multi-handled shovel are, from left to right, Philadelphia Redevelopment Authority chairman Gustave G. Amsterdam, Philadelphia mayor James H.J. Tate, Adams, Undersecretary of the Treasury Joseph W. Barr, and Assistant Secretary of the Treasury Robert A. Wallace. (Left, courtesy of *Coin World*; below, courtesy of Special Collections Research Center, Temple University Libraries, Philadelphia, PA; Joseph Wasko.)

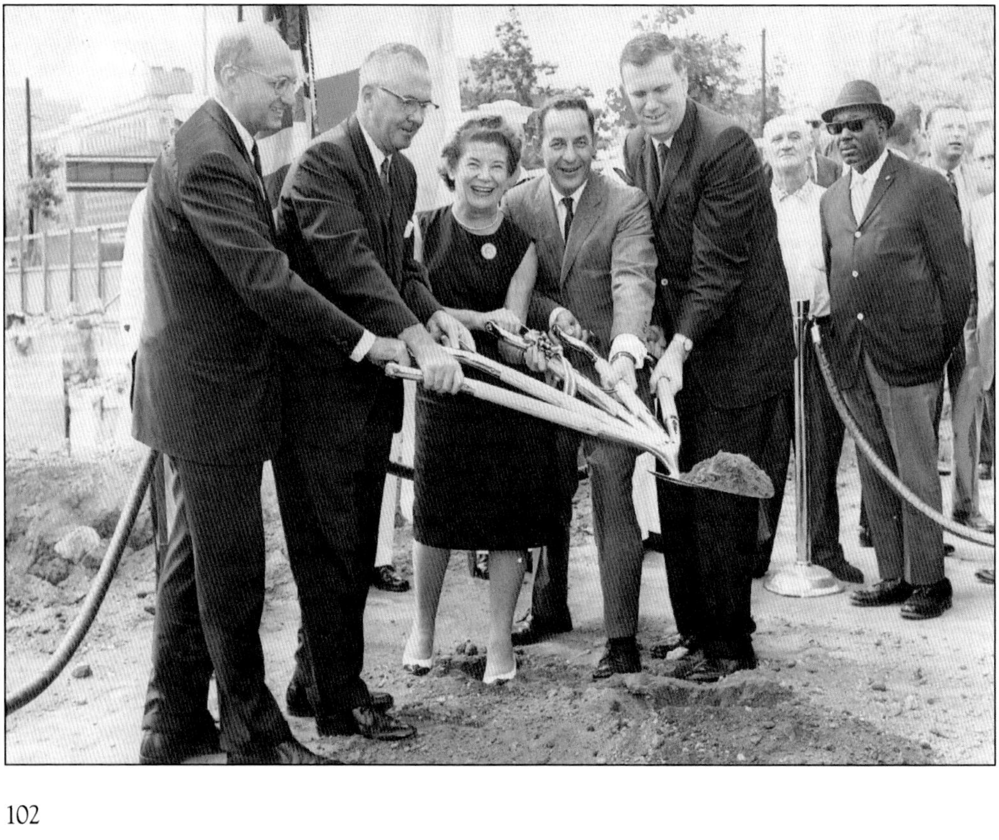

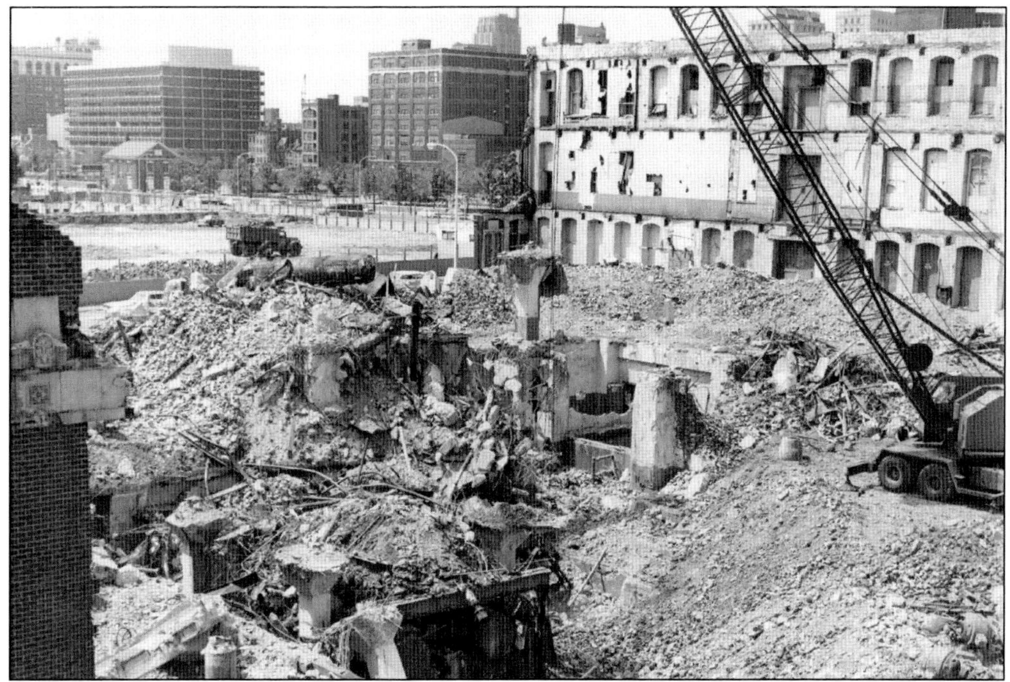

Site preparation for the new Philadelphia Mint is well underway in this 1965 photograph, showing demolition of old buildings standing on the land destined for the new facility. Following clearing of the land, construction was in full swing by the following year. (Courtesy of the Special Collections Research Center, Temple University Libraries, Philadelphia, PA; Dominic Ligato.)

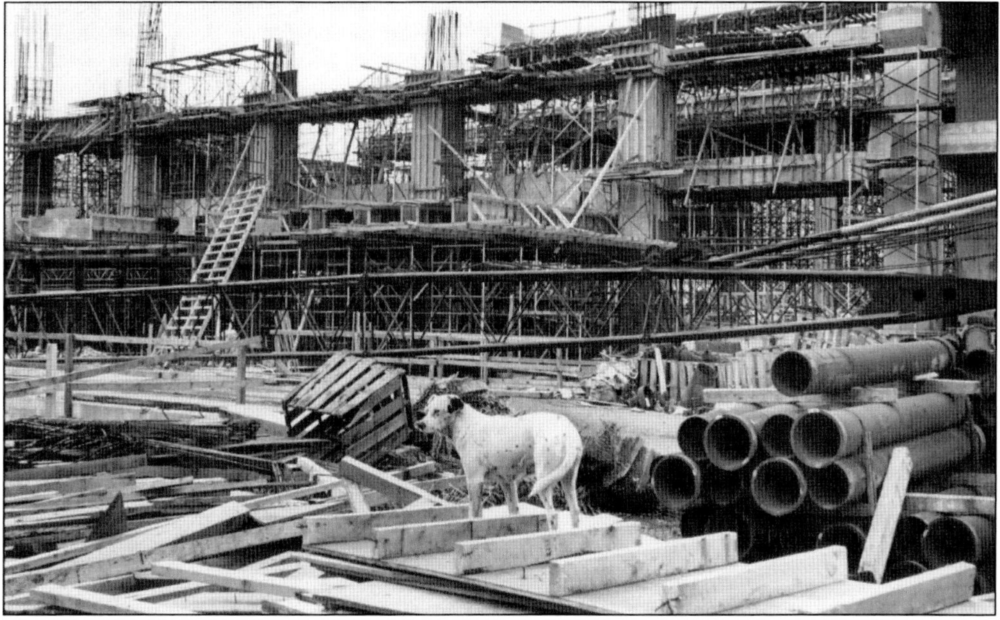

A Dalmatian steals the scene in this November 27, 1966, photograph of the fourth Philadelphia Mint under construction. It would be many more months before the first coins were made at the new mint building. Still, the massive facility was taking shape quickly. (Courtesy of the Special Collections Research Center, Temple University Libraries, Philadelphia, PA; Michael J.J. Maicher.)

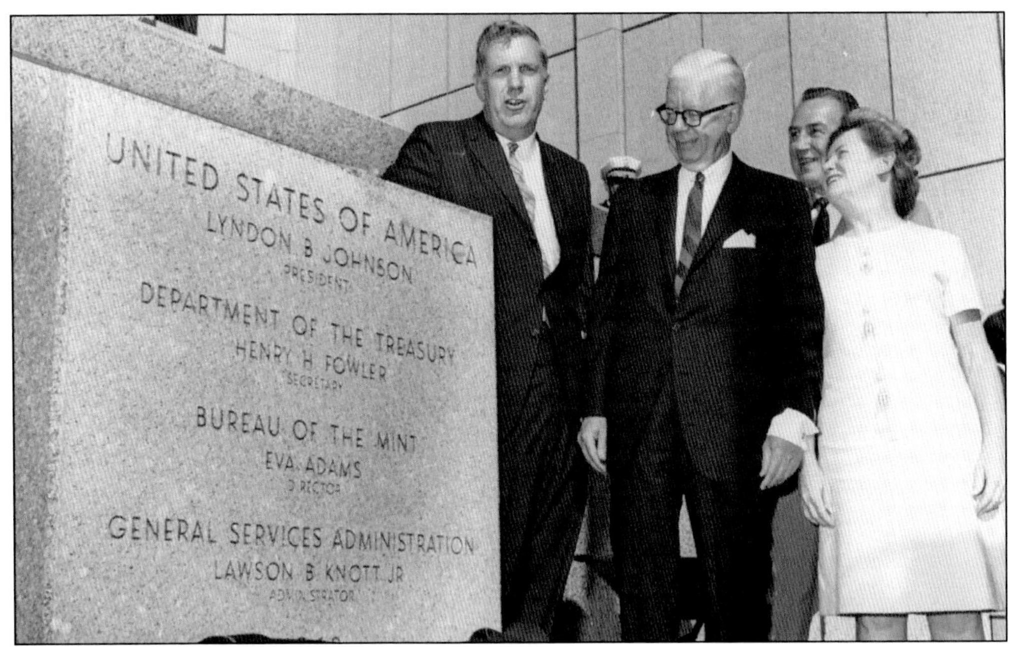

Massive crowds and the media turned out for a cornerstone ceremony at the new Philadelphia Mint on September 18, 1968. Pictured above are, from left to right, Assistant Secretary of the Treasury Robert A. Wallace, Secretary of the Treasury Henry H. Fowler, Commissioner of Public Buildings William Schmidt, and US Mint director Eva B. Adams joined with other officials to lay the mint's cornerstone, which is still visible today on the property near the northeast corner of Fifth and Arch Streets. The highly anticipated opening of the mint, which was scheduled to begin operations in early 1969, energized cornerstone ceremony attendees with promises for the new facility to accommodate 2,500 tour visitors per hour in the comforts of a modern, glass-enclosed elevated gallery high above the busy mint floor. (Both, courtesy of *Coin World*.)

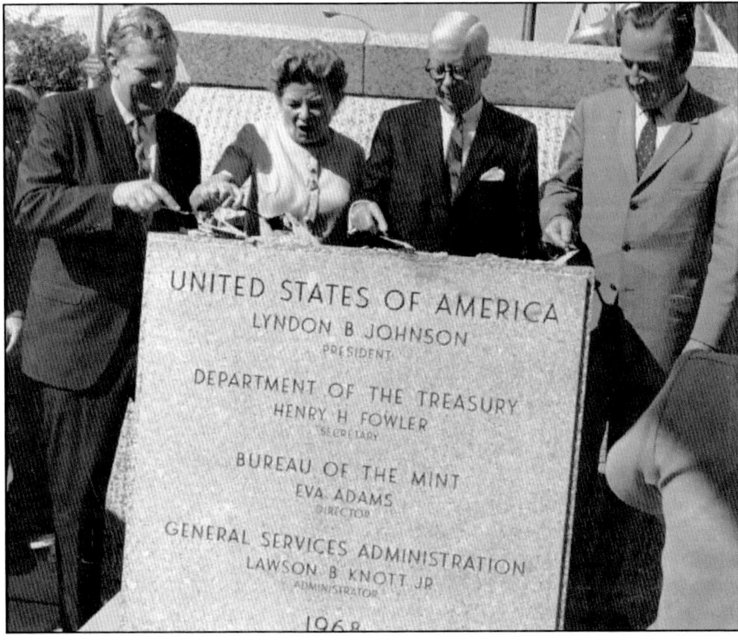

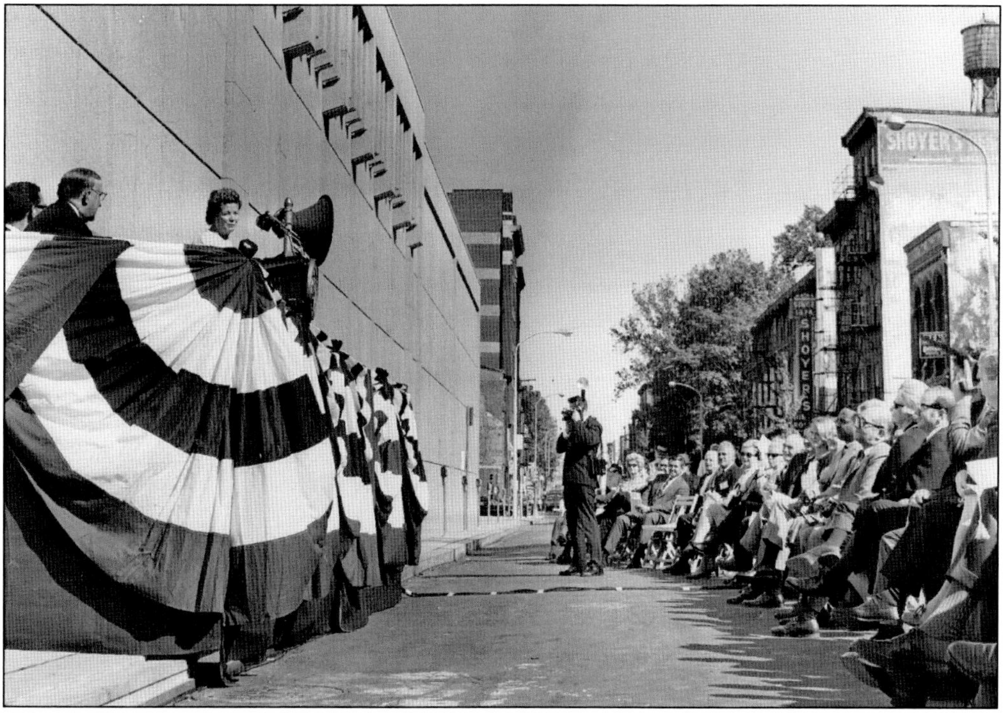

US Mint director Eva B. Adams addresses the crowds during the cornerstone-laying ceremony for the fourth Philadelphia Mint on September 18, 1968. Operations would transfer from the 1700 Spring Garden Street location to the new Philadelphia Mint at 151 North Independence Mall East over the next several months. (Courtesy of Special Collections Research Center, Temple University Libraries, Philadelphia, PA; Joseph Wasko.)

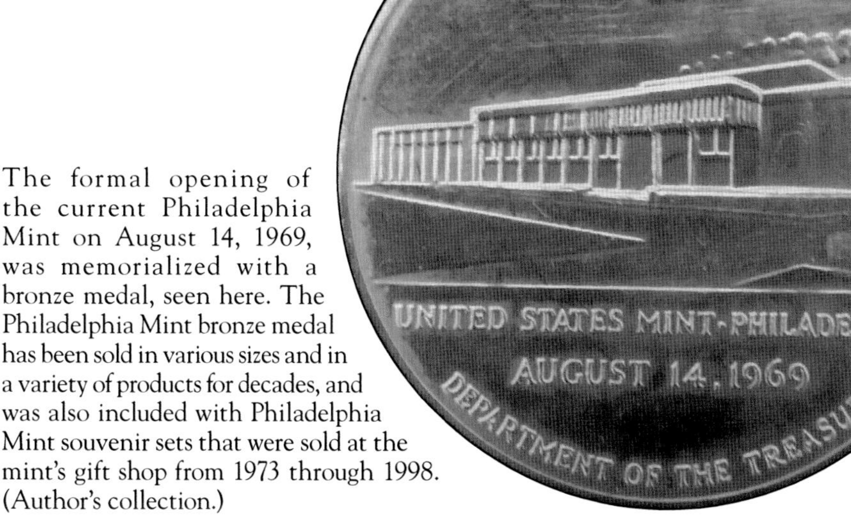

The formal opening of the current Philadelphia Mint on August 14, 1969, was memorialized with a bronze medal, seen here. The Philadelphia Mint bronze medal has been sold in various sizes and in a variety of products for decades, and was also included with Philadelphia Mint souvenir sets that were sold at the mint's gift shop from 1973 through 1998. (Author's collection.)

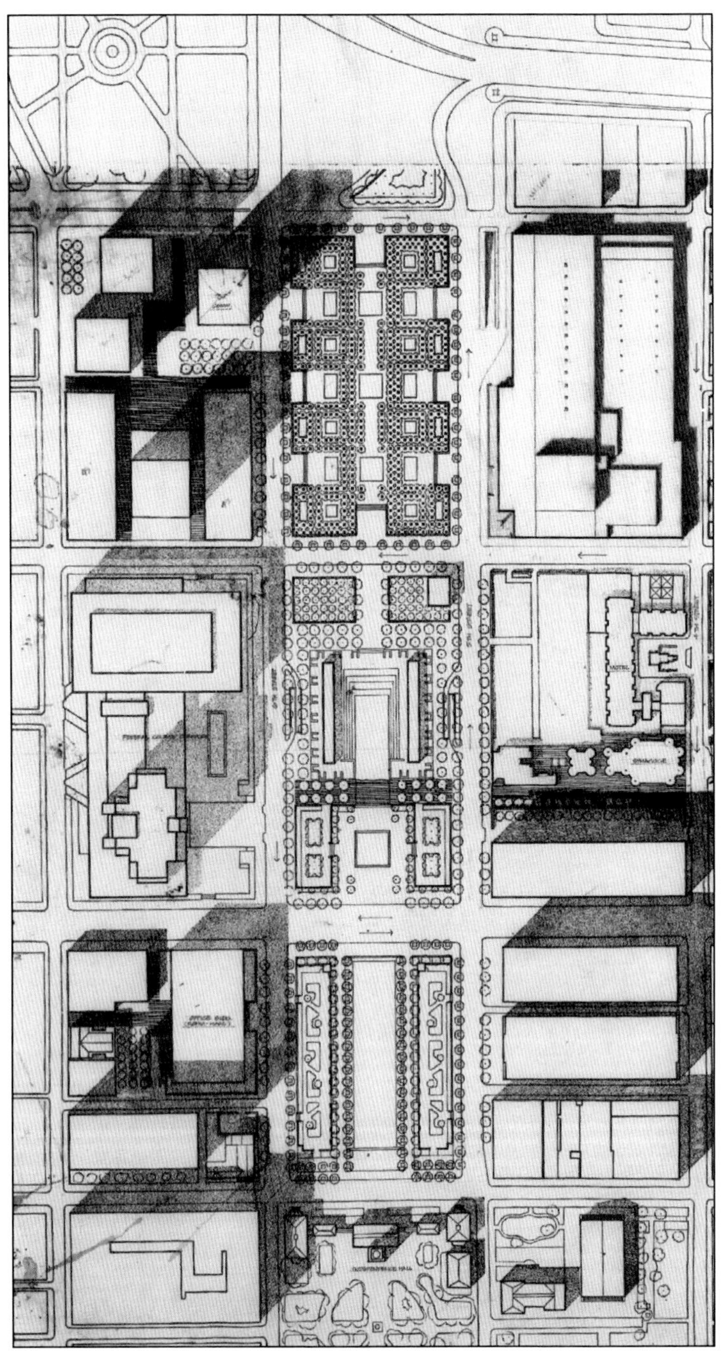

This mid-1960s aerial sketch of the fourth Philadelphia Mint (the large rectangular building at upper right) shows how the current facility is situated in the Independence Mall area at the northeast corner of Arch and Fifth Streets. Several other landmarks are noted in this illustration, including Independence Hall at bottom center. When this map was drafted, the Liberty Bell still resided in Independence Hall; it was not relocated on Independence Mall until 1976. The National Constitution Center, which would be located near the top center, was not built until 2003. (Courtesy of the Lawrence S. Williams Inc. Collection, the Athenaeum of Philadelphia.)

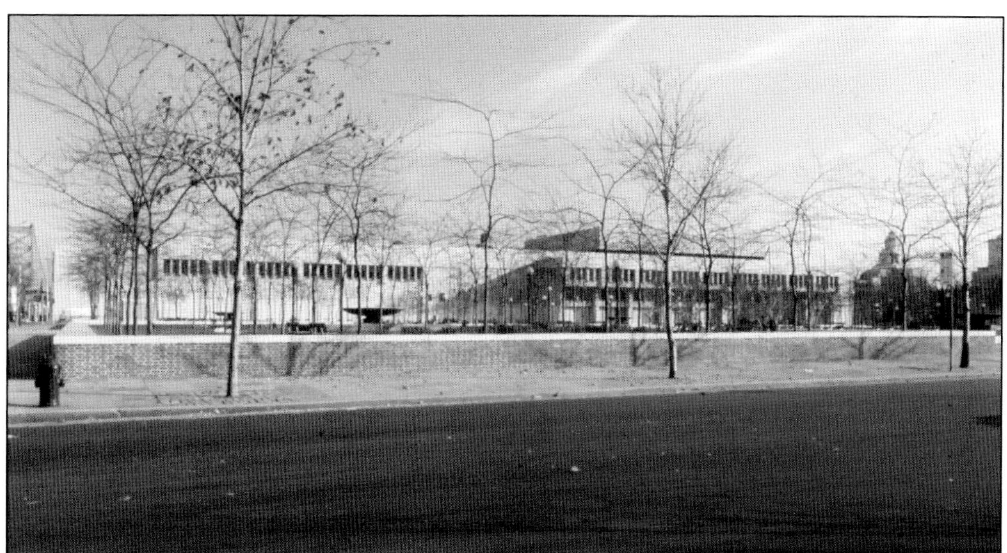

This 1970s photograph of the Philadelphia Mint was taken from the southwest corner of North Sixth and Race Streets. This particular view of the current mint is now obscured by the National Constitution Center, which today would dominate this photograph. With its creation approved as part of the Constitution Heritage Act signed by Pres. Ronald Reagan in 1988, the National Constitution Center houses the US Constitution and other historic American relics. Pres. Bill Clinton attended the center's ground breaking in 2000, and the long-awaited landmark opened on July 4, 2003. (Courtesy of the Lawrence S. Williams Inc. Collection, the Athenaeum of Philadelphia.)

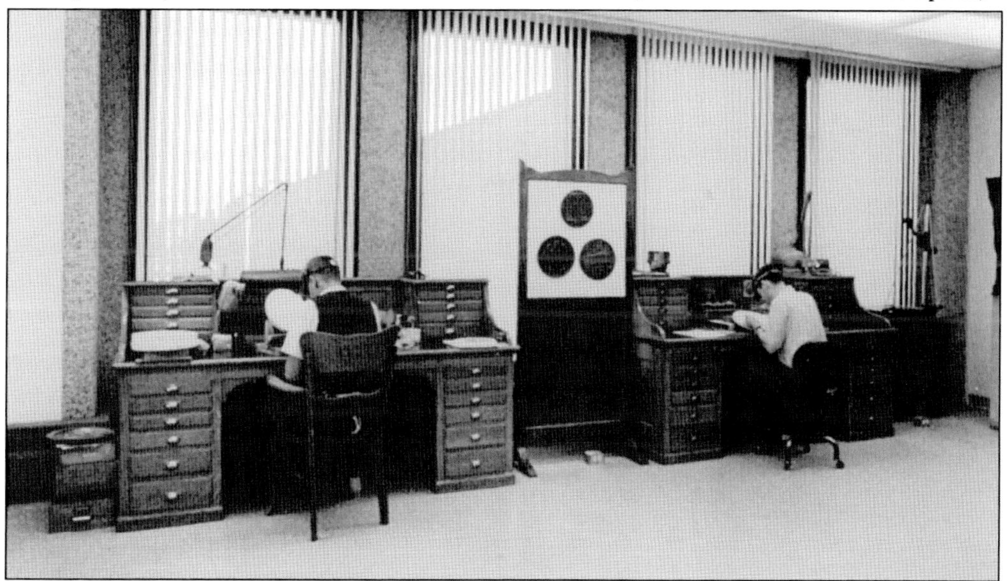

Views of the surrounding historic district are plentiful from many vantage points throughout various parts of the fourth Philadelphia Mint, as seen in this early 1970s photograph of the sculpting and engraving department. At the time, the creative individuals who designed, sculpted, and engraved were working with traditional tools of the trade that had been in use throughout much of the 19th and 20th centuries. Some coin artists still prefer using these methods; however, many also employ advanced computer technology that has emerged since the beginning of the 21st century. (Courtesy of the Lawrence S. Williams Inc. Collection, the Athenaeum of Philadelphia.)

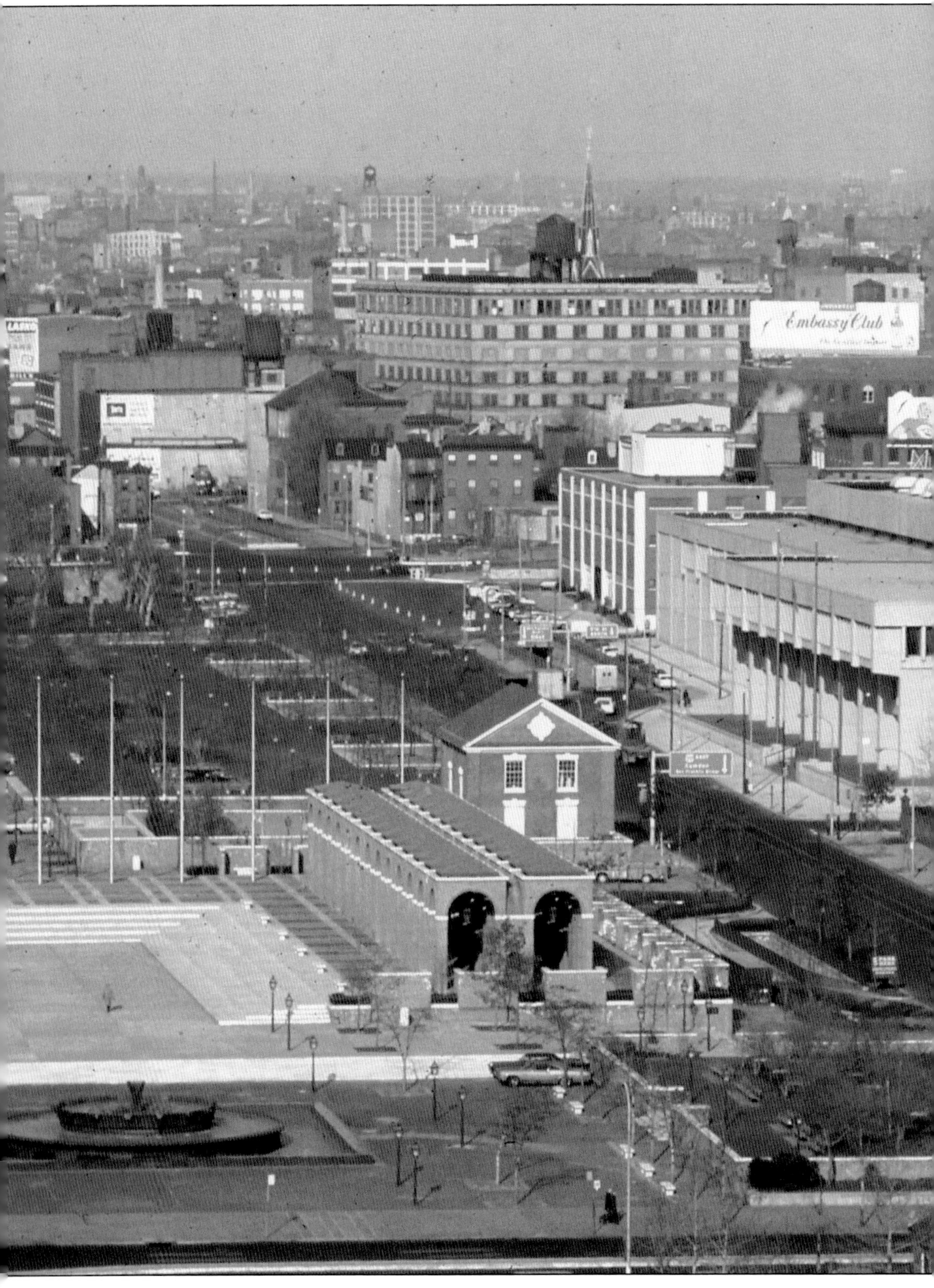
Embassy Club

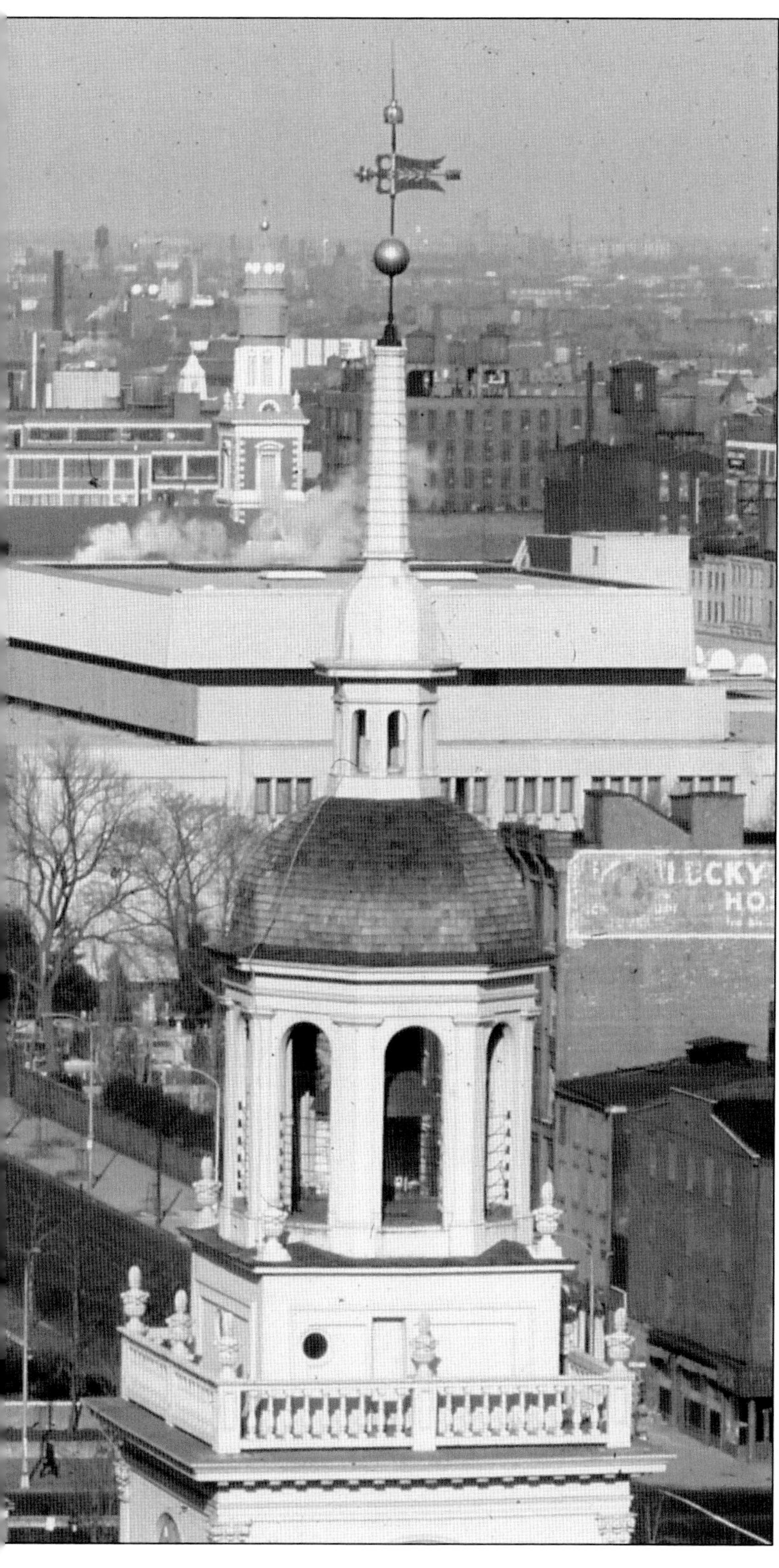

This c. 1970 photograph shows the fourth Philadelphia Mint (right) when it was still a relatively new addition alongside the sprawling Independence Mall plaza. Concepts for the park originated in earnest by the 1930s, and Pres. Harry S. Truman signed Public Law 795 for the creation of Independence National Historical Park on June 28, 1948. Development of the park unfolded in multiple phases during the following years and was complete in 1959, with the Free Quaker Meetinghouse (center) among the few survivors of wide-scale demolition to clear the land formerly occupied by numerous urban buildings. (Courtesy of the Lawrence S. Williams Inc. Collection, the Athenaeum of Philadelphia.)

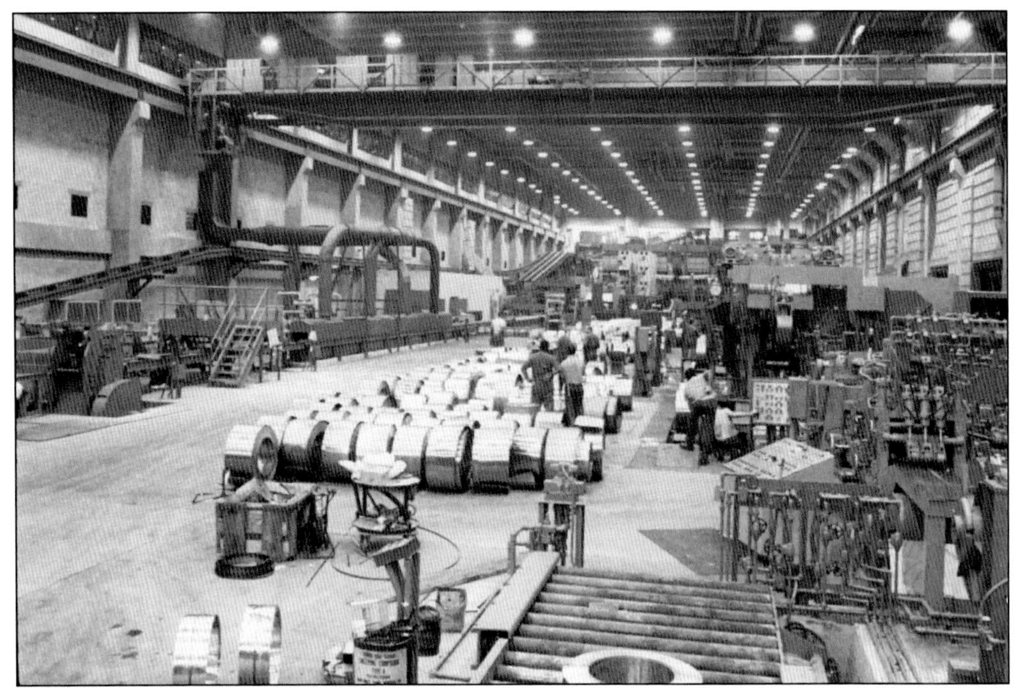

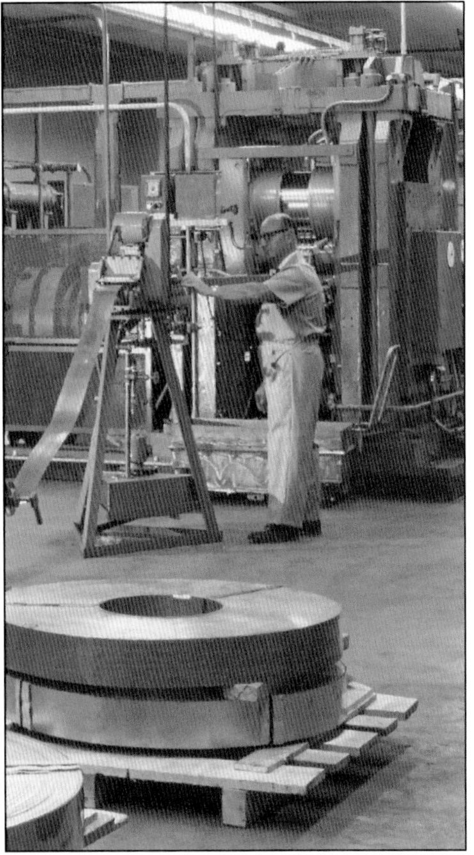

Operations at the new Philadelphia Mint were running at full tilt by 1970, about the time these photographs were taken inside the facility. Mint employees in these images are working on various aspects of metal preparation. Note the huge coils of metal in both images, which will be blanked, annealed, washed, and converted into planchets ready to be struck into coins. (Both, courtesy of the Lawrence S. Williams Inc. Collection, the Athenaeum of Philadelphia.)

Frank Gasparro was a proud son of Philadelphia who eventually became one of the most famous US Mint engravers. Born on August 26, 1909, Gasparro was a class of 1927 graduate of South Philadelphia High School and attended the Pennsylvania Academy of the Fine Arts on Broad Street. He joined the US Mint in 1942 as a junior engraver and eventually made his mark by designing the Lincoln Memorial reverse design for the one-cent coin. In 1965, he became the mint's 10th chief engraver. Among Gasparro's credits are the reverse of the Kennedy half-dollar, both sides of the Eisenhower dollar in 1971, and the first small-size dollar coin, a conceptual model of which he is holding here. Gasparro retired in 1981 and went on to design many medals and private coinage issues before passing away in 2001 at the age of 92. (Courtesy of the Smithsonian Institution Archives.)

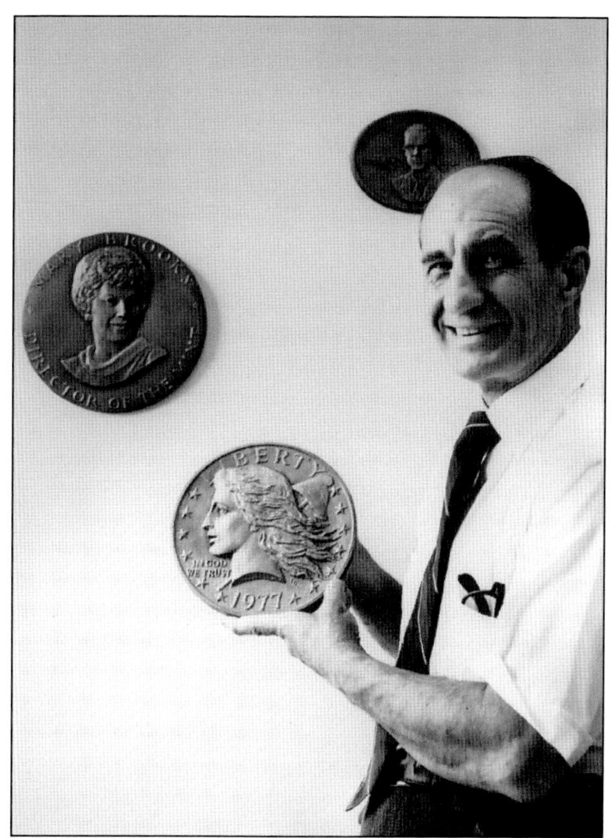

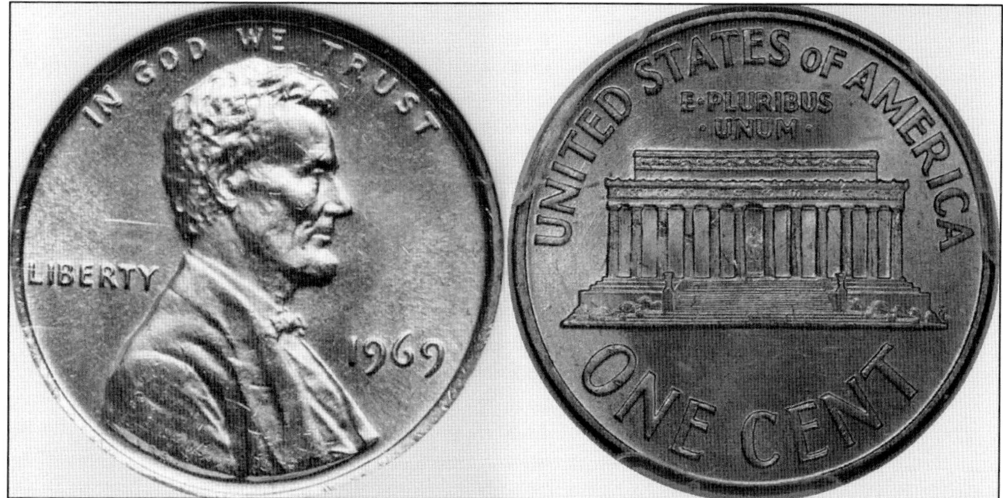

Replacing the "Wheat Ears" motif that premiered with the first Lincoln cents designed by Victor David Brenner in 1909, the Lincoln Memorial cent debuted in 1959. The Lincoln Memorial cent reverse by Frank Gasparro features a tiny image of Lincoln sitting in his chair, as seen in the actual Lincoln Memorial in Washington, DC. Thus, Lincoln Memorial cents became the first circulating US coins with a likeness of the same person on both sides. Around 150 billion Lincoln Memorial cents were struck before the design was retired at the end of 2008. Gasparro's "FG" initials appear at the bottom right of the Lincoln Memorial. (Courtesy of Heritage Auctions, www.HA.com.)

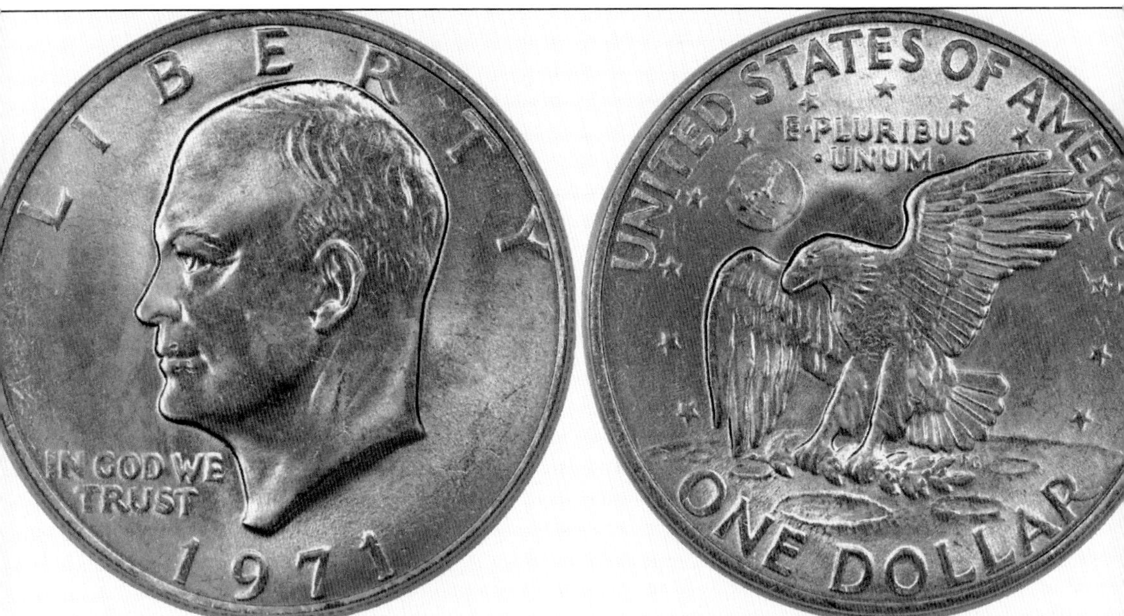

The Eisenhower dollar was struck from 1971 through 1978 and was the first circulating coin for which Gasparro contributed both the obverse and reverse design. The obverse carries a striking portrait of Dwight D. Eisenhower (left), who served as president from 1953 through 1961. He died at the age of 78 in 1969. Meanwhile, the reverse (right) of the dollar features the insignia of Apollo 11, the spacecraft that carried US astronauts Neil Armstrong, Edwin Eugene "Buzz" Aldrin, and Michael Collins on their historic voyage to the moon in July 1969. (Courtesy of Heritage Auctions, www.HA.com.)

By the late 1970s, the US government was ready to try a new concept: a small-size circulating dollar coin. Chief engraver Frank Gasparro created a beautiful concept coin with a young Liberty, seen here. Eventually, the decision was made to honor woman's suffrage leader Susan B. Anthony, a coin that Pres. Jimmy Carter signed into law on October 10, 1978. The "Susie B." dollar, measuring just 26.5 millimeters in diameter, is nearly 12 millimeters smaller than the Eisenhower dollar it replaced. (Courtesy of the Smithsonian Institution Archives.)

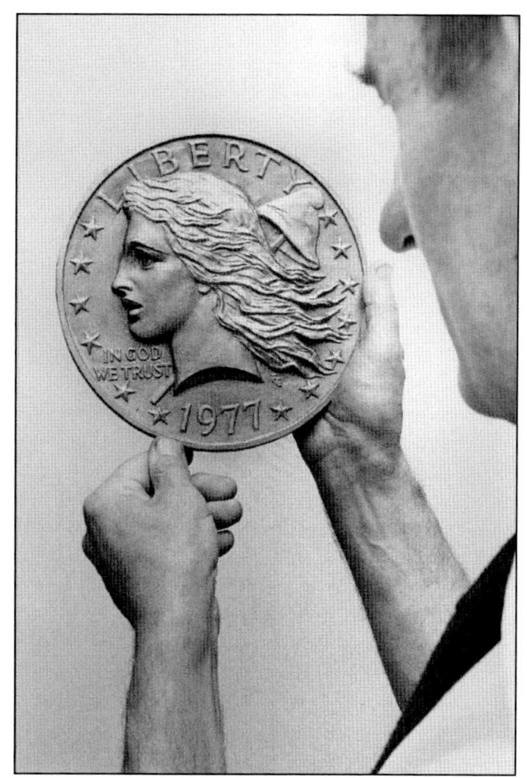

The Susan B. Anthony dollar was released to the public on July 2, 1979, but failed to catch on, due mainly to similarities in size and appearance to the quarter. Struck until 1981, the dollar languished in vaults for years until one last striking in 1999. The Susan B. Anthony dollar is notable for being the first regularly circulating US coin to bear the likeness of an actual woman, as opposed to allegorical figures of Liberty; also, it was the first issue since 1945 to bear the "P" mintmark signifying the Philadelphia Mint. (Courtesy of Heritage Auctions, www.HA.com.)

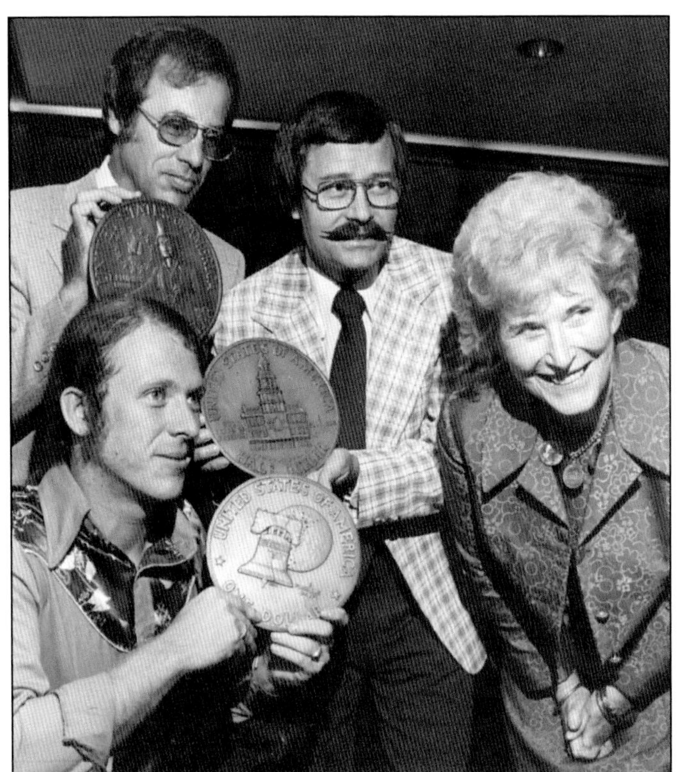

Following authorization by Congress in the early 1970s for the release of special dual-dated "1776–1976" coins honoring the nation's 200th anniversary, the US Mint held a nationwide contest to seek designs for the circulating commemorative quarter, half-dollar, and dollar coin. The winners are pictured here with models of the coins they designed, including (from left to right) Dennis R. Williams (dollar coin), Jack L. Ahr (quarter), and Seth G. Huntington (half-dollar), along with mint director Mary Brooks. The three designers gathered at the Philadelphia Mint on August 12, 1974, for a special first-strike ceremony for the new bicentennial coins. (Courtesy of *Coin World*.)

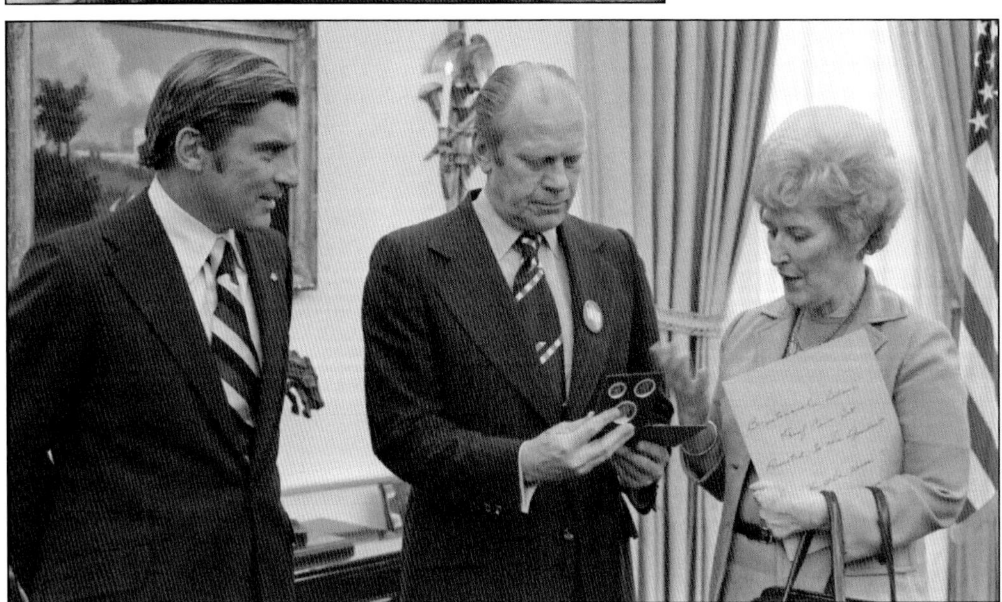

Mint director Mary Brooks presents Pres. Gerald R. Ford with prototypes of the bicentennial coins on November 13, 1974, with American Revolution Bicentennial Committee director John Warner looking on. A total of nearly 2.5 billion bicentennial coins were made, including circulating and collector versions of the quarters, half-dollars, and dollar coins, which includes the 1.6 billion Bicentennial quarters struck for circulation in 1975 and 1976 with the "1776–1976" dual date. (Courtesy of the Gerald R. Ford Presidential Library & Museum.)

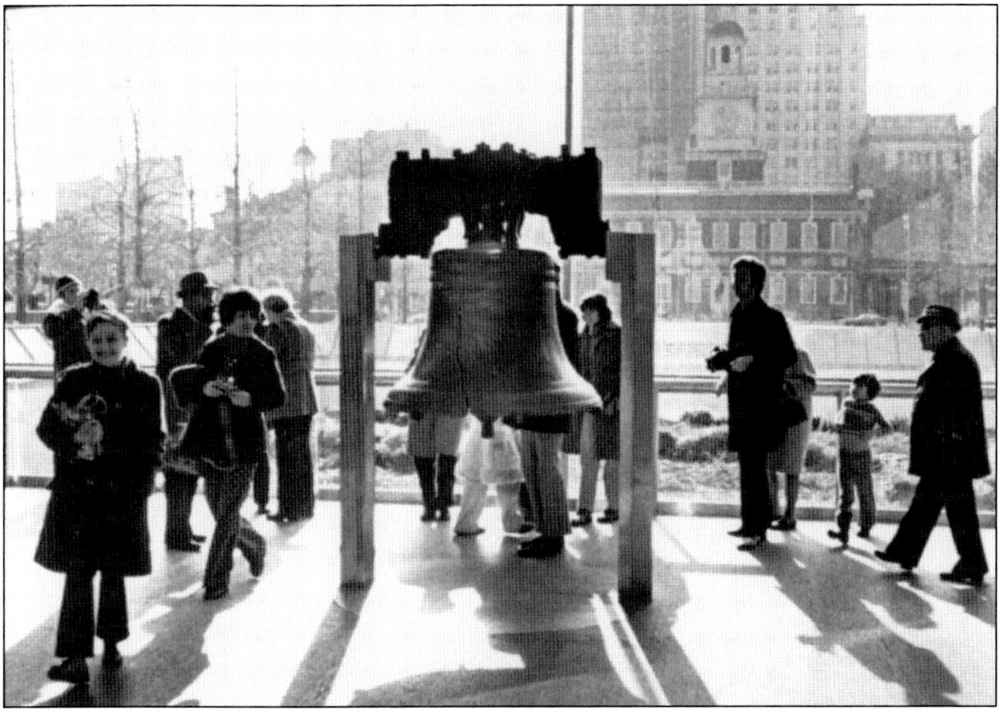

The Liberty Bell is seen here in the spring of 1976 shortly after it was relocated to its new home outside of Independence Hall, seen in the background. Both Independence Hall and the Liberty Bell, famous landmarks located near the Philadelphia Mint in Independence National Historic Park, are featured on the reverses of the bicentennial half-dollar and dollar, respectively. The reverse of the bicentennial quarter depicts a Colonial drummer. (Courtesy of Independence National Historic Park.)

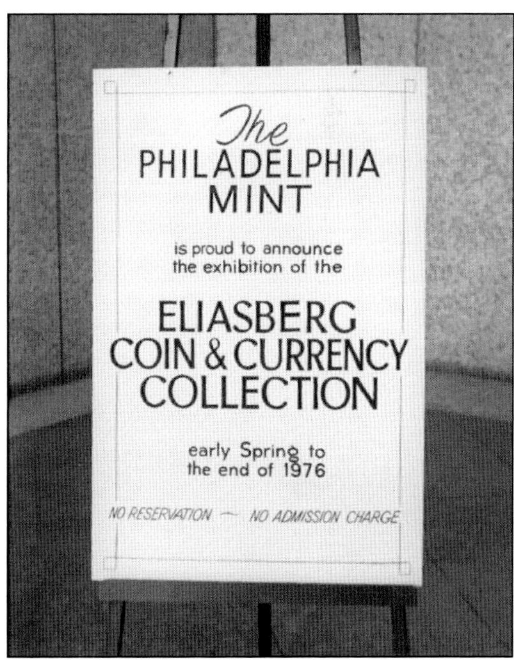

In 1976, the Philadelphia Mint exhibited the legendary coin collection of Louis Eliasberg, an American financier who in 1950 completed the most comprehensive US coin collection ever. His collection, which included some of the rarest US coins, was dispersed over a series of auctions that first took place in 1982. Among the rarities in the Eliasberg collection was the first "million-dollar coin," an extremely rare 1913 Liberty Head nickel that sold for $1,485,000 in 1996. (Courtesy of *Coin World*.)

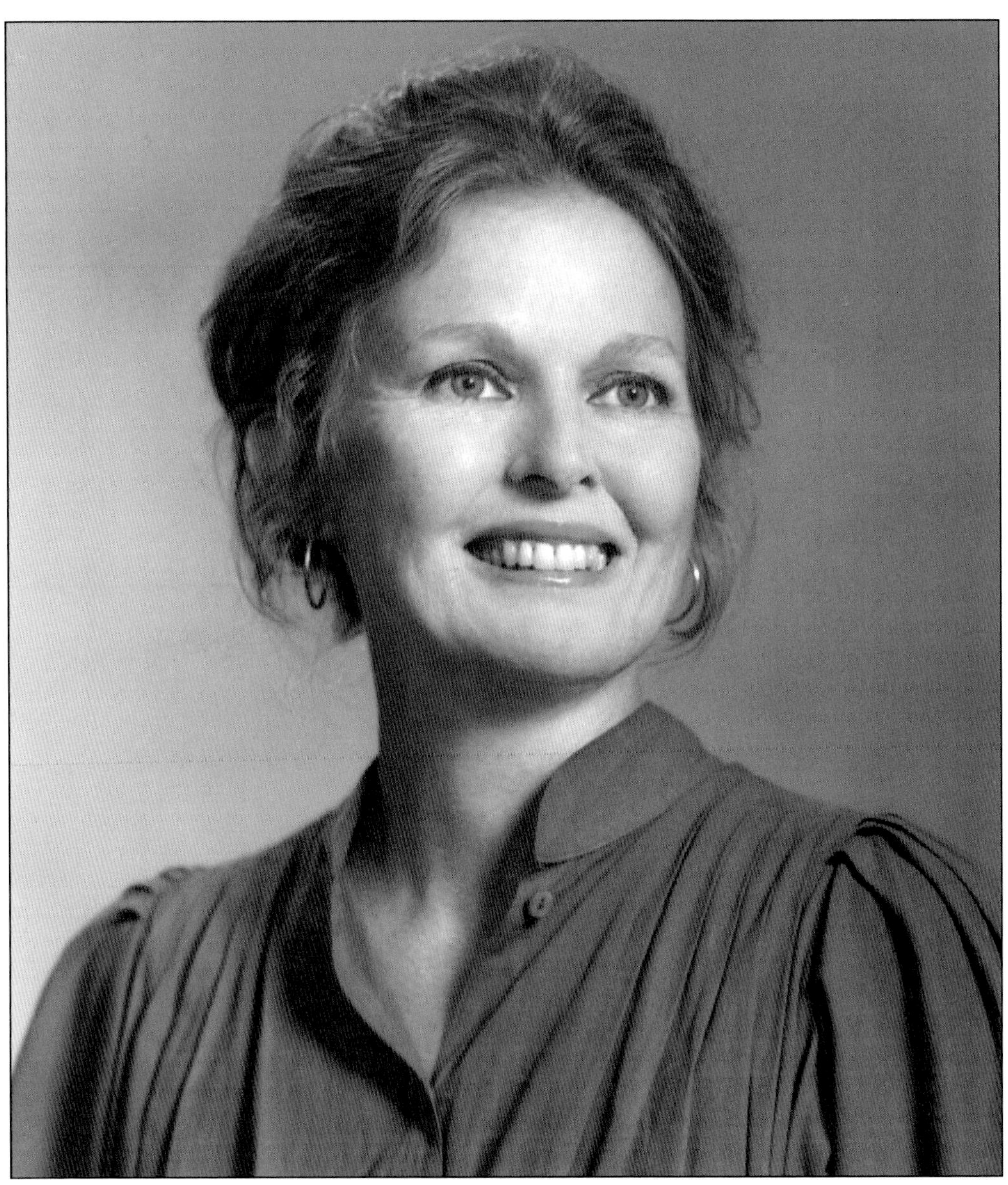

Following Frank Gasparro's retirement in 1981, newly inaugurated Pres. Ronald Reagan nominated accomplished medalist Elizabeth Jone to become the US Mint's next chief engraver. A native of Montclair, New Jersey, the 46-year-old Jones became not just one of the younger chief engravers in US Mint history but also the first woman to hold the position. Soon after becoming the 11th chief engraver on October 27, 1981, Jones designed the George Washington commemorative half-dollar. The George Washington half-dollar became the first official US commemorative half-dollar since 1954 and the nation's first 90-percent silver coin since 1964. Jones designed many other coins over the following decade, including the obverse of the 1983 Los Angeles Olympic silver dollar, the 1986 Statue of Liberty commemorative $5 gold half eagle, and 1988 Olympic commemorative $5 gold half eagle. Even after her retirement from the chief engraver role in 1991, Jones has remained active in her role as a numismatic advocate. She designed the 2001 Capitol Visitor Center $5 gold commemorative coin a decade after leaving her post as chief engraver. (Courtesy of *Coin World*.)

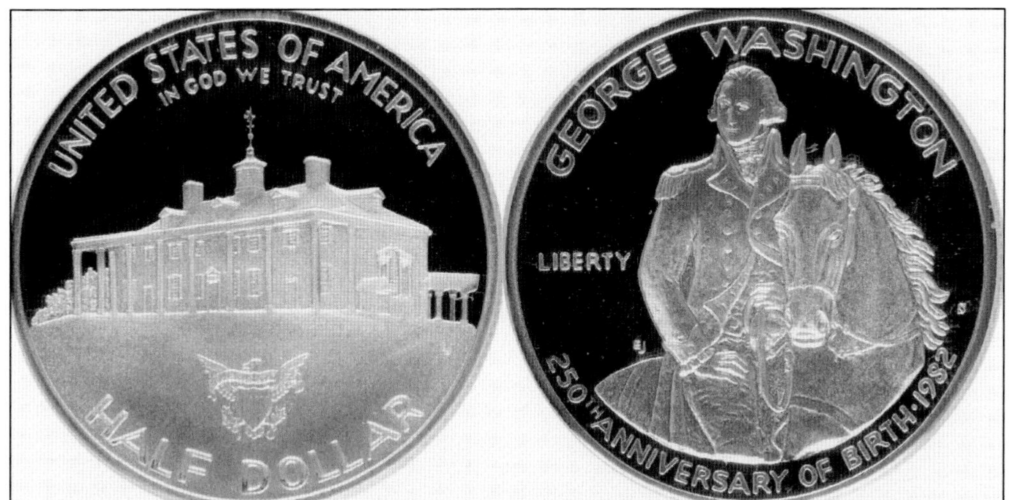

The 1982 George Washington half-dollar seen here was signed into law by President Reagan on December 23, 1981, and commemorates the 250th anniversary of George Washington's birth in 1732. The obverse (right) features Washington, who served as a Revolutionary War general and the nation's first president, on horseback. On the reverse (left) is a view of Washington's stately plantation house, Mount Vernon. The 90-percent silver half-dollar, designed by Elizabeth Jones, was popular as the nation's first commemorative coin in a generation. More than 7.1 million uncirculated and proof versions of the 1982 George Washington half-dollar were made, making it one of the most successful issues of the modern US commemorative coin era. (Courtesy of Heritage Auctions, www.HA.com.)

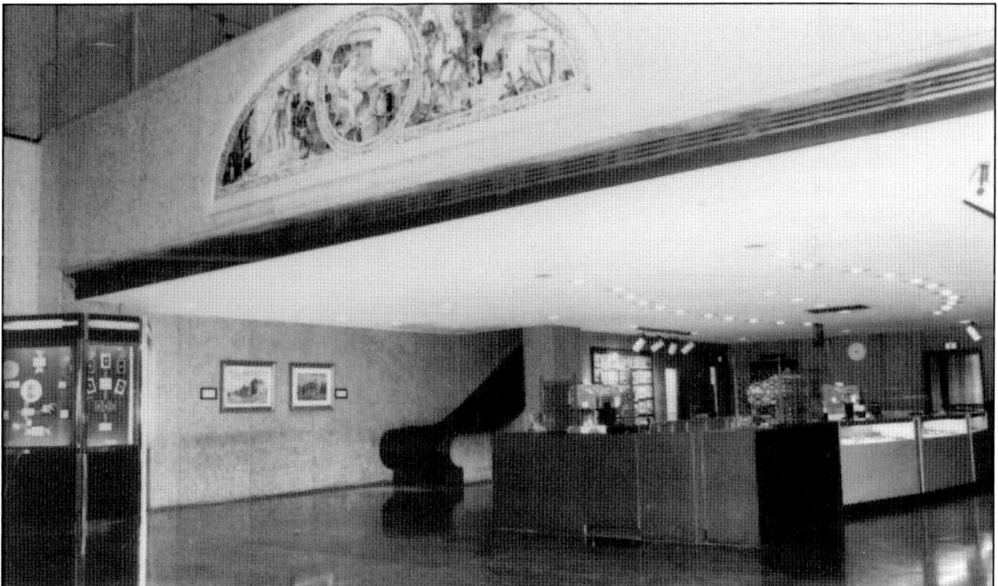

This is a view of the Philadelphia Mint gift shop in 1981, just as Congress was considering legislation on the first commemorative coins of the modern era. In addition to commemorative coins, visitors at the Philadelphia Mint in the early 1980s could buy proof sets, uncirculated sets, souvenir sets containing examples of various circulating Philadelphia coinage from the year of purchase, medals, and more. The shop has been remodeled significantly since the time this photograph was taken and includes a wide array of merchandise, including numismatic books, apparel, and more. (Courtesy of the US Mint.)

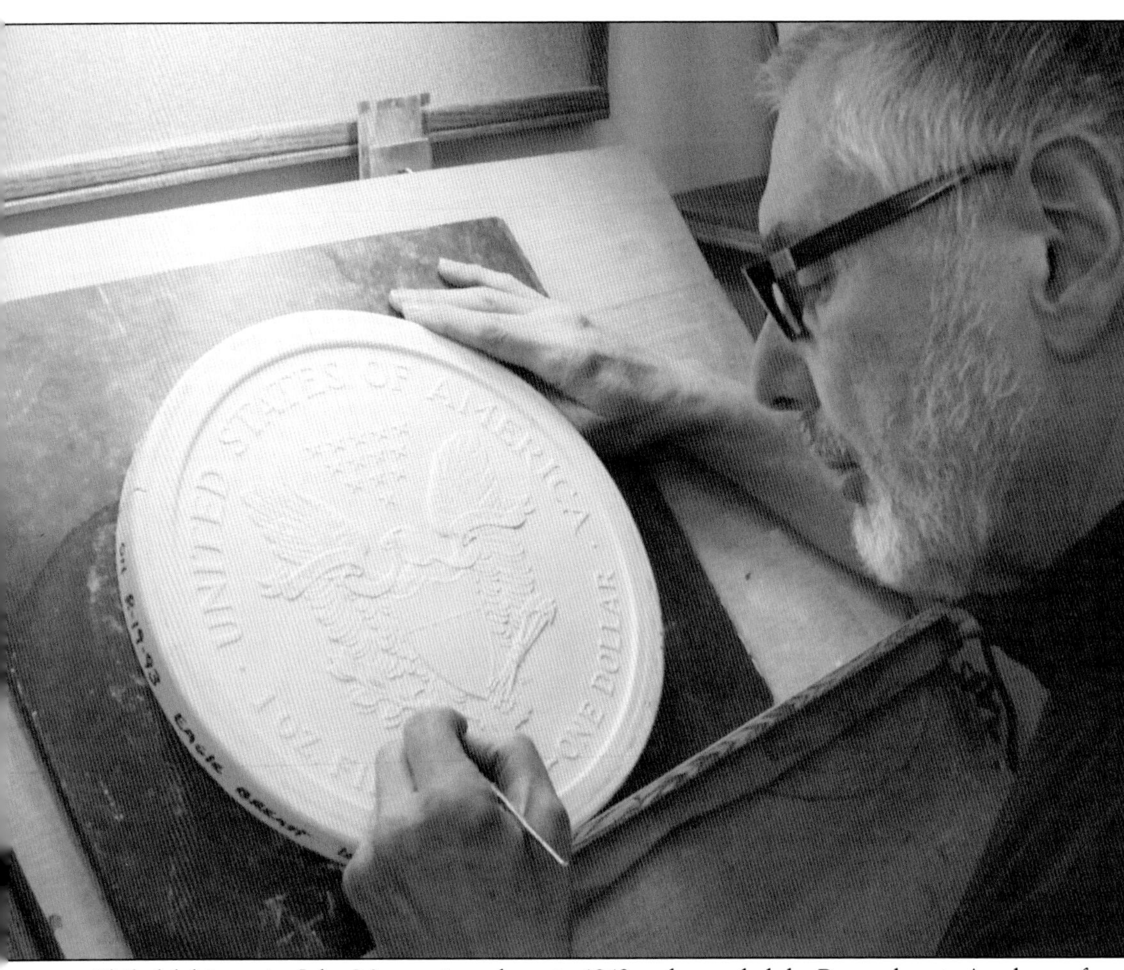

Philadelphia native John Mercanti was born in 1943 and attended the Pennsylvania Academy of Fine Arts, the Philadelphia College of Art, and the Fleisher Art Memorial School. Serving six years in the Pennsylvania Army National Guard, Mercanti joined the US Mint in 1974. While he was appointed to the vacant position of chief engraver in 2006, 15 years after the departure of Elizabeth Jones, Mercanti had already amassed an impressive portfolio of more than 100 coin and medal designs, including the 1984 Los Angeles Olympic $10 commemorative gold eagle (the first official US gold coin issued since 1933), the 1986 Statue of Liberty commemorative silver dollar, 1991 Mount Rushmore commemorative $5 gold coin, and reverse designs for several issues of the 50 State Quarters, including the Pennsylvania quarter that was released in 1999. In this photograph, he is seen working with a model of the American Silver Eagle bullion coin reverse, which he designed in 1986. Mercanti retired from his post as 12th chief engraver in late 2010 and maintains an active presence in the private-sector numismatic arena. (Courtesy of the US Mint.)

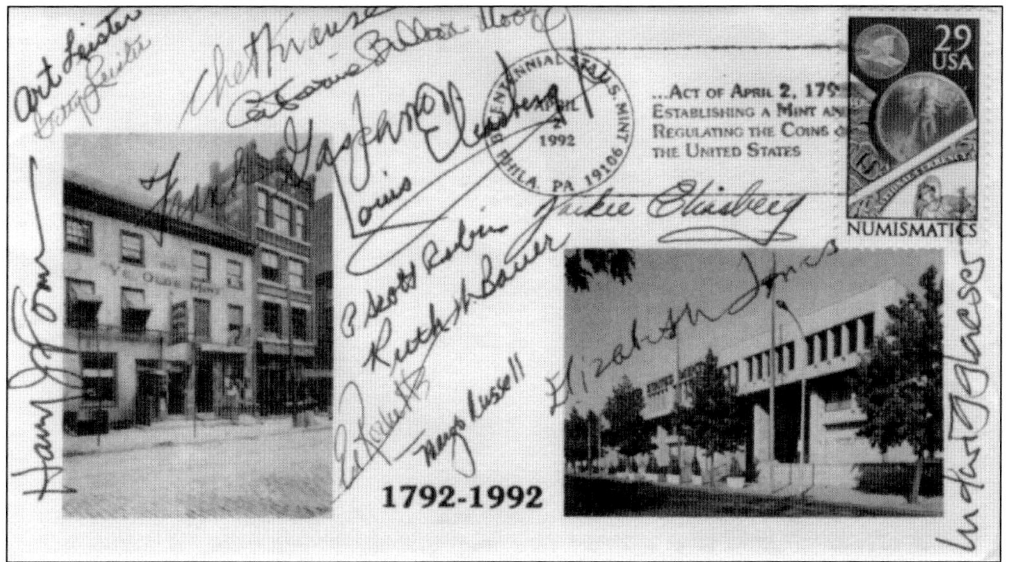

The 200th anniversary of the US Mint was marked in April 1992 in gala fashion. Below is a photograph of a patriotic ceremony involving the cutting of a large birthday cake with the image of a 1992 Lincoln cent and an icing inscription bearing the words, "U.S. Mint Bicentennial Celebration 1792–1992." Above is a special US Postal Service cover with a commemorative stamp honoring the mint's 200th birthday and signatures from several numismatic luminaries, including former chief engravers Frank Gasparro and Elizabeth Jones. (Above, courtesy of Leonard Augsburger and Joel Orosz; below, courtesy of *Coin World*.)

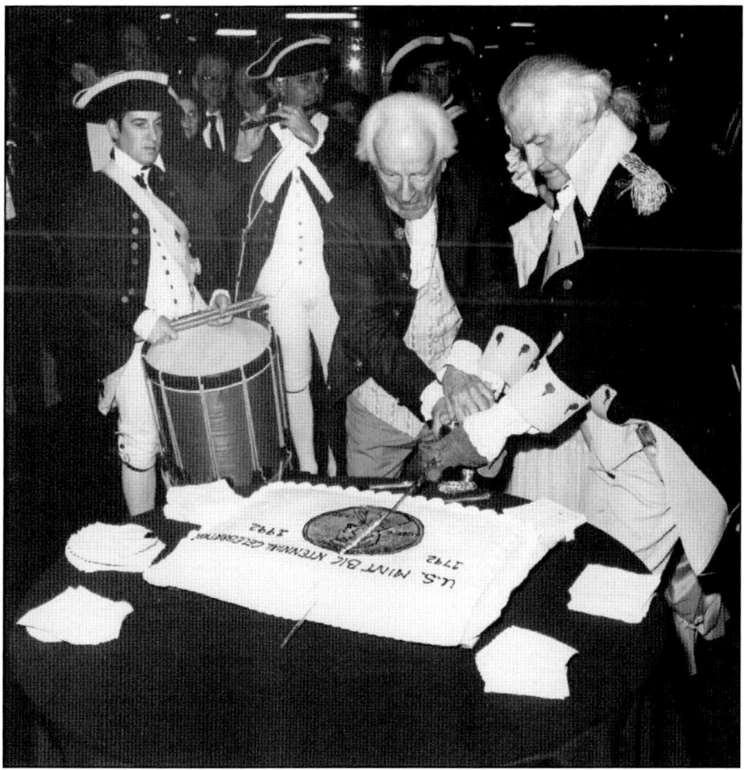

Following the January 4, 1999, release of the first 50 State Quarters issue, which honors Pennsylvania's neighboring state of Delaware, the second coin in the wildly popular 50 State Quarters series celebrated the 1787 entry of the Keystone State into the Union. The Pennsylvania quarter, the reverse of which was designed by Philadelphia native John Mercanti, depicts Commonwealth standing in front of an outline of the state. Also seen on the Pennsylvania quarter is the state motto, "VIRTUE, LIBERTY, INDEPENDENCE." A small keystone is pictured in the upper-left corner of the state outline. (Courtesy of Heritage Auctions, www.HA.com.)

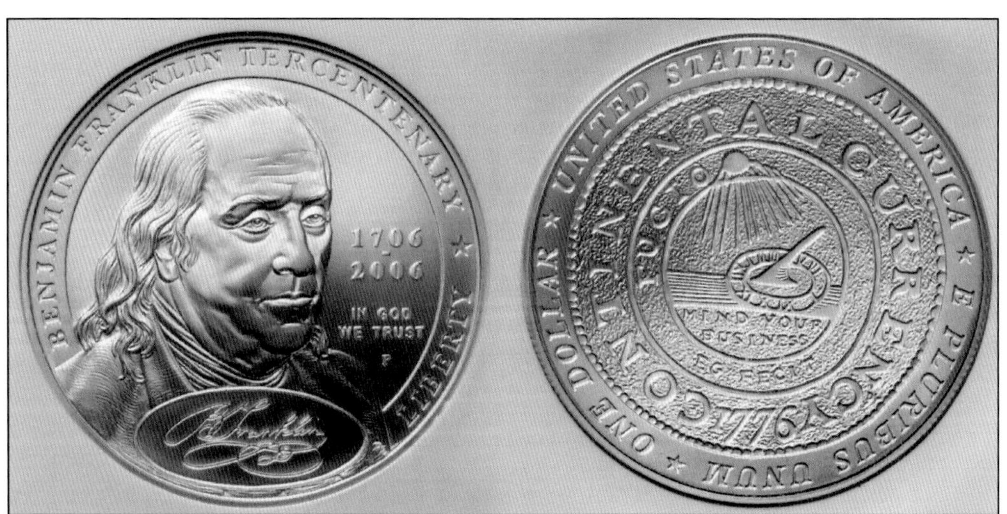

In 2006, the US Mint honored one of Philadelphia's favorite founding fathers with a commemorative silver dollar. The Benjamin Franklin tercentenary silver dollar, celebrating the 300th anniversary of Franklin's birth in 1706, features an obverse portrait of the man who was born in Boston but ran away to Philadelphia at the age of 17. By the time he passed away at the age of 83, Franklin had become an author, printer, freemason, postmaster, inventor, scientist, humorist, activist, and statesman. Franklin is interred across the street from the Philadelphia Mint at Christ Church Burial Ground. (Courtesy of Heritage Auctions, www.HA.com.)

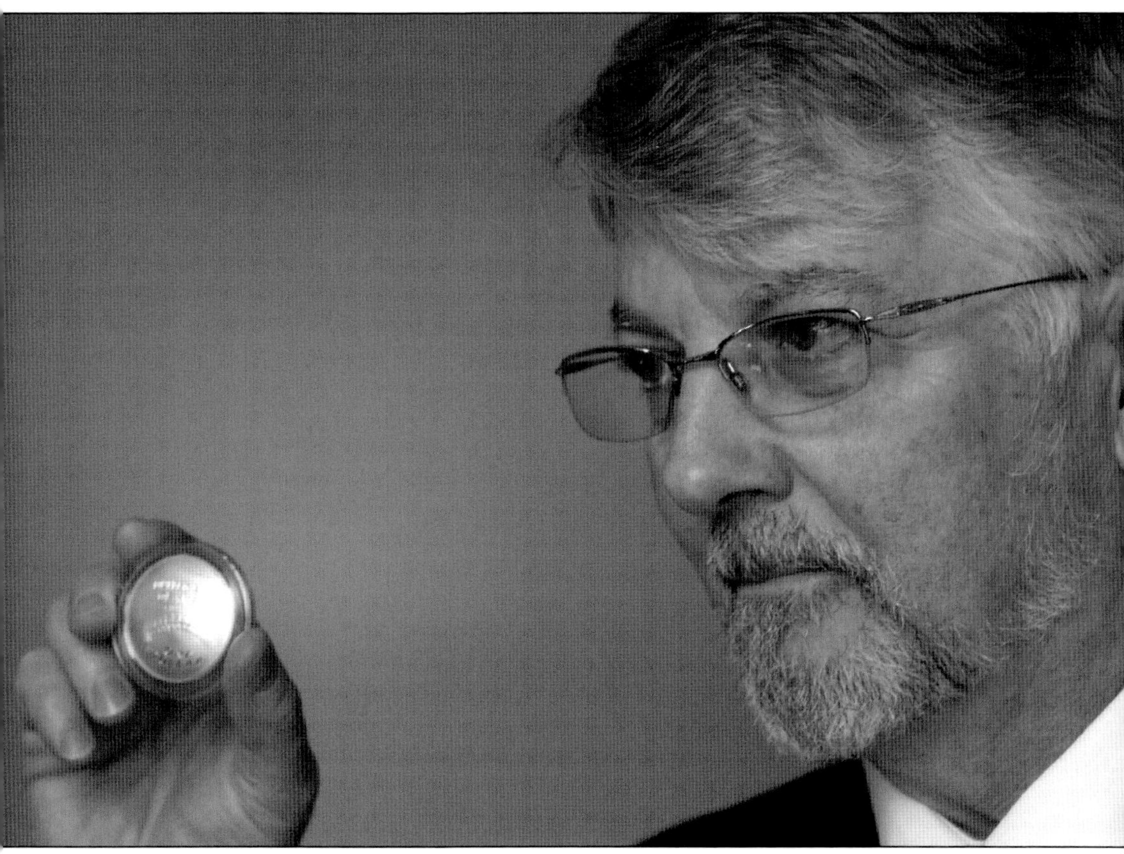

The 2006 Benjamin Franklin silver dollar is just one of many coins and medals designed by Don Everhart, a sculptor-engraver who already had built a large portfolio as a freelance designer and private mint artist before joining the US Mint in 2004. Everhart designed a multitude of circulating coins as well as commemorative issues and medals. Among these are the reverses of the 50 State Quarters honoring Nevada, Hawaii, and New Mexico. He also designed the Statue of Liberty design on the reverse of all Presidential $1 coins (2007–2016) and the reverses of the 2014 National Baseball Hall of Fame commemorative coins. In addition to his work involving coins, Everhart has designed many Congressional medals and also created the Pres. Bill Clinton Second Inauguration Medal. The native Pennsylvanian retired from the US Mint in 2017, having left a numismatic legacy that will endure well into the future. (Courtesy of the US Mint.)

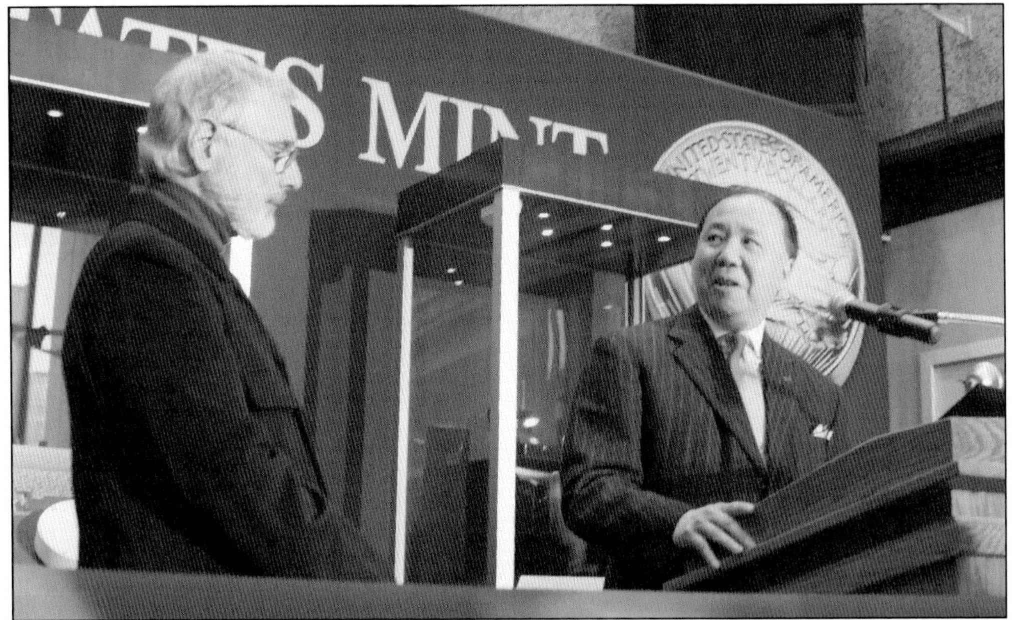

Edmund Moy, who served as director of the US Mint from 2006 through 2011, was one of the mint's most visible leaders. Here, he is seen with Chief Engraver of the US Mint John Mercanti (left) unveiling the 2009 Ultra High Relief Double Eagle gold coin. Years after leaving the US Mint, Moy continues advocating for numismatists in a private-sector role and meets eager coin collectors during public appearances. (Courtesy of the US Mint.)

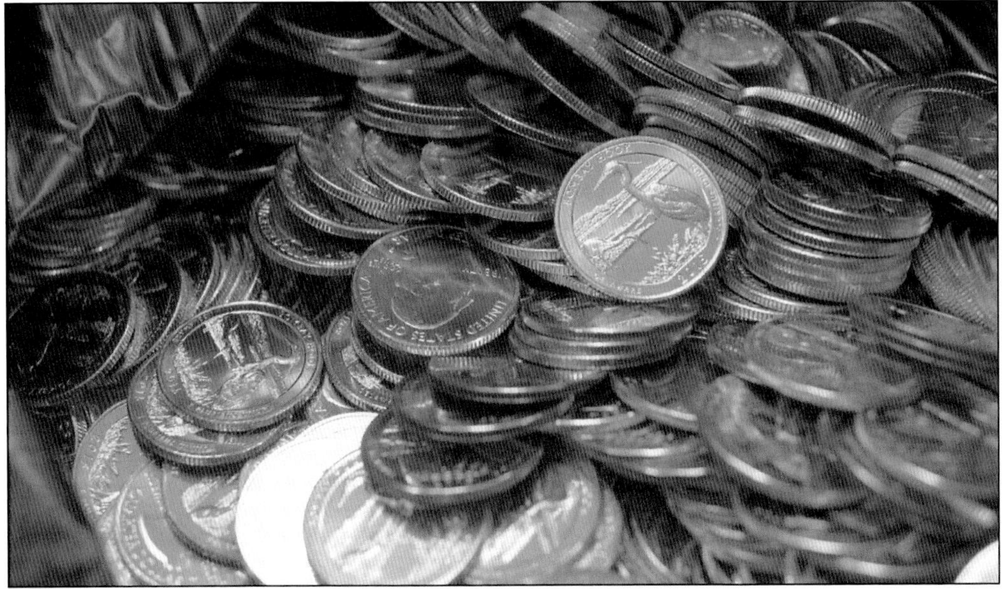

One of the most popular circulating coin series following the end of the 50 State Quarters program in 2008 is the America the Beautiful Quarters series. Beginning in 2010, the series honors national parks or national landmarks in each of the 50 states, the District of Columbia, and the nation's territories. In this photograph is a pile of 2015 America the Beautiful Quarters depicting the nearly 16,000-acre Bombay Hook National Wildlife Refuge in Smyrna, Delaware. (Courtesy of the US Mint.)

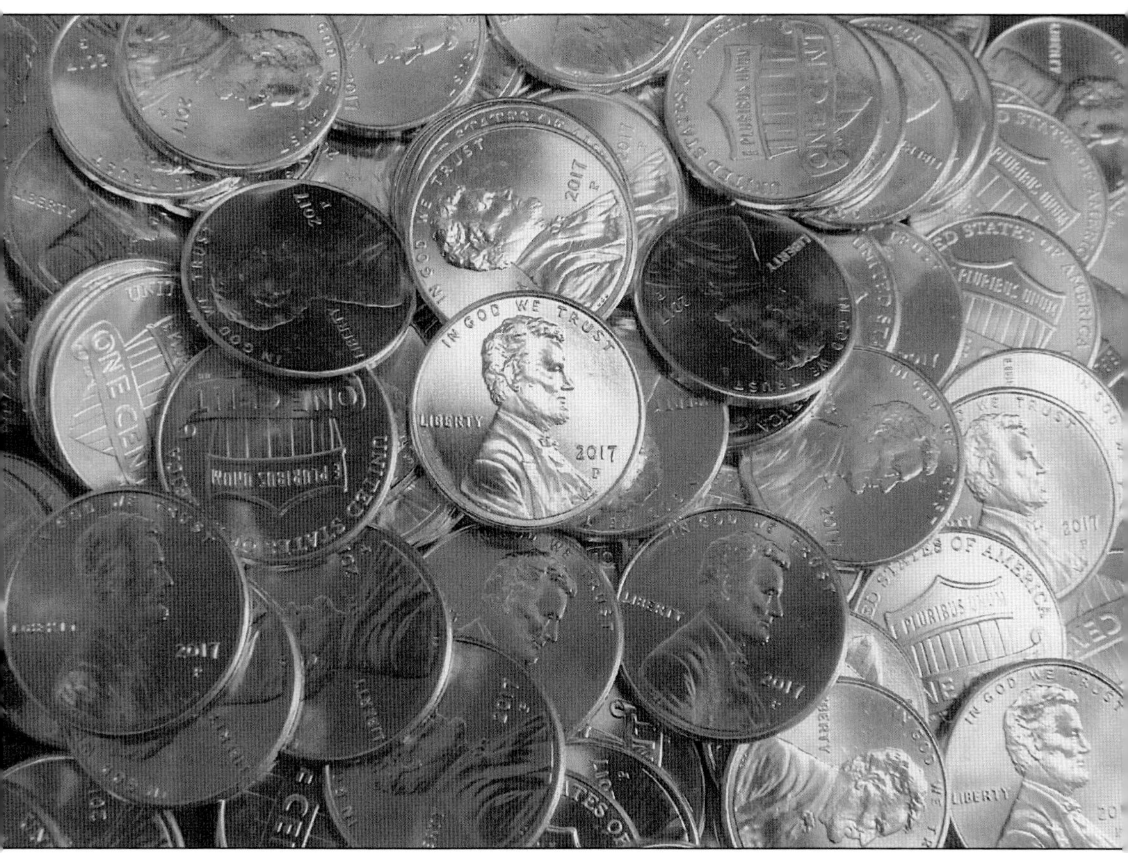

The US Mint honored its 225th anniversary in 2017 with several special releases, including the 2017-P Lincoln cent, pictured here. The 2017-P Lincoln cent is significant because it became the first US one-cent coin to bear the "P" mintmark symbolizing the Philadelphia Mint; since 1980, all circulating Philadelphia-minted US issues greater in denomination than one cent carry the "P" mintmark. More than 4.3 billion 2017-P Lincoln cents were made, so they remain affordable, yet important, collectibles as they represent a historic first for the Philadelphia Mint. The US Mint marked its 225th anniversary by creating yet another historic first with the release of the 2017 American Liberty High Relief Gold Coin. The gold coin, struck in the denomination of $100, became the first official US coin to depict Liberty as an African American woman. (Courtesy of the US Mint.)

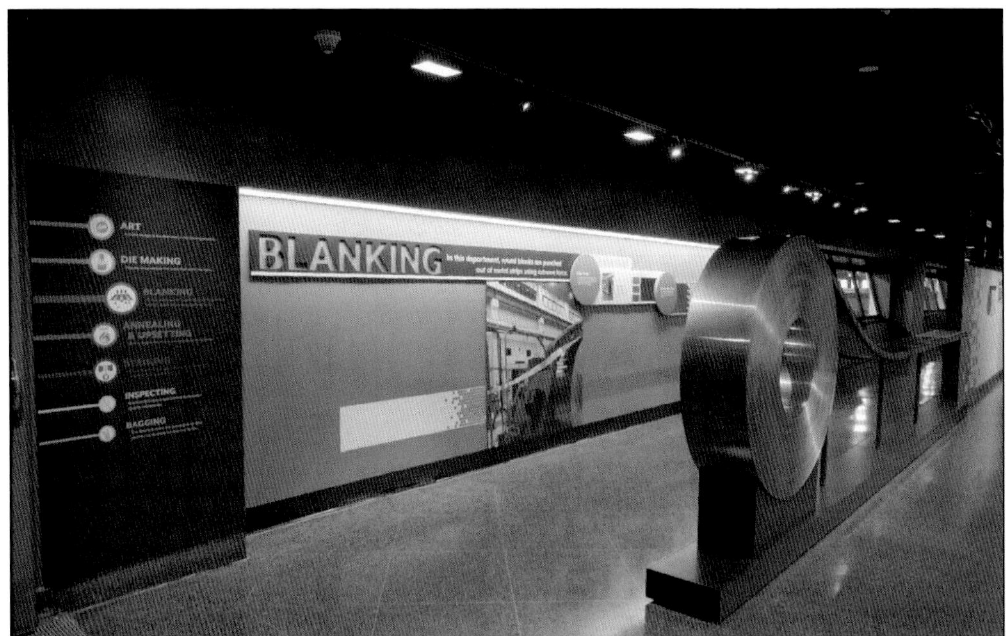

In addition to serving as the world's largest coin factory, the Philadelphia Mint is one of the most popular tourist attractions in the City of Brotherly Love. On a typical busy day, thousands will tour the Philadelphia Mint, including locals, school groups, out-of-state tourists, and international visitors. Those who visit the Philadelphia Mint encounter educational displays, as seen above, and can view coins being made on the presses, pictured below, some 40 feet beneath the elevated visitors' tour gallery. Visitors spending 30 minutes watching coining operations during a regular business day will have witnessed the birth of about one million new coins. (Above, courtesy of Quatrefoil Associates; below, courtesy of the US Mint.)

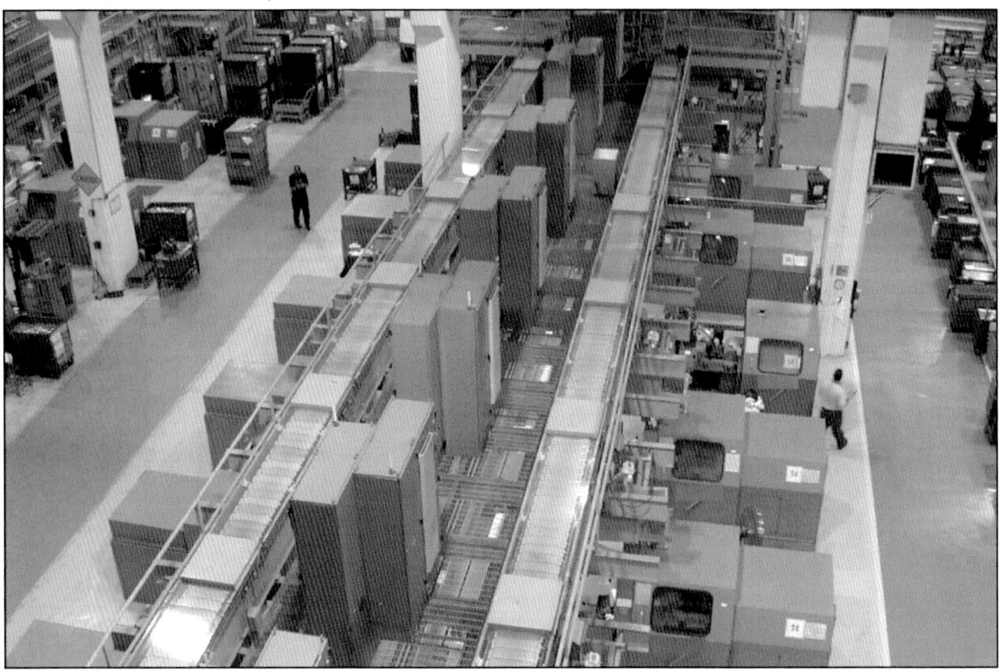

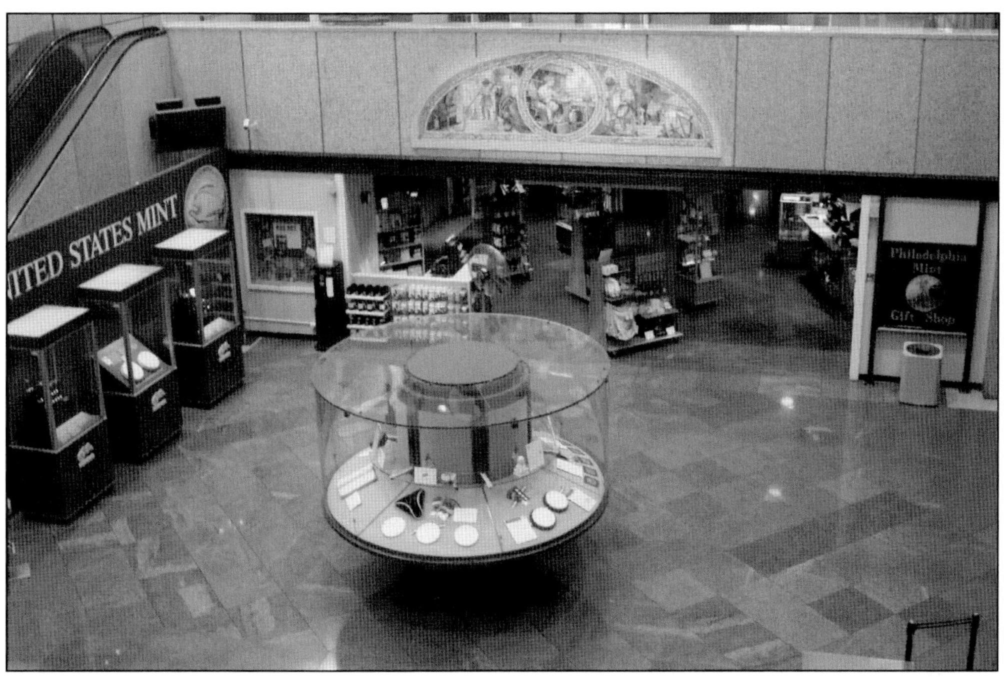

There are many historic relics that can be seen during a tour of the Philadelphia Mint, including the seven colorful Tiffany glass mosaics mounted on the mint's lobby walls. These large mosaics were created by Tiffany Studios in New York to celebrate the 1901 opening of the third Philadelphia Mint, where they were displayed until minting operations were moved to the current facility. The artistic glass masterpieces depict cherubic children minting coins in the tradition of the ancient Romans, as seen in a mural discovered during excavations in Pompeii, Italy, in 1895. The mural pictured above and in close-up below is found atop the lobby entrance of the gift shop. (Both, courtesy of the US Mint.)

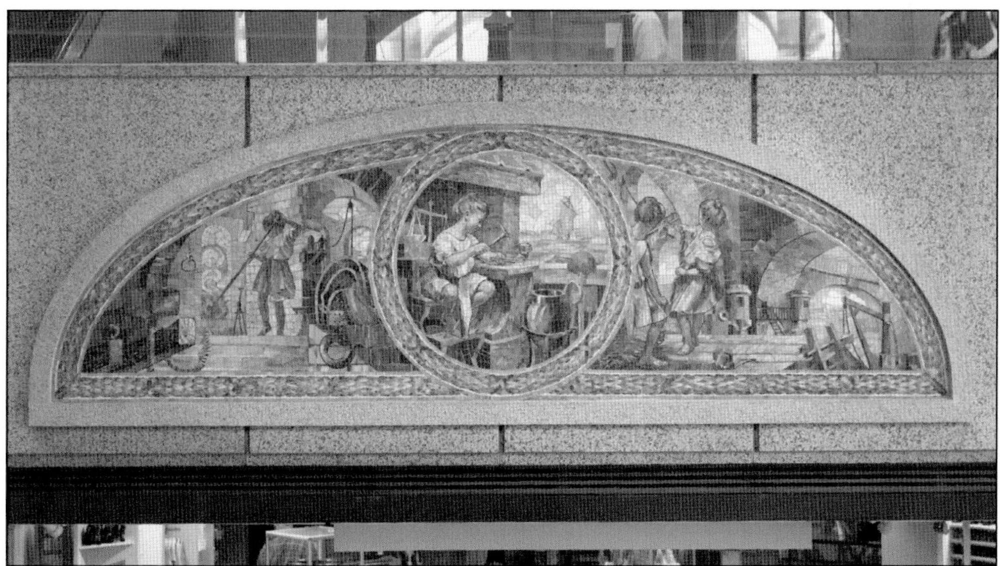

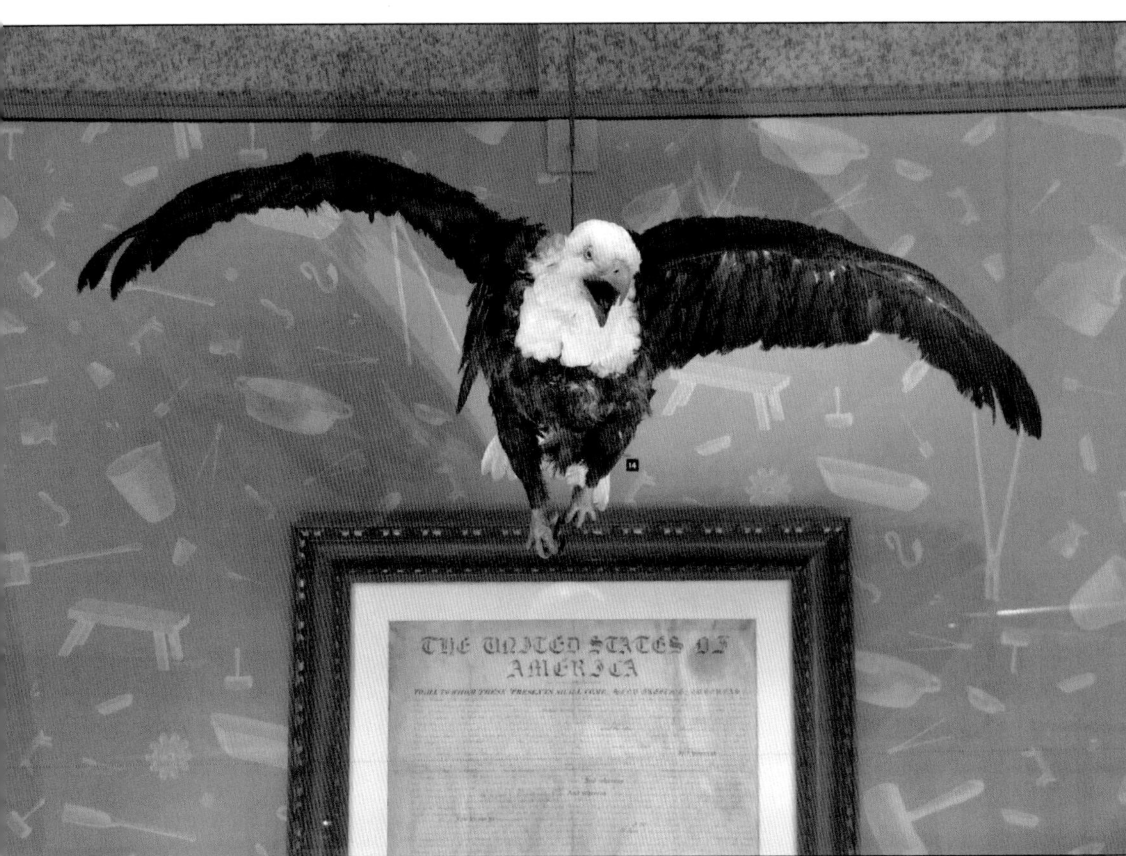

One of the biggest celebrities in Philadelphia is Peter the Mint Eagle. The famous bald eagle took residence in the roof structure of the Philadelphia Mint during a period of a few years that numismatic scholars believe occurred sometime between the early 1830s and late 1850s. Mint officials allowed Peter to come and go as he pleased, soaring above Philadelphia during the day and returning to the mint by nightfall. Legend says he inspired depictions of eagles seen on various US coins made since the mid-19th century. Though many aspects of Peter's life are memorialized only in lore, he really did live at the Philadelphia Mint, and it was there where he met his unfortunate demise when his wing was accidentally caught in the flywheel of a coin press after it suddenly started. Peter died soon after, but a taxidermist preserved the eagle's body, which has been on public display ever since at the second, third, and fourth Philadelphia Mint buildings. (Courtesy of Quatrefoil Associates.)

Bibliography

Bowers, Q. David. *A Guide Book of The United States Mint: Colonial, State, Private, Territorial, and Federal Coining Facilities*. Atlanta, GA: Whitman Publishing, 2016.

Breen, Walter. *Complete Encyclopedia of U.S. and Colonial Coins*. New York, NY: Doubleday, 1988.

Burdette, Roger W. *From Mine to Mint*. Great Falls, VA: Seneca Mill Press, 2013.

Del Mar, Alexander. *The History of Money in America from the Earliest Times to the Establishment of the Constitution*. New York, NY: Burt Franklin, 1968.

Evans, George G. *Illustrated History of the United States Mint*. Philadelphia, PA: George E. Evans Publisher, 1886.

Historical Society of Pennsylvania Photograph Collection, Philadelphia, PA.

Lange, David W. *History of the United States Mint and its Coinage*. Atlanta, GA: Whitman Publishing, 2006.

Orosz, Joel J. and Leonard D. Augsburger. *The Secret History of the First U.S. Mint: How Frank H. Stewart Destroyed—And Then Saved—A National Treasure*. Atlanta, GA: Whitman Publishing, 2011.

Records of the US Mint, Philadelphia, PA. Digital Photography Collections. National Archives and Records Administration.

Records of the US Mint, College Park, MD. Digital Photography Collections. National Archives and Records Administration.

Stewart, Frank H. *History of the First United States Mint: Its People and Its Operations*. Lawrence, MA: Quarterman Publications, 1924, reprinted 1974.

Taxay, Don. *The U.S. Mint and Coinage: An Illustrated History from 1776 to the Present*. New York, NY: Arco Publishing Company, 1966.

The Athenaeum of Philadelphia Photograph Collection. Lawrence S. Williams Inc. Collection, the Athenaeum of Philadelphia, PA.

The Eric P. Newman Numismatic Portal at Washington University, Saint Louis, MO.

Travers, Scott A. *The Coin Collector's Survival Manual Revised Seventh Edition*. New York, NY: House of Collectibles, 2015.

Treasury Department, Bureau of the Mint. *Domestic and Foreign Coins Manufactured by Mints of the United States 1793–1980*. Washington, DC: US Government Printing Office, 1981.

US Mint Photos, Philadelphia, PA. Special Collections Research Center, Temple University Libraries.

US Mint Photos, Prints. Washington, DC. Prints & Photographs Division, Library of Congress.

Yeoman, R.S. and Kenneth Bressett. *A Guide Book of United States Coins*. Atlanta, GA: Whitman Publishing, 2018.